Listening to People

Chicago Guides to *Writing*, Editing, and Publishing

Listening
to People

A PRACTICAL GUIDE

TO INTERVIEWING,

PARTICIPANT OBSERVATION,

DATA ANALYSIS, AND

WRITING IT ALL UP

Annette Lareau

THE

UNIVERSITY OF

CHICAGO PRESS

Chicago and London

The University of Chicago Press, Chicago 60637

The University of Chicago Press, Ltd., London

© 2021 by The University of Chicago

Published 2021

Printed in the United States of America

30 29 28 27 26 25 24   4 5

ISBN-13: 978-0-226-80657-0 (cloth)

ISBN-13: 978-0-226-80643-3 (paper)

ISBN-13: 978-0-226-80660-0 (e-book)

DOI: https://doi.org/10.7208/chicago/9780226806600.001.0001

Library of Congress Cataloging-in-Publication Data

Names: Lareau, Annette, author.

Title: Listening to people : a practical guide to interviewing, participant observation,
data analysis, and writing it all up / Annette Lareau.

Other titles: Practical guide to interviewing, participant observation, data analysis,
and writing it all up | Chicago guides to writing, editing, and publishing.

Description: Chicago ; London : The University of Chicago Press, 2021. | Series:
Chicago guides to writing, editing, and publishing | Includes bibliographical
references and index.

Identifiers: LCCN 2021003591 | ISBN 9780226806570 (cloth) | ISBN 9780226806433
(paperback) | ISBN 9780226806600 (ebook)

Subjects: LCSH: Sociology—Methodology. | Social sciences—Methodology. | Social
sciences—Fieldwork. | Interviewing in sociology. | Participant observation.

Classification: LCC HM517 .L37 2021 | DDC 301.01—dc23

LC record available at https://lccn.loc.gov/2021003591

♾ This paper meets the requirements of ANSI/NISO Z39.48-1992
(Permanence of Paper).

For my students at
University of Pennsylvania,
University of Maryland,
Temple University,
and
Southern Illinois University,
with gratitude.
I have learned so much from
all of you.
And,
for all novices who want to
do their own study one day.

Contents

1

Introduction

The Emergent Nature of the Research Process

Interviews and participant observation studies deepen our knowledge of people, institutions, and social processes. These approaches draw us into the *meaning* of events in the everyday lives of individuals, showing how people are affected by social structural forces. Well-crafted studies can make us feel as if we are close to the social events being vividly described. For example, while surveys of victims document the size and scope of disasters, in-depth interviews and participant observation can help us grasp unexpected ramifications. In *Everything in Its Path*, Kai Erikson demonstrates how the collapse of a poorly maintained dam in West Virginia not only released a torrent of water that swept away homes and killed 132 people. The catastrophe also—in part because of how the disaster relief was organized—dissolved key social bonds and feelings of community.

Relatedly, ethnographers show how people simultaneously live in different overlapping social worlds and reveal how these worlds collide in unexpected ways. For example, professionals routinely enact policies that do not consider multiple institutional pressures, but family members feel the cross-pressures keenly. In *Trapped in a Maze*, Leslie Paik describes the "multi-institutional maze" that confines families such as Ms. Catherine, an older woman living with her two teen grandsons and nephew. Ms. Catherine interacts with eleven different institutions; the colliding institutional rules create havoc.[1] Many times, qualitative studies offer a "local point of view" regarding the meaning of events. This perspective can challenge taken-for-granted assumptions. For example, in his study of defendants going through the criminal justice system, Matthew

Clair notes that lawyers were surprised when Black defendants sometimes voluntarily declined an offer of probation and chose instead to
go to jail. Clair's study, *Privilege and Punishment*, illuminates the logic
behind this choice: since the working-class Black defendants were re-
signed to a high level of police surveillance in their communities, they
viewed probation as too risky. Other times scholars can show how very
different groups of people have similar experiences, as anthropologist
Katherine Newman used interviews with displaced homemakers, air
traffic controllers, blue-collar workers, and managers to illuminate the
pain of downward mobility.[2] Because in-depth interviews and participant observation can uncover processes that were previously unknown
or underdeveloped in the social science literature, these methods are
especially helpful in improving our conceptual models.[3]

Many people want to learn how to do high-quality in-depth interviews and participant observation.[4] In my case, when I was beginning
to learn how to do this kind of research, the literature I read left me feeling stumped. I could not find the advice I needed. The books seemed
overly prescriptive. They informed me that I should sensitively "probe"
in interviews, but they didn't describe what that looked like, nor did
they seem to recognize sufficiently the difficulties inherent in probing.
As I read methodological appendices, I was especially frustrated when
researchers who had carried out a participant observation study described gaining entry into a field setting as the result of a serendipitous
event. How was I supposed to replicate such serendipity as I sought to
break into a setting? Books about interviews and observation made it
seem like doing a study would be relatively smooth sailing, but in my
experience, it was not. I yearned to read a book that was more realistic
and practical.

In pursing my interest in a deeper understanding of how people
think, act, and make sense of their everyday lives, I also have been
struck by studies that had wonderful, unrealized potential: the authors
designed great projects, gained impressive access, spent a great deal
of time collecting data, either by interviewing many people or writing countless field notes, and wrote clearly. Despite all of these very
promising elements, the final products fell short. How did that happen? What went wrong? In some cases, the works didn't have data of
sufficiently high quality to offer readers the rich, vivid feeling of being
there. The lack of in-depth data made it hard to assess the basis for

the authors' claims. I was bothered by researchers who essentially told readers to "trust" them because they had collected a great deal of data since I wanted these authors to *show* their readers the data they found to be persuasive. In other cases, authors provided plenty of data, but their arguments lacked focus. Sometimes, the arguments were clear, but the research questions were narrowly conceived and, worse, the authors had not considered alternative explanations. In a few instances, a single error—whether in design, data collection, or analysis—was so consequential that it dramatically reduced the value of the study. How could similar studies yield work of such wildly different quality? The qualitative methodology books I read didn't answer this question.

These challenges—that methods books are not practical enough and that potentially wonderful studies can flounder—led me to write this book. In *Listening to People*, I give concrete, practical advice for actually doing a wide variety of studies including class projects, theses, articles, and books. After all, novice researchers can encounter very hard problems and still manage to produce outstanding studies. In addition, since even experienced researchers inevitably face difficulties, I offer a more realistic account of the research process than appears in many other works. I also stress the inherently uncertain nature of the research process, and the importance not only of talking to others but also of listening to feedback from others while conducting research. As the title of this book suggests, I consider listening to be the core of in-depth interviewing and participant observation. You must listen to people as you collect data, listen to feedback from others as you describe what you are learning during data collection, "listen" to the findings of others as you delve into the existing literature on topics that interest you, and "listen" to yourself as you sort through and prioritize some aspects of your study over others. As you engage in listening in these different ways, you will discover connections, reconsider assumptions, catch mistakes, develop and assess new ideas, weigh priorities, ponder new directions, and undertake numerous adjustments, all of which ultimately will make your contribution clearer and more valuable.

What Does *Emergent* Mean? Thinking as You Go

In analog photography, the film is developed, and prints are made in a darkroom. There, you use a machine to enlarge and then briefly expose the image onto white photographic paper, and subsequently you immerse the paper in a chemical bath. At first, the paper is completely blank. But then your photograph begins to take shape — very gradually and unevenly. It may even be hard to recognize the image when it is beginning to emerge, but very slowly the picture comes to life. If the image is too light or too dark, you return to the machine and change the amount of time you "burn" (give the image more light) or "dodge" (withhold light on part of the picture) to create a balanced photograph. Then, you put the new paper into the chemical bath, watch for the image to emerge, and finally plunge it into a "stop bath" when you are satisfied with the picture.

There are important differences between developing pictures and allowing insights to emerge from your interviews and participant observation research, but the slow taking shape of focus is similar. In addition, in interviews and participant observation, there is a lot of adjusting and changing as you go along — particularly in the first half of the study process. Thus, it is common for interviewers and participant observers to not really know what they are doing for a long time. If this happens, you may feel confused and uncertain. You may not quite understand how your study fits into the intellectual debates in the field. You may not know what is new and exciting. Or, you may feel overwhelmed and be convinced that your study is a big mess. All of this uncertainty and worry is normal. As you do interviews or hang out in a setting, many new questions surface. You have to make many decisions based on incomplete information — should you probe this or that, should you spend time with this person or that person, why are you doing this study, and what do you hope to learn? Since social life is complex, there are always multiple intellectual pathways present within any given study. As a result, you need to be constantly "thinking as you go."

As I explain in a discussion of data analysis in chapter 8, there is also not only one right way to sculpt your study. In that chapter, I present the case of a student who was doing a study of dog owners and was struggling to choose among multiple reasonable research questions. He couldn't address them all, and for a while he was uncertain. Gradually, however, he settled on one intellectual direction, and he let the others go. In my own case, when I was a doctoral student and met regularly with Arlie Hochschild to discuss my research, she would listen attentively as I described another new idea I had, but then she would say kindly, "You know, that is a great idea! But why don't you set that idea aside for another paper. *Let's focus.*" As I learned to develop a focus, the core ideas of my study emerged more clearly.

Why is focus so important? It is hard for readers (or for any audience) to absorb a story that is really four or five different stories. When a writer hops from point to point, or when a speaker presents a lot of examples that are interesting but don't fit together clearly, the audience can become confused, bored, or impatient. As a reader, you may have had the experience of reading a long paper and not really understanding why the author wrote it. (Was there a key idea? What was it?) Or, you may have read something with so many different ideas and examples it was hard to get the overall argument straight. Do not underestimate how difficult it can be for readers to simply follow an argument. If you have a clear focus, it helps your audience understand what key idea you are trying to convey.

When you first start doing interviews and participant observation, however, finding a clear focus is difficult. Sometimes it is impossible—even if you have read other relevant studies very carefully and thought a great deal about your topic. Normally it is only by collecting data, and thinking about the literature, honing your question, and collecting more data, that your focus slowly takes shape. Similar to the image in a darkroom, your focus emerges over time.

One more point about the emergent nature of interviewing and doing participant observation: You often have to *act* as if you know what you are doing. To gain access to a research setting and research subjects, you must explain the purpose of your study. Furthermore, people who read and review research proposals, funding applications, institutional review board (IRB) applications, dissertation proposals, and so forth usually expect you to tell them the purpose of your study. At this stage, they want to know what you are thinking, and they want to make sure that you haven't overlooked anything. They may be especially concerned that you think through the impact of your study on the research participants. What you say in applications and proposals is, by definition, inherently speculative, since the true focus of your study can only become clear as you move through data collection and data analysis. Adjustment and change are integral to the process of interviewing and participant observation.

William Strunk Jr., author of the classic English usage guide *The Elements of Style*, once advised his students at Cornell University, "If you don't know how to pronounce a word, say it loud!" The writer E. B. White, who later revised *Elements*, endorsed this guidance and added: "Why compound ignorance with inaudibility?"[5] In the case of preparing a proposal or funding application for a study using interviewing and participant observation, you want to clearly state your preliminary research question and then outline how you plan to proceed: you will gain access, collect data (specifying your methodological approach), be sensitive to particular problems (listing examples), and use these possible solutions (listing examples) to the possible problems. You will consult with advisors. It is also important to express tremendous enthusiasm and excitement about your study. It will be valuable! You will learn important things! You are aware of possible hiccups, but you have a plan for addressing those!

Although in some ways the entire exercise of writing a research plan is deeply contingent, it is also the best you can do. You are sharing what you know when you know it. As you learn more, you will adjust your study. The emergent nature of the work also means that you don't want to wait too long before you start collecting data. Once you start that step, many things will shift, and you will have new questions. This is all normal and appropriate. At some point, ideally around halfway through your data collection, you want to settle on your highest intellectual priorities, begin to focus your data collection on your central research question, look for data to support your emerging argument, seriously consider alternative explanations, and begin to think about the kinds of data you need to nail your argument. As I explain in later chapters, your research question, understanding of the literature, and focus of data collection will all evolve. You don't want to get to the end of the study without a clear focus. But, at the beginning, you want to loudly and confidently act as if you have a clear plan. That plan is to get permission to do the research, begin your study, and do the best you can. That is good enough.

Organization of This Book

I begin, in chapter 2, with planning. Despite important differences, interviewers and ethnographers face many similar challenges. I take up the thinking and decision making that happen in the earliest stages of a project, particularly designing the study, choosing whom to study, and making difficult trade-offs. I also provide an overview of the research journey. Chapter 3 is about preparing by getting ready. Here I discuss navigating the IRB as well as practical matters such as handling food, clothing, and safety while collecting data. I also discuss the tricky issue of recruiting people for your study and gaining access.

Then, I devote two chapters to interviewing. Chapter 4 is about "everything but the interview," including planning before an interview, constructing an interview guide, packing an interview bag, and thanking study participants. Chapter 5 takes you through two real-life interviews, using long excerpts from an interview done by a novice and one done by a more experienced interviewer. The excerpts are accompanied by boxed commentary where I point out what probes worked well and which were less successful.

Chapter 6, which begins a two-chapter discussion of participant observation, takes up some of the key challenges associated with doing participant observation: introducing yourself to people at your study site, defining your role in the field, scheduling fieldwork, and avoiding common mistakes (e.g., forgetting to eat before going into the field, putting off writing up your field notes for more than twenty-four hours after a visit). I also take up other challenges in terms of what to talk about, how to respond to participants' requests for help, and the reality that it may be hard to get yourself out the door to do fieldwork. Chapter 7 offers concrete examples of high-quality and low-quality field notes and shows how underdeveloped field notes can be improved dramatically.

One theme running through this book is that you have to think as you go. It is best to carry out data analysis at every point in the research project—as you design your study, collect data, refine your focus, collect more data, code, and write up the results. But, despite the ongoing nature of the work, it is helpful to pause and systematically compare and contrast what you have learned through coding. Chapter 8 focuses on this formal phase of coding in data analysis. Chapter 9 turns to the challenge of writing, clearly stating an argument, providing ample data to support your claims, discussing disconfirming evidence, and building a conclusion. In chapter 10, the book's conclusion, I revisit the value of doing this kind of work, the limited impact of most mistakes, and the gift that the inexperienced bring to the table. I offer some final words about the importance of having faith throughout the process.

How to Use This Book

Listening to People is intended to be read from beginning to end and to be revisited when you are facing a particular task or wrestling with a specific problem. As a result, I usually briefly define key terms in each chapter so that they can be understood in that context. Throughout, the focus is on doing in-depth interviews and participant observation. Although these two approaches are arguably the most common qualitative methods used in the social sciences, they are not the only methods. Other related, and overlapping, methods include focus groups, autoethnography, content analysis of documents, portraiture, the extended case method, and mixed methods—to name only a few.[6] Due to space constraints, these methods are not taken up here. Many forms of qualitative research, however, feature key elements—including research design, aspects of data collection (e.g., probes in interviewing), data analysis, and writing—similar to those of interviewing and participant observation. Thus, I am hopeful that *Listening to People* will be widely helpful.

Since writers are often told to "write what you know," in the chapters ahead, I have provided a number of examples from my own research in the field of sociology. These studies, which have used participant observation and interviews, often focus on the influence of social class and race on key aspects of family life, including child rearing, family-school relationships, and school choice. I have also been involved in studies of wealthy families, the upwardly mobile, and refugee families. Of course, in addition to studying individuals, interviews and participant observation methods are excellent for illuminating organizational dynamics, political groups, and broader social systems. I hope that as you read, you will focus on the topics of interest to you within your discipline; many of these likely will attend less to the daily lives of people and more to the functioning of organizations across the globe.[7]

You will find that in addition to examples from sociology, *Listening to People* draws on work from other fields. Moreover, I asked colleagues in other disciplines for their advice and gathered helpful insights from outside academia, as well. I share these tips and suggestions in boxes throughout the book. Across the social sciences, there are excellent studies using interviews and participant observation, and, unfortunately, there was room to list only a fraction of them here. To broaden the available repertoire of resources, I cite excellent older, less frequently read works along with a very small number of current works. The bibliography also contains works on methodology that have helped me; the index is a valuable roadmap to general topics and specific discussions. Since this book is meant to be a practical guide, I don't explore the theoretical roots of in-depth interviewing and participant observation, nor do I examine issues related to these methods that are frequently discussed in the literature. Theoretical models also vary across disciplines, and the role theory can effectively play in guiding your research is not taken up here.[8] Nor do I enter the debates on the relative merits of interviews and participant observation.[9] The vigorous discussion of the proper use of social science research in public life is also set aside.[10] Furthermore, while it is clear individuals enter the research process from different, and unequal, social positions, these important issues are also not the focus of this book—though they do surface in a variety of ways.[11]

This book seeks to be a friendly companion as you learn how to design, begin, collect data, analyze, and write up a study using in-depth interviews and participant observation. Your journey carrying out this kind of research can be exciting. While many important studies can be done in an office sitting in front of a computer, crucial aspects of interviews and participant observation are done out in the world, listening to people, by hanging out with them or by formally interviewing them, or by using both of these methods. Just as traveling to and exploring a new place can be thrilling because you are immersed in a different social world, doing this research can be a powerful experience that is different from your usual life. There are, however, many potentially challenging aspects to interviewing and observing, including significant imbalances between researchers and participants with respect to power and status.[12] These are issues that require you to be both vigilant and deeply sensitive to the way you conduct your research and to how your study affects your participants and the communities they are a part of. Ethnographic work also is contradictory at times since, as I show in subsequent chapters, you need to be systematic and rigorous with respect to key aspects of your study but sensitive and highly flexible in other areas. The work also can be tiring, even exhausting. Still, in-depth interviewing and participant observation studies not only deepen our understanding of crucial issues. They can also be a memorable and transformative life experience for those who use these methods. If you would like to carry out a study, I recommend doing so. You can learn a great deal about yourself and others. More importantly, the knowledge you generate—about people, groups, institutions, and social processes—can change how others understand the world.

Before You Begin

Dreaming and Thinking

Beginnings are exciting—the moments when everything is ahead of you and filled with possibility. Beginnings are also a time for key decisions. Studies using interviewing and participant observation face common challenges from the very beginning, and this chapter takes up these earliest moments. Doing some daydreaming is a very important first step. As you begin to focus your daydreaming, you choose a topic from your list of enticing potential studies, frame a preliminary research question, and consider a number of important design decisions. Then, it's a good idea to assess, realistically, the other obligations in your life—obligations that might shape the breadth and depth of the research you are able to undertake. This chapter takes on these initial design decisions and provides an overview of the research journey. Since one of your goals is to create excellent work, I also briefly discuss widely established criteria of outstanding work. In the next chapter, I take up the various steps in translating your plans to reality.

Dreaming: Conceptualizing a Study

But first, the dreaming. What would you love to do? Whom do you want to study? What kinds of studies do you find satisfying? Why do you admire some studies? What studies do you find unsatisfying? Why are they problematic?

In answering these questions about other research, you can begin to assess your dreams in light of the existing field. At this stage of the process, as long as your project is ethical, nothing is out of bounds. Even if the goal seems outlandish because access to a site is highly restricted (e.g., following around a professional football team, seeing how network news is produced), it is important to elucidate your private hopes and dreams—the rumblings inside your soul—to give them careful thought. As noted earlier, there are many forms of listening. Here, you are listening to your own inner voice. You also want to talk to others and listen to the expertise they share. Reading other studies also helps you "listen" to established knowledge. As you daydream about your future study, it is helpful to identify studies that can act as role models. But you also might want to do something that has not yet been done. And, here, even if you get negative feedback, keep in mind that the naysayers are not always right. For example, when I was starting my second project, which involved visiting families with young children inside their homes on a daily basis for almost a month, many people, including colleagues, friends, and graduate students, told me flat out that it could not be done: families would not give me permission. Their harsh assessment scared me. But they were wrong, and the research I completed led to my book *Unequal Childhoods*. Similarly, when Rachel Ellis was a graduate student and wanted to do a one-year ethnography in a women's prison for her dissertation, one famous professor told her it would be "very difficult and maybe even impossible."[1] But it was not impossible. Colleagues scoffed at the idea that Katharina Hecht would be able to interview high-income earners in London, but, by working with their personal assistants, she gained access.[2] If I were really excited about a possible idea for a study, I would not necessarily listen to naysayers. I would try to begin the study three, four, or five times, try to trim your focus to one key aspect, or tailor it in other ways before I truly gave up on it. As always, however, you want to daydream about a question that you want to answer and are able to answer through the distinctive strengths of interviewing and participant observation, which are understanding social processes and their meanings to participants.[3]

Thinking: Developing a Research Design

After the dreamy "all things are possible" time comes the consideration of the cold, harsh facts. As I explain shortly, there are many trade-offs in designing a high-quality study, and you need the *time to be there* in a field site or to conduct interviews. The nature of the study design varies—undergraduates do different studies than graduate students or senior scholars. Although the key issue is what you want to learn, you want to consider how much time you have to conduct the research, and working backwards, when your written product needs to be done. You also will weigh the relative merits of doing interviews (described in more detail in chapters 4 and 5) or participant observation (discussed at length in chapters 6 and 7).[4] A key decision will be whether you choose to study one group or do a comparison of the experiences of two or more groups.[5]

Put differently, you need a research design. As you begin to mull over a possible study, you might reflect on what you hope to be doing in your study. For example, what exactly do you want to observe and why? What is most important? If you are visiting a site (such as a school), why are you there? What are you hoping to learn? As a participant observer, how much will you aim to be a participant and how much will you aim to be an observer? If you are interviewing people, whom do you want to interview? Why do you need to speak with them? What can they teach you? What don't you know? There usually are not right or wrong answers to these questions. Rather, it depends on your goals. In the beginning, you might not be sure of the purpose of your study, but you will have some thoughts. Gradually, you can figure out your central goal.

Since interview and participant observation studies almost always unfold over time in unpredictable ways, any research design will need to be flexible. Making an ideal plan ahead of time is reasonable, and it can be helpful for others who are helping you (e.g., advisors, granting agencies). That said, it is appropriate to adjust the plan once you begin since often things do not work out as anticipated. And do make adjustments rather than persist with a problematic course. For example, in an interview study, you might revise your questions in the middle to drop ones that prove to be "tone deaf" or add new questions that allow you to explore an important, emerging issue. In a participant observation study, you might find that things are unfolding very differently than expected, or you might not end up focusing on what you originally intended to study, but you have gained interesting insights on a related topic and earned the trust of others. There is nothing problematic or shameful about adjusting as you go along. It is normal.[6] Indeed, a strength of interviews and participant observation research is that you can be responsive to what you learn in your setting.

Sometimes this means that, in reality, you do not ask the first one-third of your sample a question that surfaces as the study goes along. Clearly, this is not ideal, but it is unarguably better to deepen your analysis based on new insights. Does this mean that you may not have asked every person the same question, and when you want to make a table you might have incomplete data? Yes. Is this difficult? Yes. Is it avoidable? No. As discussed in chapter 1, it's important to remember that the findings of ethnographic research are *emergent*.

SETTLING ON A FOCUS OF YOUR STUDY

The choice of conducting interviews or participant observation depends on the research question or, put differently, what you want to know. Interviews are particularly valuable for learning how people understand key aspects of their lives. Participant observation is especially helpful for unpacking social mechanisms. Of course, some studies use both. For sensitive topics that require deep trust, having an ongoing relationship with participants (through participant observation) can be valuable, and, in some cases, essential.[7]

In interview studies, researchers focus their questions and recruit people who can teach them what they want to know. Interviews often center on meaning making: how people understand their social positions, barriers they believe that they have faced, worries they have about their children or their jobs or their health, or accomplishments that have generated pride. In organizational studies, interviews can help you understand how the organization does, and does not, work. In conducting interviews, you want to choose a group of people who are best positioned to help you understand the topic that interests you. Your interviewees must be experts on your chosen topic. For example, doctors can talk knowledgeably about providing care but not about how patients experience medical care.

For a participant observation study, you want to be sure to choose a research site that allows you to observe people interacting with others. Hence, doing an observation of people watching a movie is not usually an ideal choice because the people in the study are not generally in teracting with each other in an observable fashion. (Studying a group of people creating a video would be better.) If you are interested in how people develop romance and sexual relations, it would be ideal to follow people on dates. Such a study, however, would be extremely intrusive, and it would be difficult to not influence the interactions you are observing.[8] It might be better to "hang out" in bars, fraternity parties, or other places where budding romances and flirtations can be observed.

In a different vein, if a researcher is interested in religion, attending religious services is only a preliminary step. For example, to understand an evangelical congregation, it is important to be able to "hang out" with people as they do missionary work, feed the homeless, study the Bible, or otherwise interact in small groups. The critical point is that the site must be a place where people are there to interact. If you are interested in understanding social interactions that are not tied to a specific location, it might be better to embed yourself in a group of people rather than in a specific site (you may even choose to follow members of the group across various sites), such as joining a group of birdwatchers, a sorority, or a campus religious group.

THE RESEARCH DESIGN: YOUR STUDY AND ITS
CONTRIBUTION TO THE WORLD OF IDEAS

One study cannot do everything. Both before beginning, and during the study, you will need to make hard choices. Broadly conceived, each research project is limited by specific key resources (time, money, accessibility, and so forth). And, as I elaborate shortly, there are many conflicting priorities in choosing both a group to study and a location to study them (at least initially). How do you decide? The answer, I believe, is connected to the tentative idea of what you want to study. What is your research question? What are you trying to learn? What steps will you take to gain the knowledge you seek? For help in navigating these issues, think about the broader ideas that will guide your work, as well as your theoretical goals.

Indeed, researchers differ in their relationships to the world of ideas. Partly, you can gain guidance in making these (hard) decisions by considering the kinds of studies you admire. Many people admire studies of topics or groups. You might think, "I want to study homelessness." "I want to study sororities." "I want to study doctors." "I want to study engineers." These are examples of research topics. Some people are very comfortable doing a rich, descriptive study of a group. There are influential studies of communities or organizations such as Andrew Deener's *Venice*, about a beach community in California; David Grazian's study, *American Zoo*; or Gary Alan Fine's books on the culture of restaurant work (*Kitchens*), debate teams (*Gifted Tongues*), or baseball teams (*With the Boys*). These studies contain deep questions about practices and processes; they teach us how social groups, communities, or organizations function. This is a goal in and of itself. Broadly conceived, these studies often help us understand nuances and processes in how these organizations work, particularly in terms of how organizations meet, or don't meet, their mission.

Other scholars use their study as a *springboard* to focus decisively on one theoretical question. They see their tightly focused research as contributing to the development of more general ideas of social processes. Hence, while they often start from the same point—a research topic—they work to hone the question more narrowly. Ultimately their goal is an explicitly defined, theoretically based research question, as when Michael Burawoy asked how workers ended up breaking rules to help meet the goals of their employers in his book *Manufacturing Consent*. Kimberly Hoang, in *Dealing in Desire*, showed how the role of hostesses in Vietnam facilitates economic transactions in the global economy. In a different vein, Maia Cucchiara, in *Marketing Schools, Marketing Cities*, explored how publicly funded programs supporting school reforms end up yielding unequal benefits for students. Karolyn Tyson showed how organizational dynamics, particularly the number of African American children in gifted classes, shaped racial dynamics in schools in *Integration Interrupted*. In these studies, researchers ask a clear analytic question that offers competing answers; they reject some answers as they put forth their intellectual position. Using theoretical concepts, they connect their empirical details to a set of abstract ideas in their discipline. By engaging with these ideas, the researchers in this approach highlight an intellectual contribution.

HOW READING HELPS YOU CHOOSE YOUR TOPIC

Reading widely before you begin data collection will help you focus your interests in your project. There are no hard and fast rules here, and it varies if you are an undergraduate or a doctoral student. Undergraduates may have read a handful of articles before beginning a class project. For a doctoral student, I normally would suggest that students read at least twenty articles in the core area as well as a few of the key books. It is ideal to read the most widely cited pieces in your topic, and also read classic works, gradually over time. When you read articles on a topic, you want to be familiar with many of the articles being cited (although you will not know all of them). But, the problem is that there are dozens and dozens of articles that are somewhat related but seem important. For example, for my book *Unequal Childhoods*, there were countless related topics such as doctor-patient interaction, teacher-parent interaction, families and religion, the long-term benefits of extracurricular activities, racial socialization, and so forth. If I spent time reading for each topic, I would have never completed the project. In the end, I developed a "rule of thumb" to read two or three pieces: usually one review essay, one classic piece, and/or one recent, high-quality piece. I also sometimes read about a topic in an encyclopedia or handbook. After that, I stopped even though there were vast holes in my knowledge. I decided that if the topic became more important, I could read more later. There is a risk of being "terrorized by the literature," as Howard Becker notes, so after you have read in some depth for your central topic and superficially for your side topics, you will need to stop reading and start collecting data.

Your contribution to the literature will also become clearer if you continue to read while you are collecting data (or, if you are too tired or busy to do this every week, carve out a couple of days every few weeks where you slow down data collection so that you have time to stop, read, and think). Good studies are developed in light of other studies. Of course, sometimes you go far afield to learn more. Robin Leidner did participant observation in McDonald's and with insurance salespeople, but, really, she was interested in the concept of rationalization.[9] Others might have been drawn to study McDonald's to understand other topics such as food consumption patterns or work-family balance. No matter what you have chosen to study, reading some of the literature is essential and—usually—helpful (even if it is intimidating). (Chapter 9 contains a longer discussion of how much to read.) Sometimes, depending on your research focus, it can be difficult to find your "conversation partners" in terms of finding an intellectual debate that seems apt and finding your critique in the equally messy literature. In a book on qualitative research, Kristin Luker helpfully imagines the literature as a "bedraggled daisy," suggesting you draw a Venn diagram of the various literatures that are relevant to your study.[10]

RESEARCH DESIGN DECISIONS: WHO, HOW BIG, AND HOW LONG

As you plan your study, you will need to make some key decisions, including *who* you are studying, *how long* you will study them, and *where* they are located. What age of people are you studying? Are you studying people who have had certain experiences? Are you studying people of one racial and ethnic group or multiple groups? Do they need to have been born in the US or can they be first- or second-generation immigrants? Most of these decisions are case by case. But, other things being equal, unless the research question demands it, it is often helpful to study more than one racial and ethnic group, to restrict the age of the people you study to five years (for young people under 18) or two decades (for adults), and to have some clarity on the role of the country in which people were raised and are citizens. Yet, there are good reasons for studying only one racial and ethnic group or restricting a study in other ways. As always, it depends.

You also need to think about how long you will collect data. Of course, you want deep and dense data. The goal of data collection is "saturation" or, as Howard Becker put it in his book *Evidence*, "when you don't learn anything new for a while, your study is complete."[11] Ideally, if you are doing participant observation, you want to go to your site regularly during the week and remain in this setting for a good while. (The amount of time depends on your point in life. For an undergraduate in a one-semester class, it might be two visits a week for two months; for a doctoral student it might be two or three visits per week for nine months.) For interviews, you need to interview enough people until you keep hearing the same things over and over again. Since doing this type of research is rarely a lucrative business, you also need to figure out how you will pay the bills while doing fieldwork. Also, you need time to conduct the research *and* write field notes or notes on an interview within 24 hours of each visit or, for an interview study, find time or funds to transcribe the recordings. Ideally you should have a minimum of 9 to 15 hours per week, if not more, to devote to the enterprise, although some people have done it with much less. Many more hours per week would be better. Thus, one of the first cold, hard facts to consider is whether or not you have the time to carry out your study. Sometimes you can rejuggle your schedule to "make" the time; for example, parents with children might seek additional family support and childcare during data collection. You want to "count" as work the many different tasks connected to your study: traveling to do the research, managing the logistics of future visits, doing the interviews or participant observation, writing field notes, transcribing data, and writing memos reflecting on what you learn. For example, if you write field notes for 2.5 hours for each hour of participant observation, then 10 hours of field-work (over three visits) would "cost" 25 hours in writing field notes; this does not count the 1.5 hours of logistics and perhaps 3 hours of travel time. You also want to spend 3 or more hours writing memos and reading. Thus, around 10 hours of participant observation quickly multiples into a 43-hour week. Interviewing also has comparable parameters: arranging the interview, preparing, traveling to the location, uploading the recordings, writing a reflection, and sending a handwritten thank you note. Plus, many respondents cancel and reschedule. A week where you conduct three interviews is a good week.

In addition, you want to think about the goals of your study and the duration of the work. Longitudinal interviews can be valuable. Some researchers do "check-ins" or follow-up research after the intensive period of data collection has ended (e.g., six months or one year later). Given the emergent nature of the data process, a common approach is to take a pause in data collection, particularly in interviewing, do data analysis (discussed in chapter 8), and then resume interviewing with a clearer focus.

THE RESEARCH DESIGN:
THE SIZE OF A STUDY AND TRADE-OFFS

Before you can file an IRB, you need to make important decisions about your study. These decisions should be based on the purpose of your study. One study cannot do everything, and you almost always have to limit not only the size of the study but the number of groups you are studying. Small, rich studies can be extremely valuable. In thinking of the scope of a study, there can be tremendous pressure to "do it all" and have very large samples. Yet, interviews and participant observation have a distinctive logic, and your deep grasp of the data strengthens all aspects of the study. The scope of the study depends on many factors, but it is very appropriate for undergraduates (or people in intensive summer courses) to have highly circumscribed studies (i.e., "mini" studies.) Here, people will have a limited number of interviews—usually under 10, and a limited number of visits, often only one per week in the term. Mini studies proceed through all of the preparatory steps but spend less time doing the work since their timeframe is constrained. For other scholars, very thoughtful articles and books have been based on a limited amount of data.[12] Indeed, Robert Weiss, author of *Learning from Strangers*, reports that he can easily keep 50 people in his head to think about. In avoiding the "arms race" to go bigger and bigger, the goals of the project should be the deciding factor, as Mario Small notes in his valuable article "How Many Cases Do I Need?" Furthermore, most of the largest studies have been done by researchers who had staff and funding. (For example, my book *Unequal Childhoods* was based on an overly ambitious study and had a large grant and research assistants helping with data collection.)

Also, in a study based on interviews or participant observation, researchers always make compromises. Your knowledge of the literature and your own self-knowledge can help reveal which compromises are ones "you can live with" and which are "completely unacceptable." It is still with deep regret, however, that you may need to leave out some groups you would like to study in order to gather more detailed and rich data on a smaller number of people. Here, think again about studies you admire. Are you comfortable with a study of one racial group? Have you read a study you liked with this design? Is having a comparison essential to you? Of course, the contours of a group are not obvious. What matters is what you think. In addition, whatever decision you make, you want to talk to others whom you respect, and *listen* to what these other people are telling you. (If you listen to other people, they can also possibly anticipate how others, for example, in the publication process, might assess your design.) You don't need to share with the people you are studying all of the ins and out of your study, and they may not, in fact, agree with your categorization in all ways. (Most Americans consider themselves to be middle-class, for example, so working-class families may have objected to my putting them in that category if they had known about it.) To some extent, you can make adjustments as the study moves along, but other crucial elements need to be fixed so that the study is systematic and is well designed.

Ideally, you want a study that has a method and is systematic. For example, to me, there are undeniable benefits of comparing people doing similar activities in different settings.[13] Within the constraints of the real world, it is ideal to compare groups who are as similar as possible. This "apples to apples" tendency will increase your confidence in your conclusions. For example, in an interview design, it is not ideal to have three interviews with one racial group, two with another, and six with a third group. I personally am not comfortable with having only two or

Table 2.1. *Hypothetical Study of Family-School Relationships of Mothers with Children Three to Six Years of Age in Traditional Public School or Charter School*

	African American mothers	White mothers	Total
Upper-middle-class	7 to 11	7 to 11	14 to 22
Lower-middle-class	7 to 11	7 to 11	14 to 22
Working-class	7 to 11	7 to 11	14 to 22
Total	21 to 33	21 to 33	42 to 66

three people in one category; having five, six, or seven people in a category helps me feel more confident if I discern a pattern. Thus, if you have a comparative design, you want to be reasonably systematic. Of course, in the end, you may have slightly varying numbers—such as 11 in one group and 13 in another. You may create a simple table of your groups (with the squares in the table termed "cells") as you compare, for example, white and African American families who have children three to six years of age who are upper-middle-class, lower-middle-class, and working-class. (See the sample table 2.1.) You might restrict the sample to all US citizens or people who arrived by the age of five to avoid the distinctive experience of being an immigrant. Further, in interview studies, it is ideal to triangulate by having multiple interviews for each person in a subsample (for example, parents of a college student or a partner of a worker). Or, you might do an ethnography and then do detailed interviews with a subgroup of people you observed.[14]

Still, you will then need to make numerous other decisions. To give one example, I did a study (with a racially diverse team of research assistants) on variations in child rearing, summarized in *Unequal Childhoods: Class, Race, and Family Life.* The study was based on months of participant observation of classrooms in two elementary schools; separate, in-depth interviews with 137 parents (distributed among a total of 88 white and African American families); observations of countless children's activities; and intensive family observations, usually daily for three weeks, with a total of 12 families from the interview group, categorized as either middle-class, working-class, or poor. In my recruitment of families for the intensive observations, I faced difficult trade-offs. I was asking families for permission to visit them, usually daily for two to three hours per day, for around three weeks. (For being in the study, the families were paid $550 in current dollars.) I interviewed a number of middle-class African American families who were single-headed households. I was recruiting one family at a time, and I had completed observations of two white families before I recruited the African American middle-class families for the observation phase. In deciding on the four middle-class families for the intensive family observations, I held firm that the two African American families needed to be two-parent families (as were the two white middle-class families I had already observed) since I was worried about confounding family structure, race, and class. The school where I had observed and recruited the families was a predominantly white, suburban, public middle-class school; the school enrolled only about three African American children per grade. All of the African American families with children in the third and fourth grades graciously agreed to be interviewed, but the two families who were two-parent homes declined to take part in the intensive home observations (which involved daily visits for almost one month). As a result, the middle-class African American families who agreed to be in the intensive study were not from the public schools where I had completed months of observations. This meant, among other things, my observations in public schools could no longer be a central, defining feature of the book. This was a difficult choice, particularly since there was a single-parent African American middle-class family from the public school where I had done observations who probably would have agreed to be in the study if I had asked. Although I had always envisioned the project as based around school observations, my desire not to confound family structure with other factors meant I needed to make a significant adjustment. The study became less about school life and more about family life. In short, sometimes you have to move past incredibly promising people to study or enticing sites for observation because they will not yield a systematic comparison. Throughout, you have to figure out what is most important to you (in my case, race and class) so you can "hold constant" other factors. If the groups are comparable in crucial ways, it helps you focus on key mechanisms, and it increases your confidence in your findings.

In addition, the more restrictions you have, the harder it can be to recruit people for your study. Does the child need to be the eldest child in the family? In a study I did with Elliot Weininger about school choice, the age of the eldest child was important, but in other studies it might not be.[15] Does it matter whether the participating family has only one child or more? What about family structure? (We did not specifically recruit on this issue, but we made sure to have two-parent families [including blended families] as well as comparable numbers of single-parent families in each race and class category.) Does it matter if the mother works outside the home full-time or part-time? (In our study, we did not recruit on this factor, but, as it happened, we did have variation on this issue.) You continue to think about all of the factors that matter. You decide which ones are essential. Often you focus on a couple of key issues and then allow other factors to unfold with the sample. Keep your eye on the other ways in which study participants vary from one another. If a pattern turns out to be important, then you can adjust the sample to increase the number in a particular category.

In juggling all of these competing priorities, it is easy for the number of interviews to skyrocket very quickly. For example, in a hypothetical study of mothers of children three to six years of age comparing two racial groups and three social classes, having seven people per cell would yield a study of 42 people, which is much easier than 11 people per cell for a total of 66 people.

Limiting a study to two racial groups, one gender, and three social classes is difficult. (What about Hispanics? What about immigrants? What about fathers?) In addition, historically, some (dominant) groups have been studied more than other, equally important groups. As Amy Steinbugler notes, "When dominant groups are chosen again and again and again, it has long-lasting consequences for our discipline[s], about whose habits and experiences become normative."[16] Of course, you respect the groups you have omitted, and you believe that your study would be better if you included more groups. But making hard choices is necessary. You want to avoid collecting interview data and then ignoring it. The meaning of the data is often in the words of your study participants. Why conduct in-depth interviews only to reduce the patterns to numbers? After all, the samples are usually nonrandom. In my experience, doing the interviews yourself allows you to probe deeply, connect with people in your study, and learn a great deal. But one person can do only so much. In my study looking at class and race differences in family life, I sought a minimum of somewhere between seven and nine people in a cell. With only three or four people in each cell, I worry that I might have someone idiosyncratic enough to throw off the findings. If you have more than nine or ten people per category, then the study can become unwieldy.

I also realize that, realistically, much of this research is done by young people who are just starting out. They don't have big grants to pay for transportation or transcribing dozens of interviews. They need to be pragmatic. It is easy for you to feel that your study is inadequate. Yet, small is good. Small is reasonable and practical. Small means that in order to keep a study a reasonable size, you often need to limit the number of groups you study. One study can do only so much, and multiple studies will inform each other. And, the good news is that, as Mitch Duneier pointed out, the best ethnographies are often done by young people as doctoral dissertations.[17] For example, many classic ethnographies, including *All Our Kin*, *Streetcorner Society*, *Urban Villagers*, and *Tally's Corner*, were originally produced as doctoral dissertations.[18] In fact, many ethnographers do only one participant observation study in their lifetime, and they do it when they are early in their careers. For, while not famous enough to get large grants, young researchers have critical advantages: they have the gift of time, they often (but not always) have few family obligations and thus have more free time than older ethnographers, they can blend in more easily than older ethnographers in settings with adolescents and adults, and they have "fire in the belly" to make the study happen. It is a winning combination.

SELECTING THE STUDY SITE

In addition to considering whom you will study and how many, you need to think about *where* the people will be, the communities where you hope to find people to study. Be practical! You want to be able to visit the site frequently enough to understand the lived experience of people or, if you are interviewing, you want to study people close to their homes *and* close to your home. Concretely, this means that your field site should be close to where you live (or where you move to live to carry out the research). Ideally, you should be able to visit the site frequently and relatively easily.

If you do not own a car, the site should be accessible by public transportation. If you do own a car, the site should be no more than 30 minutes each way, and you need to have a concrete, reliable travel plan or, realistically, you may need to choose a different research site. There are rare circumstances when it makes sense to do a study of a setting over an hour from home each way, but usually it is vastly better to choose a slightly less desirable field site that is closer to home. Of course, don't forget to budget for traffic congestion in choosing a site. If it is critical that you study a field site far away, then you should try to organize your life so that you can move there for several months. Before you begin to think concretely about a research site, you need to think about how you can get there.

> **GETTING THERE**
> Could you borrow a car from a family member or friend? Does your university have a car you could use? Could you ride a bike there? Could you arrange a barter with a friend where your friend drives you there and then you do something for your friend? Can you get a grant to pay for rides?

Remote Data Collection

In 2020, the global pandemic Covid-19 swept the world. Universities around the United States abruptly closed down many operations, including in-person research, and moved to online classes. Responses varied across the states, but most states restricted movement and called for social distancing. The crisis produced a national tragedy with countless deaths as well as widespread unemployment and food shortages. While the full impact of the pandemic has yet to be understood, the consequences will be vast. For researchers, a host of new challenges developed regarding how to conduct interviews and participant observation during this national crisis. I struggled with this in my own work. Since the 2020 pandemic came in the middle of my data collection for a study interviewing families of high net worth (i.e., usually over ten million in net worth), I paused my study for two months before resuming interviewing online (using video recording techniques). Online interviewing was better than not progressing on my data collection. But, as I explain shortly, this move came with challenges.

Researchers seeking to navigate this highly varied terrain can draw on an extensive, and growing, literature on conducting qualitative research online that includes "net" ethnography (which is defined as "ethnography adapted to online communities"), digital diaries, "re-enactment videos," electronic support groups, online focus groups, political activities, online videos, and tweets.[19] Historically, some face-to-face contact has been critical in developing the kind of research relationships that yield deep, rich data, but this field is rapidly evolving. There are also numerous methodological pieces on online qualitative research from a variety of disciplines.[20] In their writings, scholars discuss gradually building trust and then gaining permission to share profiles.[21]

There are also extensive methodological discussions of online interviewing.[22] Some insist that in online interviewing "the quality of responses gained through online research is much the same as responses produced by more traditional methods."[23] My own experience of online interviewing has been mixed. In some cases, with a gregarious respondent, I found the results of a two-hour semi-structured interview to be comparable in quality to a face-to-face interview. More commonly, however, in an online interview I find that the quality is roughly about 75 to 80 percent of what I believe I would get in a face-to-face interview—particularly in terms of the depth I gained on sensitive matters. It is more difficult to build rapport; my connection with the participants is weaker than in face-to-face interviews. Then, when I encounter sensitive matters, I feel uncomfortable probing more deeply since there were not the same "signals" that the respondent is at ease. In some cases, the respondents have been, in my opinion, less forthcoming. In addition, interviews can end abruptly in a way that would be unlikely if you were in person. As I discuss in chapter 5, when you are face-to-face and a sensitive issue comes up, you are often able to "read" the situation and then "dig deep" to get more details (if the person is comfortable with you doing so). However, some nuance is lost when you are interacting through video conferencing. Online interviewing is vastly better than nothing, but I find the resulting interviews are usually not as high quality as interviews done face-to-face. Others have a different experience. And some populations, such as undocumented populations or refugees who are deeply skeptical of potential harm from institutional figures, may not feel safe doing an online interview and having it recorded.

There are advantages to conducting interviews and observations online. As noted, in some historical moments, such as a pandemic, it is one of the few options available. In addition, online interviewing eliminates travel and data collection costs, the inconvenience of being away from home for research, and other expenses. Some participants may find an in-person interview too formal, uncomfortable, and nerve-wracking. The method enables you to reach populations, for example, on other continents, who would otherwise be nearly impossible to reach. Online activities are a crucial part of daily life for many groups, particularly youth. A study of youth that did not include online activity would be incomplete.

Remote data collection is a topic that generates strong views, as people distinctly vary in their enthusiasm for it. Just as members of the university community have had vastly different levels of enthusiasm for teaching through online education, there are varying responses to using online techniques for data collection. Thus, the use of online technologies to carry out data collection in the social sciences is still unfolding and being understood.

WHO YOU ARE SHAPES THE STUDY

In doing a study, your own identity matters because conducting research raises complex questions about the authority and legitimacy of researchers to convey the lives of others.[24] As Peshkin put it, "One's subjectivity is like a garment which cannot be removed."[25] Rather than being able to preclude challenges in your research connected to your identity, your task is to understand the strengths and weaknesses of any pathway. These issues come up at many different moments in a study, especially with participant observation, but they are also present in interview studies. Commonly, these issues are framed as the insider/ outsider debate.

Insider/Outsider Issues

Broadly conceived, the "insider" perspective suggests that the experience of having grown up in a community, having a shared racial or ethnic membership, or having some other kind of shared experience increases the quality, legitimacy, and value of a research project. For example, Victor Rios in his book *Punished: Policing the Lives of Black and Latino Boys* and Randol Contreras in *The Stickup Kids: Race, Drugs, Violence, and the American Dream* highlight the unique advantages they had from having grown up in the communities they studied and, when they were young, having had some involvement in key activities. Although Rios observes that he was both an "outsider" and an "insider," he notes that "the fact that I also encountered harassment by police ... looking like the boys allowed me to embody a keen sense of what these young people were experiencing."[26] The young men in his study referred to him using the highly respected status as "O.G. Vic," where O.G. stood for "original gangster." This status helped him to gain trust and facilitated access. Still, he also writes, "I acknowledge that my insider status limited my observations" as the young men might have sought to please him, and he may have made assumptions based on his (negative) experiences with the police. In his comment here, Rios acknowledges a classic issue that the insiders bring advantages in terms of access and trust. Nonetheless, these advantages may create a vision that takes for granted key issues and misses others. Insiders may also have difficulty forging relationships with others in the community who are outside of their normal realm.[27]

Others cite the fresh perspective that outsiders bring. In her book *The Dignity of Working Men: Morality and the Boundaries of Race, Class, and Immigration,* Michèle Lamont cited the benefits of having a "not readily identifiable" accent from being raised as a Québecoise who has lived in France and the United States. As she interviewed American men, "Most ... were aware of my foreignness ... which allowed me to question them on taken-for-granted notions (e.g., the meaning of the concept of *phony*) that a native researcher could not have explored as freely."[28] Outsiders are often presumed to be ignorant of cultural mores, and they can ask more freely than others. This can be an advantage.

In this hotly debated issue of insider/outsider, which is particularly contested in the arena of race and ethnography, I generally take the position that "outsiders" can do a high-quality study of "insiders." Outsiders' deep respect for the people being studied is crucial along with their curiosity and openness.[29] I believe that women can do outstanding studies of men, straight people can do very strong studies of gay people, and members of one racial and ethnic group can do an impressive study of people of a different racial and ethnic background. Of course, there are always risks that an outsider will misunderstand what it is like to be someone else, especially when it involves barriers of race and class; researchers need to accept this reality as well as not assume, as Duneier points out, "that you have trust or even special rapport with the people you are trying to write about, even when it seems you do."[30] Nonetheless, outsiders also can bring fresh insights. They can see things that an "insider" status may prevent others from recognizing. The outsider restriction, the idea that only people with the same membership can study each other, also has the unfortunate consequence of restricting people in one social position to studying only people like them. (For instance, this position implies that you could study only your own community, whether that is in terms of your racial and ethnic background, social class, sexual orientation, gender, religious affiliation, and so forth.) Furthermore, in the end, any study is limited. Creating a research design where you study multiple groups has many benefits. Although it creates more work, it helps to defuse some of the criticism on outsider/insider issues. That said, excellent work has been done from both outsider and insider perspectives on the issue of racial and ethnic membership.

Although the "insider/outsider" quandary has gotten the most attention around issues of racial and ethnic membership as well as gender, there are also major challenges when you (i.e., the researcher) are middle-class and the people you are studying are economically disadvantaged. Of course, there are also challenges when you "study up," researching people who are wealthy if you are not. And there are challenges when you study people like yourself.

Given the charged nature of the insider/outsider debate, whatever position you take you will be open to criticism by those who hold a different view. A key goal is to create a number of studies completed by insiders and outsiders where the imperfect knowledge accumulates, eventually achieving a more and more complete picture. Still, it is important that you read deeply about the insider-outsider debates and think through your view. You also want to cite methodological pieces defending your position. Make a decision that makes the most sense for this project, and the limitations you face, and when you are inevitably questioned on the matter, you can convey a thoughtful, nuanced defense of your position.

Your Research Journey: An Overview

Carrying out a study is an intellectual journey. Here, I provide a brief overview of the key steps, recognizing, of course, that each study unfolds somewhat differently. As table 2.2 shows, there are dis-

Table 2.2. *An Intellectual Journey: An Evolving Focus*

Typical Steps in a Journey	Research Question	Literature	Data and Analysis	Examples of Research Questions[a]
Beginning of the study	An initial research question	Knowledge of the literature: you have a hunch of something that bothers you or you see the literature as incomplete.	Create a plan for collecting data, an IRB, permission.	How does social class shape kids' lives outside of school?
First steps of the study	An emerging research question	Revisiting of the literature: using your data, you consider what is missing from the literature.	Collect data. Think about what you are learning. Begin to focus. Think about your contribution.	Are middle-class kids busier than working-class kids?
Middle of the study (The middle section may be repeated a number of times: *seeking feedback* from others and listening carefully	A number of emerging research questions that are headed in different directions

Revise the research questions in light of your deepening | Revisit the literature: using your data, sharpen and focus your critique of what is missing from the literature. | Focus your data collection to answer the research questions you have posed.

Begin to build an emerging intellectual position (i.e., an | Many questions: How does gender shape kids' lives by class? How does race shape kids' lives by class? Why do parents differ in their strategies? |

is critical during this time.)	understanding of the literature and of your emerging findings so that the question, literature, and data are all in sync with one another. Set priorities.		argument) from your data. How do your findings contribute to the literature? Look for disconfirming evidence for your thesis. Systematically code your data.	How do parents' cultural tastes vary? How do parents interact differently with professionals in institutions? What role do kids' preferences play in their activities?
End of the study	An ultimate major research question (Other questions are subordinated to the main question or "spun off" for separate papers.)	A focused statement of how your study enhances the literature.	On the basis of your data, develop a final argument (or thesis) that is your contribution to the literature	Question: How does social class shape the cultural logics of child rearing? (Answer: All parents want their children to be healthy and happy, but middle-class parents engage in concerted cultivation and working-class and poor families engage in the accomplishment of natural growth.)

a These research questions are based on Lareau, *Unequal Childhoods*.

tinct parts of your intellectual journey. First, in the "beginning" you have a preliminary hunch or critique of the literature, an initial research question, and a plan to begin the collection of data. Then, in your "first steps" you collect data, think about what you are learning, and begin to focus. As you move into the "middle of the study" your data collection leads you to revise so that you have a number of research questions. You consider what your data are showing. You revisit the literature to sharpen your critique. You begin to develop an intellectual position (i.e., a thesis) that captures what you are finding. Once you have this thesis, you look for disconfirming evidence to challenge your thesis.[31] (This process repeats the steps in the "middle" of then considering your research questions, sharpening your critique, looking at your data, assessing the strength of your evidence, looking for disconfirming evidence, and, drawing on your body of evidence, developing your argument about what you are finding.) Often one study could go into multiple directions, but you have to make choices based on where you have the strongest data, what *you* are most interested in studying, what others see as your strongest contribution, and other factors. Finally, in the "end of the study," you have an ultimate research question, a critique of the literature, a focused body of data, and an analysis of how your data offers a fresh contribution to the literature. The critique, data, and analytic conclusions constitute your final argument. Methodological appendices sometimes provide a vivid account of the researcher's intellectual journey.[32]

In this book, chapter 8 has a focused discussion of data analysis, but, realistically, data analysis is "baked into" the entire data collection process by writing memos, talking to others, listening to people who give you feedback, and focusing.[33]

In sum, it is common to start with one question, have the project swell to multiple questions (heading in different directions), and then, based on the strength of your data, your priorities that you have developed by listening, and the feedback you have received, end with one central, revised research question. (The remaining questions are subordinated to your primary question or "spun off" as side projects.) As you collect data, you keep trying to clarify your research focus. At the end of your study, your findings ideally contribute to the literature by describing a group or, even better, addressing an analytic question. Hence, even in the earliest stages of data collection, you begin to consider what you are learning. Usually your data set is uneven. You have a lot of excellent data on some points; you have more sketchy data on other points. Your data collection process reflects your intellectual priorities. In the early stages of your study, your preliminary research question, literature, and data don't usually fit together perfectly. This is normal. (Chapter 8 discusses this challenge in depth.) Sometimes you need to radically change your research question in light of what you have learned.

RESPONDING TO CRITICS: SCRIPTS TO ADDRESS THE 4 R'S

Jack Katz coined the phrase the "4 R's" to characterize four questions readers repeatedly raise about qualitative studies: representativeness, reactivity, reliability, and replication (see table 2.3).[34] It is helpful for you to consider the 4 R's for two reasons: you want to take stock of your own views and you want to prepare answers for when you are asked challenging questions by others about these enduring issues. Although your response will depend on your project and your views, I very briefly share possible responses to these concerns. Regarding the worry of representativeness, to the best of your ability, you should compare your study to comparable populations to see whether there is anything deeply unusual about your study population. (If it is atypical, then clarify why this deviant case is illuminating.) Since this is arguably the most common question qualitative researches are asked, I address it at length in chapter 9. The issue of reactivity is also a concern, particularly in participant observation, but if you visit frequently in a participant observation study, people will get used to you and probably revert back to more typical behavior. It also helps to ask in an "exit interview" with your research participants how things were different when you were there. (Children or people who are unusually forthright are especially good to ask.) To address reliability, you want to keep interviewing until you stop learning new things; visit your site many times over several months to see whether you learn different things when you are there. Ideally, you will also vary the time of day, day of week, and, if possible, people you hang out with at the site. You also want to seek disconfirming evidence that might undermine your thesis. In terms of replicability, you can note that there are often common patterns in research findings regardless of who conducts the research. For example, ethno-

Table 2.3. *The 4 R's*

	What you can say in response to these questions
Representativeness— "With such a small sample, how do you know that that your results are representative?"	"My study seeks to go deeper to understand the meaning of the events. The goal is not to generalize. Instead, I am trying to improve our understanding of key social processes. I focus on unpacking the factors that matter—often these processes are missed by other studies."
Reactivity— "Doesn't it change things to have you be there?"	"Yes, the researcher is inevitably part of the data collection process; this piece is unavoidable. Still, it is tiring for people to act differently than they normally do. In a participant observation study people can't have their 'golden manners' for long periods of time. Usually they adjust. (You see this on reality TV too.)"
Reliability— "Don't your results vary a lot by when you go or who you interview? Are the results unreliable?"	"Reliability is about whether you will get the same results if you do a study on a different day. This is less of a problem using my method than other methods since my participant observation is not a one-shot survey, but ongoing for a while. You look for consistent themes across time."
Replicability— "Can your results be replicated?"	"Not exactly since my site is confidential and each study is quite distinctive, but there is a tradition of looking across studies for similar findings. There are many different studies. Each one contributes." Also: "I would hope that a scholar in my site asking a similar question would find comparable results."

graphic studies in different locations with very different investigators often show similar patterns.[35] In addition, you can look for consistency between your findings and a range of other studies.

Sometimes the questions about the 4 R's are illuminating and sometimes the questions are difficult (since there is not a lot you can do about some of the challenges). But, not all criticisms are equally consequential for your findings. Remember that there are flaws in every single study, and yours is no exception.

You will decide what you want to say when people pose the 4 R's, but table 2.3 includes scripts I have relied on when others have queried me.

The Qualities That Characterize Excellent Work

As you are beginning a project, it is helpful to reflect on what you hope to do by the end of the study. Do you want to write something from it? What would the length and audience be for your piece? Can you find role models done by others in a similar position? In addition, will you want to share photos or film? Some ethnographers, including Mitchell Duneier, have made films on the site of their fieldwork.[36] What you envision as the final product shapes the kind of consent you need to collect. Photos are extremely powerful for audiences to see. Playing an audio of someone's voice is also very compelling. To do this, however, you need to get IRB approval to ask the participants' permission ahead of time.

In addition, it is helpful to think a bit about how others might evaluate your work, and what expectations they might have of it. Although there is some disagreement among social scientists, they tend to agree more than they disagree about the standards for excellence. There are many different ways of discerning these standards, including Lincoln and Guba's discussion of the "trustworthiness" of a research project.[37] But many of these standards essentially pose the question: so what? For example, guides to proposal writing stress it is important that you set the context, explain the "payoff" of the proposed study, and situate it in the literature.

As the authors of one influential guide to writing a proposal state: "Help your reader understand where the problem intersects the main theoretical debates in your field and show how this inquiry puts established ideas to the test or offers new ones. Good proposals demonstrate

WHAT ARE KEY CHARACTERISTICS OF EXCELLENT WORK?

- clear contribution to new knowledge
- succinct assessment of previous literature that shows the holes in the literature
- a research question that can be answered with the data in hand
- breadth and depth in the data collection
- clear exposition of the results
- deep analysis that links the evidence to the interpretation
- acknowledgment of disconfirming evidence
- a discussion that uses the case as a springboard to reflect on more general concerns
- discussion of implications for ideas and practices

awareness of alternative viewpoints and argue the author's position in such a way as to address the field broadly, rather than developing a single sectarian tendency indifferent to alternatives."[38] Similarly, the guidelines for the National Science Foundation emphasize that award-winning grants will "suggest and explore creative, original, or potentially transformative concepts" and "benefit society or advanced desired social outcomes (i.e., broader impacts)."

As part of your reflection on the key elements of excellent work, you should also line up the articles and books that you have read and admired (as well as award-winning works in your field) and make a list of the qualities these works share. (You can also do a similar list for some of the worst pieces you have read. It is instructive.) These exercises help you map out your goals on your journeys. Unfortunately, although you will have done some "quality checks" of your own work as you go along, and you will have a sense of the value of what you have done, you may not always be the best person to evaluate whether you have reached the goals you set for yourself. Only others will be able to provide this assessment. So, get feedback early and often. Don't wait! Both peers and those who are in a position of power over you are helpful. The feedback will help you take stock of where you have been and where you are headed on your journey. Of course, you want to think about the works you admire, the theoretical ideas you find exciting, and the kind of piece you would like to write. It is helpful to have a role model to guide you. You will want to return to the goals for your project—your "North Star"—throughout the journey but especially during the data analysis and writing stages.

Summing Up: Beginning a Study

The earliest stages of a new study are full of paradoxes. You want to be familiar with other studies, but you don't want to be too bogged down by them since, after all, you are trying to do something new. You need to have an initial research question, but you want to accept that it will change as you collect data. You want to make a plan for your study, and you want to have a reason for the (hard) decisions you are making. But, you don't want to worry too much about adjustments and trade-offs as there is no perfect study. You want to be sensitive to your social position and how it shapes what you see. But worrying about your position in a global fashion (such as your racial and ethnic background, social class position, and age) is less valuable than being attuned, concretely, to how your position shapes your study. Finally, each study is unique, but there are widely shared criteria of what constitutes excellent work. And, although uncertainty is challenging, it is valuable to accept the intrinsic uncertainty of the situation. There are many things you don't know. That is why you are doing the study. It is also exciting to begin a study, and it is ideal to try to enjoy this anticipation and pleasure as you embark on your journey.

3

Preparing

The Early Steps in a Study

Somewhat surprisingly, research studies have a nontrivial number of logistical elements. You need to find and gain access to the people you are studying, figure out what to tell them about your study, and decide whether the actual name of the study location will be masked. On a more personal level, you must consider your safety, transportation, and attire. Once you collect data, you want to create a system for organizing the research materials, so you can easily retrieve them. Regular memos will help you think as well as focus your data collection. Since there are many uncertainties in the process of doing interviews and participant observation, the research process is anxiety producing. In this chapter, I discuss all of these issues. But approval by the institutional review board (IRB) for the protection of human subjects is essential, and so I begin there.

Institutional Review Boards

Any journey inevitably runs into obstacles. Doing participant observation research has a particularly significant headache: getting permission from the IRB for the protection of human subjects to carry out the work. In addition to the IRB office at your college, an organization you are studying may have their own IRB (e.g., hospitals, school districts, and Native American reservations). IRBs grew out of past abuses, when researchers acted in unconscionable ways (e.g., the infamous Tuskegee syphilis study where key information was withheld from the low-income African American men in the study, and they were not treated with penicillin even after it became available).[1] Briefly, the IRB is intended to protect research subjects (i.e., human subjects) from harm by requiring researchers to advise their study participants of risks, and to ask them to give their informed consent. The IRB has a simple but important set of rights that it seeks to uphold: people have the right to not be in a study, they cannot be coerced to be in a study, they can stop their participation in a study any time, and they must be told the nature of the research. The ethical principle of beneficence (where you, the researcher, have the welfare of the research participant as a goal in the study) is another important priority. We do not intend or want our research to harm people. If the research might possibly cause harm, participants need to be told about this in advance so they can give informed consent. If you were participating in a study, you too would want to know about potential harm so you would be able to give your informed consent.

NOT AN EASY MARRIAGE: WORKING WITH THE IRB

Not everyone has to file an IRB application. Usually, students in a class who do not want to ever publish results can skip applying for clearance from an IRB. For the rest of us, it is mandatory. Unfortunately, since IRBs have their roots in a medical model, they are particularly ill-suited to research using participant observation and, to a lesser extent, in-depth interviews. There is a culture clash in the bureaucratic gatekeeping demands of the IRB and the emergent "figure it out as you go along" character of ethnographic work. IRB offices have application forms for you to fill out, and when you submit these forms you are creating an "IRB protocol" (which means that you are following an official procedure). IRB policies are established by the federal government, but the norms around implementation vary enormously across local institutions.

> **IRB APPROVAL TAKES TIME**
> Going through IRB is like going through airport security before a flight. Since almost everyone eventually gets through, you will likely too.
> But you can't be in a hurry.

I have included an appendix for this chapter where I provide a deeper discussion of how to successfully meet IRB requirements and gain approval for your project. For now, here are the key points:

- You can't be in a hurry, so you should start early; allow one semester ahead of time to get your application approved.
- Always have an IRB protocol on file for a study (unless you are

a student in an official class, and you are sure that you will *never* publish the study).

- File an IRB protocol for an interview study, begin to do interviews, and then file an "amendment" to incorporate future participant observation. Processing amendments is usually faster and easier than the original submission.
- You should state your study's central questions more broadly than more narrowly, so you have more flexibility as your project evolves (e.g., "I am studying the challenges people face at work" rather than "I want to study power and authority at work").

Decide about Confidentiality

I was introducing a speaker once at a small, "brown bag" seminar; the speaker was there to discuss a recently published second book. Before the seminar I was in a rush, and I (foolishly) relied on a CV, but I didn't look up the details. I had gone to graduate school with this scholar, and I heard many people discuss the particular organization that was the focus of the first book. So, in my introduction, embellishing my prepared comments, I named it. The speaker turned pale, and abruptly interrupted me to say the name was not public information. I was deeply embarrassed. As I reflected on this social gaffe, I realized that part of the problem was that the name of the organization had been common knowledge around the department. Since a number of people mentioned it, it didn't dawn on me it was confidential. Hence, before you begin, you should decide about the confidentiality of the site or whether you will "mask" the community and the people. If you are going to protect the identity, you should tell very few people—your advisors, and, if necessary, a partner. Everyone else—other students, friends, relatives, employers, neighbors, and colleagues—should be told the code name. This means that you need to choose the code name extremely early and always refer to your community and participants using the code name. (You can change the code name, however, as many times as you want until you publish.)

People disagree about the practice of masking the name of the research site. While it was historically common for social scientists to obscure the name of the research site, that practice is the subject of a vigorous debate.[2] (Journalists, by the way, vehemently disagree with the idea of hiding the identity of the focus of a study.) Some take a hybrid approach. For example, scholars name the city since it makes it more accurate, allows the reader to understand the context, and provides valuable details, but then keep the identity of the organization or school district (and local school) confidential along with the actual names of people in the study. Of course, some scholars feel strongly they should name the people they are studying so that they can voice their concerns. Others, equally vigorously, disagree. But, no matter what you decide, make this decision early and make it clear to the participants in study materials.

I follow the tradition of concealing the identity of the people I study. I do not want my findings to embarrass or harm people. By offering confidentiality, even if people guess the identity, research participants can deny that they participated. And, many research participants make confidentiality a condition of their participation. In my latest study, which involves people with over ten million dollars in assets, I am asking deeply personal questions about the nature of their wealth and their plans for bequests. The study would be impossible to do if I had to name the respondents. Indeed, the people promoting the virtues of not giving people confidentiality have, at times, been urban ethnographers studying public spaces. Family life is more intimate. It is also good to protect children from possible embarrassment in the future.

If people are connected to one another, revealing the name of one organization or community can inadvertently reveal others. (Often, it is easy to connect the dots.) Also, citing documents that are searchable via an online exploration also can be revealing. One possibility, as Jessica Calarco suggests, is that you "mask to the level necessary to make it sufficiently difficult to determine who any one individual might be."[3] If you are masking the community you are studying, it is helpful to think of a well-known "sister" neighborhood or city that is comparable to the site you are studying. Then, when people ask where you are doing the research, I suggest that you breezily tell them something like this, "Well, the name of the community is actually confidential, but the area is an upper-middle-class affluent suburb similar to [name of a comparable site some distance away]." Some people can be extremely aggressive, badgering you to divulge the name of the actual site. Even if you have had too much to drink or you are having a heart-to-heart conversation with someone with whom you feel close, you should not share where you are doing the research if you have promised people confidentiality. If someone is pestering you, you need to be firm, make a joke ("What are you, the CIA? Is this an interrogation?"), and then change the subject.

Whom Do You Ask? Recruiting People to Your Study

Researchers recruiting people to interview and gaining access to a field site usually rely on "the strength of a weak tie" (i.e., an acquaintance).[4] In other words, your network of friends, relatives, and acquaintances can help you begin. The reason why this is a good idea is that the person can vouch for you. Figure out whom you want to study. Then, ask everyone you know whether they can connect you with a potential study site or study participants: neighbors, relatives, friends you haven't seen in years, Facebook friends, peers, professors, alumni from your earlier educational institutions, and anyone else you can think of. (Of course, you want to sound out your contacts first to make sure that they are comfortable making a request on your behalf.)

How you make the request varies: you should do what seems most comfortable for the person you are recruiting. Texting is especially valuable for younger people; for older populations, emailing, phoning, and letters all work. If possible, ask your contact to reach out to the person for you, and gain permission for you to reach out to the potential respondent. When you reach out, wait a week the first time for an answer. Then, I would touch base with my contact or, possibly, reach out a second time. If there is still no answer, I would give up, or wait months before trying again.

Not everyone is appropriate to be included in your study. Do not ask people whom you supervise or over whom you have some other form of power. For various reasons, it may not be appropriate among some groups such as family members, in-laws, or work colleagues. If so, steer clear. Also, my rule of thumb is to never interview someone with whom I would cross paths socially in the future. (The reason is because studying, especially interviewing, is not a reciprocal relationship since the person is doing the revealing to you. In this regard, you have something in common with a doctor, counselor, or social worker.) For example, when I didn't have enough Black middle-class parents of a ten-year-old child from my school observations for *Unequal Childhoods*, I started asking everyone I know whether they knew a family in this criteria or if they knew someone who might know someone who qualified for my study. If I was introduced to possible respondents who were in my current (or likely future) social world, then I declined to pursue the possibility of an interview, but I usually would ask them if they knew someone. In a different approach, researchers can get permission to hang out in a waiting room of a doctor's office (or other suitable kind of office); the receptionist can give the patient a flyer and direct them to a member of the research team or the researcher can simply approach the patient to explain the study.[5] Others recruit via online groups and use a "screener survey"; potential respondents fill out the survey. If they qualify, the researcher reaches out to them for an interview.

If you are hoping to study an organization, turning to your networks is also vastly faster, and usually more successful, than gaining access to an organization without sponsorship. In addition, in some settings it is the only way. Here is what you should do. You should have a very brief description of your study—four or five sentences. Ideally it should be on letterhead (which can be electronic) from the sponsoring university or organization. Ask everyone you know whether they know anyone in the organization or know anyone who knows someone affiliated with the organization.

Notably, at this stage, I do not describe the study in detail or ask for a 90-minute interview or to gain access to doing observation. Instead, I ask for a brief phone call. By agreeing to a fifteen-minute phone call, a potential participant is not agreeing to being in the study—only to learning more about it. It is crucial that "the ask" for an interview or to do observations be face-to-face, or in a phone call, or be after someone has "vouched" for you to the respondent. You want to avoid a "cold call" by email, text, or online since these have lower rates of success than if you have someone vouch for you. For example, in my study "Choosing Homes, Choosing Schools" with Elliot Weininger, we wanted to find three school districts to allow us to recruit parents. We needed permission from the superintendents. I did not know a single superintendent. I did, however, know someone casually who worked in an educational nonprofit. I asked whether we could have coffee to "learn about the lay of the land" in the educational sphere for a new study. We met. We recounted the goals of the study, and she very helpfully told us about possible districts or people we might approach. She knew an educator, John Larkin, who ran a group of superintendents who met regularly. She emailed him and did an introduction. I asked whether we could come to meet him in his office for 30 minutes. He agreed. In our subsequent meeting, we described the project. Mr. Larkin immediately asked me to come give a lecture to his group of superintendents. He then also graciously agreed to introduce us to some other superintendents (after asking us additional questions of whom exactly we wanted to meet). We divided the list up. I then emailed the superintendents on my list with the email subject greeting: "John Larkin suggested I reach out to you," thereby relying heavily on Mr. Larkin having vouched for me. I asked each superintendent for a face-to-face meeting about a project I was beginning "on how parents decide where to live." The email was brief. This is a slightly revised version:

> Dear Superintendent Smith:
> John Larkin suggested that I reach out to you. As I believe he mentioned, with Professor Elliot Weininger (SUNY Brockport), I have been conducting a study called "Choosing Homes, Choosing Schools" which has been studying how parents decide where to live.
> As part of the study, we are interviewing Superintendents. All of the names of the districts are confidential.
> Would you, per chance, be able to talk by phone about this in the next week? The attached paragraph provides a bit more information about the study.
> With your permission, I will contact your office next week to see if we can set up a fifteen-minute phone call. (In case you would like to reach me, my cell phone number is 555-232-2222.) By agreeing to speak with me, you are not agreeing to do the interview, but only to learn more about it.
> I know that you are a busy person. Thank you so much for considering this request.
> Yours sincerely,
> Annette Lareau

Attachment:
I am writing today because I am doing a study, with another professor, Elliot Weininger, of how parents with young children go about selecting a home. We are interested in learning more about

the factors that influence parents' decisions to locate in a particular catchment area. We are especially interested in learning about the process for parents with young children. Your name, the name of the school, community, or families will never be revealed. The community will be described as a suburban community of a large Northeastern city.

After I sent this letter, I had meetings with the superintendents. They would ask me which kind of school I wanted to study. I would give them some general criteria, and then they chose the school and introduced me to the principal, and I followed up with the principal to ask for a face-to-face meeting. All of the emails were extremely brief.

Usually, you can get your institution to give you letterhead; then you can embed the letter inside an email or attach it to the email. In addition, it can be helpful to add your position (e.g., "I am an undergraduate student at x university taking a class"). Although some people have their published works at the bottom of their email, I usually do not put a link to any published materials. But in my phone call with the potential research participant, I briefly explain prior work (i.e., "I am a sociologist who has studied the family, and I have written a couple of books about families, child rearing, and schools"). I also do an online search to see what someone will see if they search my name and review my website. In some cases, I create a specific website for a study complete with my photograph (as well as photos of research assistants), a short description of the study, and contact information. I also upload stock photos of images connected to the study.

This strategy also works in finding people to interview. You ask everyone you know whether they know anyone in the category you need. Referring to the person who vouched for you, you text or email to ask for a phone call. You phone to see whether they are willing to be in the study. Then, at the very end of the interview, you ask whether they know anyone else you can interview. I also ask them (often a few minutes later when we are walking to the door), "Would it be okay if I connect with in you a bit, maybe a few weeks, just to touch base about possibly getting connected to some folks?" You can joke about doing a little "nudge" without being a pest. If you write a handwritten thank you note or send a little gift, that will nudge the person to do the introduction. In this "snowball sample" (i.e., where research participants recruit others or provide referrals), some people restrict the number of respondents they take from one person (particularly if the topic is social networks or something where you need a variety of people).

Still, there are times when you cannot find anyone who knows someone. In that case, depending on whom you are studying, you might be able to reach out to them via a social media platform. For example, Sangeun "Shawn" Kim, a senior at Penn, contacted 20 high school graduates on public Instagram accounts of graduates of Lincoln High School; since eight of them agreed to be interviewed, he was quite successful. He had an informal, friendly approach:

> Hey! I know this is kinda random, but are you a Lincoln alum?
>
> Yep!
>
> Oh, clutch! I'm actually a rising senior at Penn. And I'm working on a project about [a program on racial literacy]. I've been talking to a lot of Lincoln alum and interviewing them virtually. I was wondering you'd be interested in sharing your perspective?
>
> Yeah, that'd be cool.
>
> Sangeun "Shawn" Kim

He created a new, public Instagram account for the project with two smiling photos of himself and one with a caption: "this account is for research—if you are an alum from xxx high school, pls HMU [hit me up]!"

Other times, you might need to write a letter. Receiving postal mail is increasingly rare, and so it may get more attention. Although slightly odd, in the letter you can say, "With your permission, I will reach out to your office to see if I can set up a phone call for 15 minutes." Then when you call the office, you say, "I am following up on my letter, and I am touching base to see if I might set up a very brief phone call with Mr./Ms. X." Another possibility, however, is to call and ask to speak to the assistant of the person you are trying to talk with and then ask the assistant whether you can set up a short phone call. If it is possible to drop by, you can hand deliver the letter. In other office settings, it is possible, and desirable, to follow up a letter with a personal visit. In some cases, if it seems comfortable for you, you can bring a very small gift such as home-baked cookies in the holiday season, tomatoes from your garden in summer, or brownies (from a mix) that you made. This is intended to be an honest gesture to smooth the transaction; although certainly strategic, it is critical that it be given without any expectation that the person will help you. (You can say, "I like to bake, and I had a bunch extra, and so I brought these along—hope you don't

mind. Maybe there is someone in the office who might be interested?")
For example, Rachel Ellis wanted to study a woman's prison, and she
needed IRB approval from both the internal review board of the prison
and the university.[6] After Ellis's original proposal was rejected by the
prison without explanation, and the revised proposal was languishing,
Ellis dropped by the Department of Corrections' administrative office.
She knew the name of the person who had received the application,
and she brought by oatmeal chocolate chip Christmas cookies (saying
they were "extra") and asked whether they knew when the proposal
might be reviewed. Ultimately, she was admitted. When you drop by,
you don't ask for an answer to your request. You ask only whether they
know when they might review your request and whether they need any
additional information. At times, it is helpful to have a résumé or curriculum vitae with the letter and list of references. For example, when I
was asking families to be observed for my book *Unequal Childhoods*, I
listed the minister at my church as a reference.

But, before you start asking, you want to practice telling people
about the study.

What to Tell People

Most people are not that interested in what you are doing. In
addition, although all studies have bias, you want to minimize the impact you have on the behavior of people you are studying.[7] Hence, you
want to accurately tell respondents the goal of the study, broadly conceived, but it is better not to provide too much detail. It is good to come
up with an "elevator speech" to describe your study. It is essential that
the speech is accurate. But, as I show in the table below, the speech
should be extremely brief—only seconds in length. Since your focus
will likely change over time, the speech should be *vague but accurate.*

Creating this speech is harder than it might seem. You want to avoid
jargon. You also don't want it to be overly detailed. For example, given
research that shows that researchers have an impact on a setting (see
classic "Hawthorne effect" from studies of a Western Electric Plant),
you want to minimize your impact on the community.[8] It is not possible
to eliminate your impact, but you do not want to present a great deal
of detail lest people might, unconsciously or not, end up altering their
behavior in order to help you. For example, if you are interested in "invisible labor" that women do in taking care of family life compared to

Table 3.1. *Sample Introductory Speeches*

	Bad introductory speeches	What are the problems?	Revised speeches
Description of study	*Social class is correlated with educational achievement. I want to decode the mechanisms through which these processes unfold.*	Jargon (social class, correlated, achievement) Focus is unclear	*I am interested in understanding the school experiences of children from different walks of life.*
Request to carry out a study	*I am beginning an ethnography of a school where I will be a participant observer.*	Jargon (i.e., ethnography, participant observer) Also unclear what you are asking from them	*I am trying to understand how family life spills into school life. If it is okay with you, I'd like to visit your classroom twice a week for two or three hours at a time that works well for you.*

men, you might be tempted to be extremely honest with people and say, "I want to know all the planning you and other women are doing to run the family that men are spared." This statement gives the research participants a great deal of information, and they may protest that there is no need for them to be in the study since they don't plan. In addition, respondents may try to please you by discussing more the planning that they do or, even more importantly, think that they should be planning and so increase the planning that they take up. Thus, you want a speech that is *vague but accurate.* You might say, "I am interested in how much work it takes to make family life happen and help people get through the day" or "I am interested in work-family balance."

Most importantly, if you are recruiting people to the study, you want to be clear about what you are asking them to do. (This is, by the way, what the IRB wants you to do, too.) Work on your speech until you've got it down pat. Practice it standing and aloud in front of friends. It is common for people to shift uncomfortably while they give their speeches, look down, fiddle with their hair, glasses, or hands, or otherwise exude nervousness. If possible, you want to avoid doing those things. To help you get the hang of it, you should practice your speech at least fifteen times (i.e., when you are making coffee in the morning, as you do exercises, or in other routines of daily life). After you say the speech, it is a good idea to show interest in the person and begin building rapport. You might ask the person a question (i.e., "Do you work here?" "How long have you been at the company?") or offer a comment ("This seems like a really nice place" or even "Nice weather we are having these days"). You want to make people feel comfortable.

What to Wear

The presentation of self in research is an issue, especially in participant observation where you visit often. Although you are observing, you are part of the context.

How the participants perceive you makes a difference in the level of trust that they extend to you. Often the researcher is a different race, class, and gender than the people in the study. As sociologists have taught us, our class positions are inflected into our cultural tastes and dispositions.[9] Clothing is one way that people reflect their social positions and taste. Many studies have shown the importance of race in shaping social interactions, identity, and other crucial issues. Gender plays a role; women are often under social pressure to wear a wider array of decorative clothing than men. In addition, clothing (and hair) are tied up with your identity. Being a fieldworker involves the contradictory challenges of blending into a new social setting and yet remaining authentic to your core identity.

A friend who hired people to do face-to-face surveys for a university research institute always hired people who dressed in extremely clean and crisp clothing. The clothing did not need to be fancy, but it needed to look fresh. Since many academics adopt a style of looking weathered and slightly grungy, this guideline is not as obvious as one might think. In addition, clothing should be relatively neutral; unless

CLOTHES TO BUILD RAPPORT

I have a pair of turquoise sneakers that I really like and when I wore them to my site one day, I got A TON of compliments on them because apparently they look a lot like another pair of sneakers designed by a popular rapper. I started planning my fieldwork outfits around being able to wear those shoes since it seemed to start a lot of productive and fun conversations with students.

Nora Gross,
Brothers in Grief

there is a good reason for doing so, your clothing should not clearly denote your social class; nor should it have a funky look. It is a good idea to choose clothes that you can wear in all social situations and still blend in well enough. Concretely this might mean wearing jeans (particularly black jeans), new looking tennis shoes, and a crisp t-shirt or sweatshirt or, in a dressier version, plain dark pants, flats, and a plain, crisp top. (The specifics will vary as fashions shift.) Sweatshirts or t-shirts that have the names of the university are a good option. Although they are class laden, they are a reminder of your identity to the people you are studying. The only exception to this is if dressing in a particular style is a really important part of your identity; in this case, the psychological cost of wearing different clothes would be too high. Some researchers, particularly people of color, may feel pressure to dress so they will be seen as legitimate. Still, issues around clothing can happen in all settings.[10] Wearing special clothes to the field can be complicated. It can mean that you have to change clothes in a bathroom at work or in your car as you leave one setting to go to another. (This may feel slightly ridiculous.)

I tend to have a few outfits for fieldwork that I always put on. Since it is tiring to do fieldwork and, as I explain elsewhere, sometimes you have to drag yourself out the door to do the work, having standardized outfits—almost a sort of uniform—has been helpful for me. When I was doing the research for *Unequal Childhoods*, I normally wore neutral, casual clothes: a crisp t-shirt and black or khaki pants. The importance of wearing these clothes was driven home to me one day when I popped by the home of a white working-class family (the Yanellis) after a meeting with higher-ups at the university. I was rushing around that day, and I did not really think much about it until I parked in front of their small row house. Looking at my expensive tailored purple wool suit, shiny black heels, and thin gold necklace, I realized how different I looked. I was wearing clothes that they would never buy or wear.

(I probably reminded them of how their employers look.) Even though it was deep in the fieldwork, Mr. and Ms. Yanelli were visibly taken aback. I also could not figure out a way to joke about it; it was just plain awkward. Thus, if you dress in a way that is foreign to the people you are studying, clothing can create a boundary. This boundary can be crossed, but it takes time and energy.

Decisions regarding attire are particularly sensitive when researchers are of a different social position than research participants. Fundamentally, researchers need to be authentic to themselves. In his book, *For White Folks Who Teach in the Hood—and the Rest of Y'all Too*, Christopher Emdin directly suggests that urban educators make adjustments in their clothing to connect with the youth in their classrooms—for example, by wearing sneakers that the youth admire. This principle—of connecting with folks you are studying through shared clothing—is a good one. Yet, you cannot pretend to be someone you are not by dressing in a contrived fashion. The clothing must be authentic: ideally it is similar to how you would normally dress with some tweaks.

Safety in the Field

Worries about safety happen in many different ways. It is always important to "listen" to yourself and your sense of risk and to act accordingly. There are contradictory patterns around safety. On the one hand, some worries of safety are exaggerated. Instead of being attacked and harmed in the course of research, the most common risks to safety are mundane ones—car accidents, motorcycle accidents, pedestrian accidents, or household accidents. For example, one interview study of Walmart workers with 20 researchers had five "minor" car accidents in one summer.[11] So, the risk of a researcher being harmed is not zero. On the other hand, danger exists. The risk of sexual assault is a particular concern, especially with acquaintances or people in positions of power.[12] Sociologists who have studied gangs, such as Randol Contreras, have also written extensively on the difficulty that can ensue for them, and the priority of sustaining trust by masking research sites.[13]

In such moments, local knowledge and guidance is helpful. Often interviewees or people in the study will provide help figuring out who in the team is vulnerable to being accosted and how to manage the context. When I was doing family observations for the study that became *Unequal Childhoods*, I was warned by many to stay away from low-income neighborhoods due to safety issues. I concluded that some of the hostility I experienced from naysayers was connected to more general patterns of systematic racial inequality and whites' aversion to entering all Black neighborhoods. Hence, I did not follow this advice. By the end of the study I concluded that the risk to my safety and that of the research assistants had been exaggerated.[14] The risks to researchers vary by, among other factors, the demographic characteristics of the researcher. Scholars of color can receive a cool reception by upper-middle-class white families, as Karyn Lacy documented.[15] Or, scholars of color can feel threatened, for example, in white communities brandishing signs of racial hostility. For these researchers, public settings offer additional advantages.

It is ideal for everyone to take precautions. Always let someone know where you are going. You don't want to flash money or expensive items around (remove watches, leave computers at home or lock them in the trunk before going to the site). You could have a friend drop you off and pick you up, or even have them go with you (you can return the favor for their study, or in some other meaningful way). A more difficult situation is when the risk is from the respondent or a friend of the key respondent; there is an extensive literature on these challenges.[16] In sum, some assessments of danger are exaggerated, but some are not. There are no easy answers, and how much risk a researcher is willing to bear is a highly personal decision. Stranger attacks are rare; attacks by acquaintances are much more common. Your safety is paramount. Hence, you want to feel free to leave a scene if you feel uncomfortable or unsafe. Of course, you can say (gripping your stomach) that "I am really sorry, but I don't feel well all of a sudden. My stomach is queasy, and I am afraid that I might be sick." Then leave immediately. You can apologize later.

Data Management

You want to set up a system of organization for recording your data accurately, frequently, and systematically before you start data collection. Indeed, as you are rushing around doing this and that, it is easy for the organizational aspect of the project to fall by the wayside. Even if you are fastidious in your organization of daily life (and many people are not), it is easy to find yourself unable to accurately report the number of interviews you have completed or number of visits because you didn't write down everything in one location. You can try to reconstruct it, but it can take hours. Further complications emerge when computers fail, and some researchers have (regretfully) not kept a back-up. (Before the days of computers, some anxious scholars used to keep their manuscripts in the freezer in case of fire.)

There are multiple forms of data that need to be organized: electronic copies (i.e., on the computer), back-up copies, hard copies, documents, and sound recordings of interviews. In addition, projects have consent forms, proposals, and other administrative paperwork. It is complex and, for some, overwhelming. Still, as Julie Morgenstern has written eloquently in the helpful book *Organizing from the Inside Out*, not having a system can create havoc as people lose data or waste hours searching for something. The key is to find a system that works for you.

There is an extensive literature, among researchers and organizers, on what to do. The system you create should be relatively simple, with only a few principal files with many more subfolders. For example, on my computer, I have only about one dozen principal files (e.g., department, teaching, students, papers, and so forth); in addition, each current study has a principal file (i.e., wealth study, refugee study, upward mobility study). For each study, within the principal folder, I have a data folder (described below). As noted, I have a folder for "papers"; here I create a new folder for each working paper on the study (with subfolders for drafts, conference power points, feedback from others, journal submissions, and so forth). For each paper I create a file called "feedback," where I put notes from conversations I have had with others, reviews, and critical assessments of the work (in addition to a "feedback" folder for every paper I write). As the project progresses, I create more folders, such as a separate folder for every conference paper I present. I always leave the original data in the home file, but then I move duplicate copies of the data into the paper file. I merrily create as many files as I wish (i.e., "extra," "good quote," and "intro") while I am working on the paper. Months later, I go back and eliminate everything except the final, published paper and the feedback that I received on the paper. The folder system has endless possibilities. You could organize it by analytic terms (e.g., social capital). You could organize it by month or year of fieldwork. It really does not matter, but the system should not be too complicated. It should clarify, rather than obscure, your data. I also have an Excel "tracking" file to keep abreast of the interviews and observations I have completed as well as if they have been transcribed, coded, and so forth. My "original data file" with the real names and code names is set aside; for the day-to-day, I only use code names.

ORGANIZING YOUR DATA

For each study, under the principal folder, I have an "organization" folder, where I keep subfolders for IRB, email correspondence, grant proposals, receipts, and so forth.

Each study also has a "data" folder that includes audio files, transcribed interviews, background information on the respondents, field notes, and documents. I organize field notes by site (or family). Then, within the folder it is by date with a descriptive file name to summarize what I observed (e.g., dinner May 8, graduation party May 9). For some studies, the data folder is broken into subfolders for different kinds of interviews (i.e., PTA, real estate agents, school admission officers, and parents).

In a large interview study, I like to have a system for my file names. For example, I include the identity of the respondent, their class, race, location, interviewer initials, and date on the file name. The information below comes from a study, "Choosing Homes, Choosing Schools," which I did with Elliot Weininger:

> Fisher MOM WC B City AL April 20. This means Ms. Fisher, a mom, who is working-class, African American, lives in the city school district, was interviewed by me, on this date.

> McBride DAD WC W Kingsley RH May 3. This means Mr. McBride, a father, who is working-class, white, lives in Kingsley suburban district, was interviewed by Rita Harvey on this date.

> Data

> Interviews
>   Middle-class parents
>   Goodwin MOM MC B City AL May 23
>   Goodwin DAD MC B City RH May 24
>   Working-class parents
>   Fisher MOM WC B City AL April 20
>   McBride DAD WC W Kingsley RH May 3
>   Field notes

School 1
   Back-to-school night AL Sept 10
   PTA executive committee AL Sept 15
   Halloween parade AL Oct 31

This system for assigning file names helps me remember the people. And it makes it easier to count how many people you have in different categories. Of course, you will create categories that are meaningful to you.

All of this avoids the use of real names and uses code names in the file names. The interview, however, is not redacted. (It is under a password-protected university server with two-step verification.) It is very helpful if the file name system is consistent.

Also, it is common to collect documents in a study. You want to "log" the documents in an Excel file (or some system), including critical information that is helpful to you (date you received it, where you stored it, relevance for your study, and so forth). You can assign a keyword or tag for the document. Most software programs have strategies for incorporating these documents into your data analysis. Some people photograph the documents and upload them.

> **KEEP TRACK OF YOUR DATA**
> Researchers should be very systematic about keeping track of their data—whom they interview, for how long, when they visit the site, how long, and so forth. Also, keep your list of pseudonyms handy. It can be hard to remember what you call people in your writing.
> Maia Cucchiara, author of Marketing Schools, Marketing Cities

As I explain in future chapters, you want to be extremely precise in your data collection. In addition, you want to manage your data in an organized fashion so you can easily access it, and you can have a good idea of what you have done. You want to keep good track of the interviews and field visits you have completed. There are some points in a qualitative study where it is appropriate to be flexible, and there are other times where you should be ruthlessly systematic. On data logging, you want to be systematic, and you don't want to fall behind.

THE VALUE OF MEMOS

Since your research process is emergent, you want to think along the way. Therefore, write analytic memos on a regular basis—through the planning process, data collection, coding process, and writing. These crucial memos allow you to take stock of the literature that interests you, your complaints about the weaknesses in the literature, the goals of your project, and your emerging findings. When you are actively collecting data, at the end of each day—after every interview or set of field notes—you want to write reflections of what you learned. These are very informal notes in which you try to process what you learned. But, as I explain later in the book, at least two to three times a month, you should plan to write out an analytic memo that is an effort to say something more coherent (one or two pages single-spaced in length) that you can share with friends, classmates, writing group members, or others working on a related topic. As we write, we think. We gain new insights. We often get clearer about what we are doing through the writing process. In these analytic memos, you step back and reflect on the big picture. What have you learned? What does the literature say? How are your findings different than what others have shown? What is new here? What is exciting? Why is it exciting? You can bring in field notes and interview quotes, link them to the concepts they illuminate, and show how your new data helps to correct a weakness in the literature. As you do this, you begin to sort out the contribution your study is making. (In addition, in memos, you can reflect on your own role in the field, and how it is shaping the research results.) It is also important to get regular feedback from others. Hence, you want to share your (chaotic) memos with others. As you talk to them, they will tell you what they think is exciting, which will help you focus on the most important parts of the study.

Being a Whole Person:
The Role of Your Study in Your Life

In addition to your work, you have a home, and you have created a life. You want your life to continue, even in somewhat altered form, during the study. Making the time is not simply about work schedules. If you are involved in an intimate relationship, it is useful to warn your partner that you will need to spend more time working in the coming months, and that you simply cannot go out on the nights when you have done fieldwork earlier that day, as you will need to spend that time writing field notes based on what you have observed, before you forget what you've seen. (Some researchers arrange for special breakfast or lunch dates with partners or other festive events that accommo-date the fieldwork schedule.) Interviewers and participant observers with children might consider additional childcare options. You might forewarn your extended kinship system that you will be able to visit less often for the period of the study. You might miss important family birthday parties. That said, you also need time to sleep, exercise, see your friends, and engage in other forms of self-care, and you do need to do some socializing to have balance and to "recharge your batteries." The trick here is to prepare people in your life to lower their expecta-tions for how much they will see you during the (limited time of) data collection, and also to help them feel loved and cared for throughout the fieldwork process. In short, you don't want to permanently dam-age relationships, so you need to nurture your personal relationships in meaningful ways and show gratitude to the people in your life for how they are supporting you.

Anxiety

Doing interviews and participant observation can be exciting, exhilarating, and revealing, but it is also stressful, in part because it is inherently uncertain. I have taught qualitative research methods at dif-ferent universities and have been struck by the high levels of anxiety I have witnessed in my students. And I myself have experienced signifi-cant anxiety in designing and conducting research. After many years, I have concluded that this anxiety, while having some unique elements, is not best understood as an individual quirk. Rather, it has social struc-tural roots; it is the product of the reality of doing this kind of research and the uncertain nature of how it unfolds. In particular, as I show in later chapters, there is a lot of rejection in doing this kind of work, and the rejection stings. People rebuff interview requests or ghost you. People in a field setting ignore you or are rude to you. And, there is always the risk that they will get mad and end the study. Of course, sometimes they are just having a bad day. They may be hungry, sleep deprived, or angry at a romantic partner. It may not be about you. But it is easy to feel as if you are on thin ice or you don't know what to do. (And, many students also experience an "imposter syndrome" that compounds the difficulty.) It is all new. This newness is exciting, but it is also stressful. Indeed, usually, by the time you figure it out, it is time for the data collection to end. And, in my experience, each new study has its own anxieties; experience helps some, but not as much as you would like.

In addition, the actual procedures for how you should carry out qualitative research are somewhat unclear. When I was a student, I found them to be downright mysterious. I was particularly hazy about the concrete information that I should know, the actions I should take, and the expected standards for success. Put differently, when should I have known better and have been able to prevent a problem in the field? When was a problem—such as someone declining an invitation to participate, a research site not working out, or being at risk for being kicked out of a research site—simply the price of doing business? Of course, this book seeks to provide additional guidance, but, even with relatively informed knowledge, you should expect some anxiety. Shamus Khan presses his students to create a "mental health plan" where they think about how they will take care of themselves as they move through the project.[17] In addition, as I discuss in chapter 9, beginning a "writing group" can provide a regular, safe space for you to share your emerging ideas, give you some accountability, and help you move ahead.

Even with the best preparation, however, these feelings of panic and doubt are hard to avoid, and they occur even in researchers who are doing an outstanding job in their studies. These feelings are also in some ways justified. Errors will happen even to the best of us. The unpredictable nature of fieldwork means that you will occasionally get into a jam that was hard to prevent. It is natural that you will be anxious and upset in trying to anticipate all of the problems that might arise, and even more so when they do surface, but the errors are not always particularly meaningful. Instead, they are part of the price of doing business. Moments of self-criticism (as long as they do not lead to paralysis) can be very valuable indeed. Anxiety, or at least the questions that lead to anxiety, can be *helpful* as you muddle through a study since anxiety alerts you to worries and potential problems in the study. Talking, and listening, to people—people who are also researchers and understand what you are doing—is essential.

To Begin You Need to Begin

It takes a while to get a project off the ground. You start to do some daydreaming, you talk to people, you make some hard choices, and you have some false starts. Most people experience a lot of failure.

It takes only one person to believe in your project and agree to participate, and you will have begun. The most common problem is for people to put off beginning. It is scary, and it is hard to start. But to do a project, you need to start somewhere. And even if someone turns you down, you will learn from describing your project out loud, and practicing. The great thing about this kind of work is that you can make adjustments. Projects can and will evolve. So, you might as well start somewhere. You can make a list of ten different ways to start, put a date on the calendar, take a deep breath, and begin.

Learning to Interview

What to Do before and after the Interview

My first job after college was working in the San Francisco
Hall of Justice. I interviewed defendants and compiled files
for their possible release without bail. Each day I rode with a
coworker in a dingy elevator and came out in a small jail cell
with floor-to-ceiling black metal bars. We rang the buzzer. The
"door man" sauntered over, let us out of the cell, and buzzed
us through a huge, clanging metal door. We entered the City
Prison. Since the police's job was to put people in jail and our
job was to aid in their release, we always received a chilly reception from the officers. Going behind the "booking desk," we
copied the information regarding individuals arrested the previous evening, and gave the list to the "door man." We then returned to the area that doubled as the families' waiting room
during visiting hours and waited for the recently arrested defendants to be called for interviews.

With fluorescent lights, cold metal seats, and huge Plexiglas
windows—with telephones as the sole communication between
those imprisoned and ourselves—the waiting room of City
Prison was not an ideal place to conduct interviews. The interviews were usually brief, less than 15 minutes. In each interview,
our job was to learn the respondent's address, obtain the names
and contact information for the respondent's references, learn
their source of (legal) income, and tell them about the release
process. Many of the incarcerated people were dazed, drunk,
drugged, or deeply distraught, and some had been injured in
circumstances that had precipitated the calling of the police or
they had been wounded by the police during the arrest. Some
were angry, asserting, "You people, you never let me out!" Over
two years, I conducted hundreds of interviews.

One of the most important lessons I took away from this experience was the need for precision and detail in interviewing. The case for release was built with evidence showing that the defendants had strong social ties in the area (i.e., close friends and relatives) and hence were unlikely to skip bail. As noted, we asked the defendants for their addresses, the span of time they had lived at these residences, their source of economic support, and contact information for people who could be "references" for them. Then, we called the references (or they called us) and asked them about the defendant's address, duration at each residence, and forms of economic support. It was very important that the information in the defendants' interviews and their references' interviews aligned exactly. Some defendants routinely gave their legal address—that of their mother or grandmother, for example. But the court wanted to know where they actually stayed (which might be with a girlfriend), and a conflict in the addresses given could delay the case by crucial hours. If there was a discrepancy, we had to wait until the next shift to reinterview and confirm the address. Since City Prison was a challenging place to be, defendants wanted to be released as quickly as possible. Interviewers could create problems by not probing with sufficient skill. Sometimes defendants grew frustrated when probed for additional information. I had to get used to the fact that not everyone liked what I was doing. Even when things went well, some moments in the interview could be uncomfortable. Of course, numerous factors went into the judge's final decision regarding whether the defendant would be released without bail, but the interview was a key component.

This first job also taught me that the first question in the interview is often just an opening gambit, and that the quality of an interview would rise and fall depending on the follow-up questions—the probes—that elicited important details. With both defendants and their references, I also needed to listen to what people were saying (including their distress about the arrest) and help them focus on the task at hand. In other words, I learned to "pivot" by listening, briefly affirming, and then redirecting. And even when people said knuckleheaded things (e.g., commenting on my body, my clothes, insisting that I begin a sexual relationship with them in the future, or alleging that I had failed to help them in the past), I needed to briefly acknowledge what they had said (usually with a brief comment or joke) and then quickly return to the task at hand without allowing myself to become distracted by my re-action to their comments.

There are many differences between interviewing defendants in prison for "free bail"—which is in the defendants' economic interest to get—and interviewing people for research where the respondent has no vested interest in the study. But there are also features common to all interviews. Politely and smoothly, the interviewer needs to guide the interview so that the interview meets the needs of the interviewer (while also being sensitive to the preferences of the respondent).[1] How-ever, respondents are doing you a favor and need to be treated with the utmost courtesy and respect. Although the interviewer has a purpose in terms of information to collect, they always need to be attuned to the concerns of the participant and willing to defer to the participant if a question makes the participant uncomfortable or if they want to stop the interview.

Although respondents are fundamentally doing you a good turn, I also think interviews can, at times, be interesting and valuable for the respondents. People like to be heard, particularly if it is without judg-ment or criticism. (How often does someone listen to you talk for over an hour, for free, without interrupting you or criticizing you?) As people talk about their lives, they may gain valuable insights. Sometimes it can be meaningful and positive, helping them process an event or life experience. It would be naive for researchers not to acknowledge that social positions in the larger society, and power dynamics, shape the interview (as many have illuminated); some even see interviews as ex-ploitative.[2] Yet, if the interviewee willingly agrees to the interview, and if the interview and subsequent material are managed with great re-spect and confidentiality is maintained, I do not see interviews as a form of exploitation.

Interviews vary in quality, with some tending to go off the rails. Some respondents talk a lot but are extremely vague, and it is difficult to get them back on track. (And sometimes *you* are truly bored and thinking, "I have to pay for transcribing this?") Some respondents are hostile or suspicious. Or, in more mundane circumstances, the interview simply can be an unpleasant chore for the respondent, particularly if the re-spondent is incredibly busy. In those instances, the interview is taking away precious time from sleep or relaxation. There are many aspects of interviewing you cannot control, but you can control crucial elements.

Your goal here is to "do no harm." And sometimes the results of your study can help others see the world in new ways.

The Purpose of Interviewing

The main goals of interviewing are to gather information from a respondent and to forge a relationship—a "partnership" as Robert Weiss terms it—with a respondent to help you learn as much as possible.[3] The two of you are collaborating; you are asking sensible questions (rather than "off the wall" questions or something that the person doesn't know how to answer). Most of the questions are open ended (they require more than a one-word response and have no right or wrong answers). The people you are interviewing are "experts" about the subject matter—they are teaching you.

As I discuss in chapters 2 and 8, you want to have an emerging research question. You have a purpose in doing the interviews, broadly conceived. And, ideally, you know something about work that has been written in this area, but there is something that bothers you about previous work. Or you are simply interested in learning more about the topic.

You also want to be curious. But, you cannot ask everything. So, guided by your emergent research question, you want to focus on information you find important as well as being open to being surprised by something that emerges that suggests a new, interesting direction of inquiry. This analytic search for information surfaces in many different stages of the interviewing process, such as design of the sample, creation of the interview guide, interview facilitation, data analysis, and writing processes. The next chapter focuses on the actual interview—especially the kinds of questions to ask in order to get high-quality data. This chapter helps you get ready by discussing the many logistical details in preparing for the interview, the interview guide, and tricky aspects of the interview such as asking sensitive questions.

The Value of Interviews

Interviews can be surprisingly intimate and revealing. Indeed, as Simmel noted long ago, a stranger "often receives the most surprising openness—confidences which sometimes have the character of a confessional and which would be carefully withheld from a more closely related person."[4] Interviews are best at showing individuals' perspectives regarding their key life events, hopes and dreams, and situations that have shaped their lives. As noted earlier, as a data collection method, the research process for interviewing is usually fewer hours than participant observation. Often, if you design your study carefully, you can collect important information and have a limited impact on your normal life schedule. In a participant observation study, interviews and observations can go "hand in hand" as something you observe can lead you to ask a question informally (e.g., "I noticed that") or formally in an interview near the end of the study.

Nevertheless, interviews have limits. If the respondent is not aware of something or cannot describe it, then effective interviewing becomes difficult. Since many important aspects of daily life are taken for granted and hard to articulate, there are significant constraints on the issues that can be effectively illuminated by interviews. (For example, parents are rarely aware whether they are warmer to one child than another.) Interviews are also subject to social desirability bias. Since people are often reluctant to admit things that are shameful, stigmatized social patterns are hard to uncover (e.g., a police department being guided by norms that favor excessive use of force).[5] Few people will volunteer ways in which they have been a terrible friend; instead, people often portray themselves in a favorable light. At times, however, very skillful interviewers can encourage people to give a more balanced portrait of themselves by including their own actions of which the respondents are not proud. Of course, it is also not always possible in participant observation to gain access to observe stigmatized behavior either. In short, all research modes have limitations. But, despite these inherent limits, interviews have been used effectively in many spheres. For sensitive matters, including observing family members, interviews are a crucial way to gain permission to conduct participant observation.[6] Interviews can also be valuable for understanding more deeply issues in the participant observation.

Getting Ready

There are a surprising number of details in making an interview happen. Some researchers will want to make a checklist, while others will just remember what is involved. There is no one right approach, as long as these details are completed before the interview starts.

DECIDING WHERE TO CONDUCT THE INTERVIEW

The first part of ensuring a good interview involves controlling where the interview will take place. If you are meeting face-to-face, increasingly, people want to meet at a local coffee shop or in a public place.[7] Although some people report good experiences in coffee shops, I believe that these settings are not ideal, lacking privacy and thus constraining what the respondent will divulge. In particular, it reduces the chance that someone will tell you something very personal or shed tears. You also can be interrupted; someone can recognize you, compromising the privacy of the respondent. The noise of a public space will reduce the sound quality on a recorder and make transcription slower and harder. But, some people (particularly low-income families) live in complicated living situations, and meeting in a public place can be better than not doing the interview. Public parks can work well, particularly if you are interviewing mothers with small children, since the children can run around. Libraries are also an option, particularly if they have a private room.

Since the setting matters, you want to think about your options when you are recruiting someone for the interview. As you set up the interview, you want to mention how long the interview will last and where it will take place ("Normally it would be in your home or another private location"). In the phone conversation with a respondent where I explain the study, I try to take the lead and say, "Normally to make it most convenient for you, I would come to you, to your home, and that way you don't have to travel." If they then suggest a coffee shop, depending on their tone of voice, I might try one more time, saying something like this: "Yes, many people do suggest a coffee shop. But, if you don't mind, it can be extremely helpful to have it in your house since it is quieter/more private. You shouldn't go to any trouble to clean up." Note that here I am pushing a bit—I suggest coming to their home—in a calm, matter-of-fact voice. Then I wait. Often there is a short pause. At that point, a number of people will agree to have you do the interview at home. Others, however, will say they prefer a coffee shop or work setting. Then I quickly and readily agree to whatever they propose; depending on how the conversation is unfolding, I also might suggest a public park. Similarly, if I set up an interview but later the respondent lets me know they are going to cancel, I might offer to do a phone or video interview, which, for some respondents, may be less stressful. In these instances, especially for low-income respondents, a video interview may be very costly on a cell phone since it may use up data. If so, a phone call is better.

If you have access to an office on campus or can reserve a room in the library, that may work as long as you can welcome the person in the lobby or outside on the street to escort them into the building; if the respondent gets lost in the building (or is not permitted to enter) then you lose valuable time. Be sure to give them ideas of where they can park or the closest stops on public transportation.

If you are traveling out of town to do the interview, avoid interviewing in a hotel room. Local libraries often have private rooms to reserve. Some hotels have conference rooms. A local university may provide a room. In one study, I was out of options, and I called City Hall. I talked to several people, and each time I explained that I was a researcher from out of town affiliated with a university, and I needed to interview a "citizen" of their community, but that the library did not have a room. In the end, they graciously allowed me to use a room for two hours.

SCHEDULE ADEQUATE BUFFER TIMES

When you schedule the interview, you want to have a large buffer zone before your next appointment. For example, I recently visited Puerto Rico to interview a wealthy man who lived a bit over one hour from the airport. I scheduled the interview to begin at 10:00 a.m. and, eager to get home, I booked a flight at 5:30 p.m., five hours after I thought that the interview would end, thinking I had plenty of time. But it turned out that with traffic it was more like 90 minutes each way to the airport. He had a doctor's appointment in the morning, and we moved the interview to 10:30, but the doctor ran late. His girlfriend let me into the large guest cottage (where he was living while his new $15 million mansion was being built outside of the cottage). She gave me a glass of water, and I sat there, waiting, admiring the many tall, profusely blooming white, purple, and orange orchids and additional tropical flower arrangements. My interviewee didn't return home until 11:00. He arrived, strode into the elegant space, shook my hand, and said, "Robert Steinburg at your service" (a pseudonym). I was relieved that he was there, and optimistic that things were back on track. However, he subsequently worked on the computer, spent 15 minutes talking with a contractor, discussed errands with his girlfriend for 10 minutes, made a cup of coffee, and spoke with his girlfriend's teen daughter about a school project. It was now 11:35 a.m.; I needed to be driving away by 2:00 p.m. to catch a flight, and I had lost my buffer zone. It took another ten minutes to get situated. In the end, we sat in chairs in the construction site, mosquitos flying freely, with an electric saw running in the background (impacting recording quality).[8] The interview began at 11:45 a.m., a full 75 minutes after it was scheduled, and ended around 2:15 p.m. For me, the hardest part of that encounter was the ongoing effort it took to keep looking flexible, cheerful, upbeat, and unstressed while I waited for the interview to begin. (While Mr. Steinburg was attending to other matters, I chatted with the girlfriend's daughter, texted notes to myself on the setting, smiled, and sipped on the glass of water I had been given.) If you book two interviews in one day, which I believe is the most you can do and be effective, there normally should be a buffer zone of at least four hours between them. In some instances, however, if you are interviewing two people in the same household, it makes sense to do them back-to-back.

CONFIRM BEFORE YOU GO

The very first research trip I took was as a graduate student where I flew from San Francisco to Los Angeles, rented a car, and drove around 90 minutes to a school district. I had scheduled the interview weeks in advance, and (foolishly) had not confirmed. When I arrived at the school district office and asked for "Mr. Hanson," the secretary turned pale. It turned out that Mr. Hanson had *died* unexpectedly two weeks earlier. It was very awkward. Further compounding my error, although I asked whether I could schedule an interview with a different administrator at a future time, I did not insist on rescheduling. The district officials felt I was owed an interview and that it should take place promptly. They rounded up a couple of people for me to talk to; the interviews were rushed and incomplete. As a result of this early and memorable incident, I always confirm an interview a day or two before the appointment.

I usually text or email the day before to confirm: "Dear xxx: Thank you very much for agreeing to speak with me as part of the UPenn study. I am very much looking forward to meeting you. I wanted to check in, however, to see if Monday at 3:00 p.m. still works for you. Of course, if something comes up, and it is a bad time, you shouldn't hesitate to reschedule."

The only time I don't add that last sentence is if I have driven more than two hours or flown to get to that interview and the change would have a significant impact on me. (Of course, if they ask to reschedule, I am cheerful, since people are busy, interviews are hard to arrange, and an offer to meet in two months can be an option that will enable the interview to take place.) Offering to reschedule, in an upbeat fashion, signals that you appreciate that they are doing you a favor. They are in control of the process.

Unfortunately, in my experience, at least 25 percent of interviews are postponed, often at the last minute. Some number of these will never take place. There is no choice but to be cheerful, accommodating, and extremely understanding, even if you are desperate to do the interview. It is also an ethical response; you do not want to be coercive. Although you, as the researcher, set goals for a study, if respondents clearly signal they do not want to participate, you must respectfully defer to their wishes.

When they cancel, it is good to say, "If you don't mind, I will be in touch later when things calm down." Or, if you feel comfortable, you can say, "Is it better to wait or is it possible to set up another time now to meet?" You can play it by ear. If someone "ghosts" you and doesn't respond to an email or text, I suggest limiting yourself to making two more requests.[9] Then, wait a few *months* or give up on them entirely. Harassing people by sending multiple texts and emails is often ineffective; it can also poison the well and make it harder for other researchers. Some respondents just don't work out. It certainly doesn't mean that you have failed. It happens to everyone. This is why it's important to recruit more people to interview than you need for your final sample.

It is also possible to keep trying to recruit someone who has ghosted you by using a different strategy; in some settings you can arrange to run into someone in a public space. In some contexts (but not others) you can "drop by," bring food, and leave a handwritten note. They may not have responded because something came up: someone was laid off, a child was sick, or there was a family emergency. Sometimes you can send a holiday card or drop by with some cookies "just to say hello." The holidays in December are a good time to bring by treats for wayward respondents. As you drop off the treat, you might say, "I wanted to say hello and bring by a little treat." The crucial element here is that the efforts to "pop by" are not moments when you are recruiting but simply trying to reestablish contact and "test the waters." Depending on how this unfolds, you might be able to take the next step. Sometimes people feel comfortable being in a study, but they don't respond because they're busy and then forgetful (just as people forget to return emails that they intend to return). In that case, if you are greeted warmly, it is reasonable to reach out about rescheduling often a few days or weeks after a social visit. Other times, however, the ghosting is because they simply do not want to participate. If you are given a cool reception, you cannot pressure people. You need to thank them and leave.

VOICE RECORDING EQUIPMENT: RUN TWO RECORDERS

Even people with an excellent memory cannot recall the details of an interview. Compared to participant observation where note taking is extremely disruptive, respondents expect you to take note of their words. The easiest way to do that is to use a voice recorder. Because of common technical failures, you should run two voice recorders simultaneously. If your IRB permits it, a phone is ideal after you put it on "airplane mode" or otherwise ensure that you will not be interrupted. For some populations who have been targeted by law enforcement, small, stand-alone voice recorders (used by police) are not a comfortable option. Phones are better. You can buy a used phone solely for interviews (i.e., does not have phone service) that will record interviews well. A microphone will improve sound quality. Some people really like when you give them a microphone to clip on their shirt. (They make jokes about being on television, and they often smile.) For others, it makes it harder for them to relax. Whether your interview is happening in person or via videoconferencing, you need to ask permission to record the interview before you turn on the recording device. (If the respondent requests it, you can also do a verbal consent or send the consent form ahead of time to have them "look it over.") Some people are uncomfortable with the video file being recorded; if so, you can record it on your phone and also run a back-up recording. Although risky, the sound quality will be better if you also ask them to record the interview using their cell phone and then email it to you. Some respondents will do this, but others will never get around to it.

You should practice with your equipment over and over again until you have it down. Most people have a technical failure at least once in a study—erasing an interview, mislabeling an interview, not turning on the recorder, having batteries die, or other (disastrous) events. (Despite my best efforts, I have lost one interview on each of the studies I have done.) That is why you want to have two recorders and an extra set of batteries. But, if you only have one recorder and no extra batteries and you lose an interview, it is not the end of the world. You will probably remember it for the rest of your life, however.

CONSENT FORMS

Unless you are asking for a verbal consent, normally you will have people sign a form that has been approved by your IRB (see appendix to chapter 3).[10] Ideally, the form will include the logo for your organization. (If you print consent forms on letterhead stationery using a color printer it gives a more polished, professional look.) The wording of your consent form should be very clear and straightforward and, if possible with your IRB, the form should not be more than one page long. It will explain clearly that this is a research study, you are asking their permission, their name will never be used (or will be used and in what context), that they may stop the interview at any time, and they can choose not to answer any question that makes them uncomfortable. (As I explain in the next chapter, I also cover these points verbally with respondents at the start of each interview.) I staple my business card to the consent form. Students can obtain inexpensive business cards printed with the logo of their university. You give them a blank consent form to keep, and you take the signed one with you.

In the signature area of the form, it is good to have lines on the page to record the respondent's home address, cellphone number, and email address (unless in the population you are studying it would be too intrusive). If it is a longitudinal study, you should also ask for the names, addresses, and phone numbers for three people who will always know where the respondent is (such as a sibling, a cousin, or their parents). However, all of these requests should be held until the end of the interview when you ask if you might keep in touch. Then, you should ask for the contact information and write it on plain paper; later you can add it to the consent form. Many universities also require a signature when giving participants cash; however, some institutions do not require signatures for a gift card. Thus, in some cases, there could be a separate form they also need to sign, but some institutions provide a waiver if the circumstances demand it.

INTERVIEW BAG

I find it helpful to prepare interview packets at the beginning of a study. I have a file folder on my computer called "interview packet" that contains a list of the materials that I bring to each interview. Then I create packets with the following hard-copy items:

- consent form with my business card stapled on it to give to the respondent
- consent form to sign
- university form for receipt of payment or gift card (if required)
- interview guide, income card, and list of experiences (discussed below)
- blank white paper for note-taking
- hard-copy directions for getting to the interview site
- contact information for the respondent including the cell phone number and address; if the person has an assistant, the cell phone number, name, and address of the assistant. (You may be able to auto-generate this information depending on how you store it.)
- any background information on the respondent, including the email or text chain from our previous communications

In a special tote or backpack, I put the interview packets and the following items:

- two voice recorders, extra batteries, and microphone, all in a waterproof bag
- thank you notes, envelopes, and stamps (in case I am inspired to write a thank you note)
- thank you gift
- protein bars, nuts, or other food in case I get hungry on the trip

Some people carry a letter of introduction on letterhead, but this kind of documentation is almost never needed. However, it might make you feel better to have it, just in case. If you are in a setting where you need permits, you should carry them along with your IRB approval letter (and a copy of your passport). In addition, I almost always send a card with a thank you note to the person after the interview (unless I believe it would be seen as strange). Although old-fashioned, people appreciate them, and it also (as I explain later) can jog their memory if you asked them to introduce you to someone.

I like the festive look of colored folders; they also protect the papers from being creased. If I am running multiple studies, the color of the file folder can have a symbolic value (i.e., manila folders for bureaucrats, green folders for my study of families of high net worth).

Usually, I try to assign a code name before I depart for the interview (or immediately after I complete the interview). The code name should be similar to the sensibility of the person's real name (i.e., Tamika for Nevaeh, Thomas for Robert, or Mimi for Tina). You can often find the ancestors of surnames, and then you can look up another name. Thus, search "last name Thompson," you can find it is a Scottish name, and then you can look up other Scottish last names. Baby name websites are also helpful as they include the most popular names in the year the respondent was born. (You can also search for names similar to the person's name.) Sometimes, especially months or years after the interview, the people you interview can become hazy in your mind. For this reason, I like to give each respondent a short descriptive tag (e.g., jazz or marathons). This descriptor, which makes sense only to me, refers to something the person adores, or reminds me of a key moment in the interview.[11] In a large study, these descriptors can be helpful.

Logistics: Ensuring Your Timely Arrival at the Interview Site

Before global positioning systems (GPS), you would have to read a map. But, if you are interviewing in the countryside, GPS may not work. Or, you could run out of power on your phone. As a result, it is good to have a written copy of the directions; you should also look at where you are going ahead of time. You might need the written directions only one in 100 times, but it will save you. To avoid getting lost and arriving late, leave plenty of extra time for public transit delays, missed trains, traffic, or rare events. If you arrive early, find a place out of sight from the interview location, where you can safely sit and read or think through the interview. (This is a good time to review the interview guide so it is fresh in your memory.) If you arrive at a work setting, it always takes a few minutes to present identification at the desk and get signed in. But you don't want to arrive too early. I aim to arrive at the front desk of an office building around eight minutes before the meeting. If I am interviewing someone in a home, I try to walk to the front door exactly at the right time.

Good Etiquette: Thanking Participants in Your Study

If possible, bring a gift or thank you present of some kind for the person you are interviewing. I give what I've brought when I arrive. For most of my career, I have brought pies. I like pies because I like desserts, and, unlike cakes—where a cake from an expensive bakery looks very different than a cake from a supermarket—pies are more generic. They generally travel well; they can be inexpensive. Participants often like them, and they look genuinely pleased when I give it to them. Or, I might bake brownies (using a mix). But there are lots of options, including ones that are less gendered, and you want to be sensitive to food allergies and other constraints. A bouquet of daisies, a box of chocolates, or a bottle of wine also make good "thank you" gifts for respondents. If appropriate, an inexpensive picture frame with a picture in it (for example, when interviewing families, of a parent and child at an event) can be much appreciated. Gift cards can be good options; the amount depends on your budget but amounts of $10 or $15 are meaningful to many people. In some cases, raising the amount (e.g., to $50) can raise response rates. I always bring a gift of some kind, even when I interview someone who has 100 million dollars. (Then the gift might be a bouquet of flowers, a plant, a bottle of wine, or, after the interview, a book that might be of interest to the interviewee.) All of these gifts must be noted in your IRB, but in some institutions, you can list a number of options, state that they will all be below a particular value, and indicate that you will choose one option. Students can often apply for grants from their institutions (with sufficient lead time), but even students on an extremely tight budget can make a plate of brownies or buy some shiny red apples. The food should look like a gift, placed on a paper plate (wrapped in plastic wrap), possibly with a ribbon or bow, and a card with a handwritten thank you. By bringing a gift, you are activating the deeply held social norm of reciprocity. All of these gifts depend on the particulars of the situation but ideally recognize the respondents' interests or values. Still, the gift should not be too elaborate, expensive, or personal, since an extravagant gift throws off the norms of reciprocity with a quasi-stranger.

Creating the Interview Guide

Interview guides are open-ended questions that help you reveal what you want to learn in the study. For an interview lasting from ninety to one hundred twenty minutes, there should be only a dozen or so main questions in an interview guide with numerous small questions (or probes) to elicit additional detail. For the follow-up questions, think about the themes or issues important in your study and the information that is crucial for you to elicit during each participant's interview. Some people create a spreadsheet with the key "big picture" issues and the subthemes. (Often, these become the themes you will use in coding as part of the data analysis.) Of course, as discussed in chapters 2 and 8, the research question, and the interview guide questions, are always related to broader issues of the goals of your study, and how you see your contribution to the literature.

I like my interview guide to begin with a general question that any respondent would be able to answer easily. When studying families, "Tell me about the family in which you grew up" is a common way for me to begin an interview. For employees, I will ask, "Tell me what you do during the day." Then I can probe their job title, the number of employees they supervise/number of supervisors, hours, weekend and evening work, exciting and dull aspects of the job, and so forth. As I discuss more in chapter 5, the interview starts at a general level and then grows more specific after the first 15 minutes. (I generally hold off asking about the most sensitive topics, such as a person's annual income, until the end of the interview.) There are numerous pesky questions about "who, what, when, where, and how" that you need to ask in order to achieve your goal of understanding the meaning your respondent attaches to life events and experiences. You want the interview to stay focused on what is important to you. In addition, an interview guide with open-ended questions can help participants feel more comfortable, reduce the implication that there is a right or wrong answer, and encourage them to share more details in their responses.

As I explain in more detail in the next chapter, you always want to ask questions about topics in which the respondent is an expert. Questions requiring speculation can lead to unexpected difficulties. For example, in the interviews with parents for my study *Unequal Childhoods*, I ultimately learned that fathers knew little about the logistics of children's organized activities. This realization was crystallized in an interview with a white middle-class father, a dentist. When I handed him a list of names of children in his son's classroom and asked him which of the parents he knew and would say hello to in the grocery story, he replied, "My wife can tell me who I know."[12] This remarkable statement showed his deep dependence on his wife. The interviews were impaired by fathers' lack of detailed knowledge about the cost of soccer, the process of signing up for karate. "That is another good question for my wife," a father would say. The fathers were excellent at describing their aspirations for their children and the powerful meaning of fatherhood (which I should have probed to learn more about). But it was frustrating to ask them about the management of children's organized activities only to discover they knew little because they didn't do much. This information was, in and of itself, important data, and the results led me to feel comfortable interviewing only mothers in future studies. But I wasted a great deal of time, effort, and money on interviews that were fundamentally not very fruitful. Thus, you want always to interview people regarding a topic with which they are intimately familiar. On occasion, you might find it useful to ask how the respondent thinks or feels about the actions of others, or even, in some instances, what they know about why someone else did something. Sometimes it is easier for respondents to talk about others than themselves. At times, when respondents start talking about what others are doing and why, they then add more about their own experiences. Primarily, however, you want to stay focused on the respondent's experiences.

An ideal interview guide does not guide answers; it asks neutral, open-ended questions. So, rather than asking, "Did you grow up in a blue-collar family?" I ask, "Tell me about the family you grew up in." As I show in chapter 5, sometimes I stutter or stumble over my words. Depending on how the interview is going, the questions might be asked differently. This is not ideal, but it is a reality. You are not measuring the respondents' answers in a precise way; rather, you are probing for deeper meaning. Interview guides evolve through a study. Some people find it helpful to do pilot interviews or a practice interview with a family member or friend (which is then thrown away). Once I begin interviewing respondents, I tweak the interview guide in the first few interviews, and then, after I have done one-quarter of the interviews, I take stock, listen to interviews, and make more adjustments to the interview guide. Then, as noted in chapters 2 and 8, the focus of the study evolves. By the time I have completed around one-half to two-thirds of the interviews, I try to be much clearer about the focus. At that time, I revise the interview guide again to capture the essential issues of the study.

A SAMPLE INTERVIEW GUIDE

Here I share the final interview guide for a study I conducted with Heather Curl and Tina Wu on cultural knowledge. Specifically, it examined tensions over cultural tastes that white and Black upwardly mobile adults experienced with their families of origin.[13] The study evolved; the guide was revised for the last time about one-half of the way through the study. All of the 30 participants were from working-class families, but the interviewees had earned two degrees (e.g., a bachelor's degree and a highly prestigious advanced degree such as an MD or JD).

At the top of our guide, as a reminder, we listed the study's key themes:

FIVE TO SIX THEMES
(1) Humor, banter, and talk
(2) The body and how people hold themselves (language, voice, presentation)
(3) Things you did not know
(4) Food taste, alcohol and consumptions
(5) Moments when you feel authentic, or inauthentic
(6) Servers, dining, and going out

BACKGROUND AND EXPERIENCE
1. Tell me about the family in which you grew up.
   a. Probes: What did your parent(s) do for a living? What was life at home like? What do your sisters or brothers do? Tell me about the schools you attended. What did you do outside of school? Who were your friends, or, who did you spend a

lot of time with growing up? What did you do together? Context: did you have an aunt/uncle/cousin who went to college?

2. How would you describe your current situation?

   a. Probes: What do you do for a living now? Describe to me your work setting. Who do you work with? What is your workplace like? What do you do outside of work? Who do you spend the most time with outside of work? What activities do you do? How do you like to spend your free time? Where do you live? Describe to me your current neighborhood. How long have you been living there? From where did you move?

CULTURAL KNOWLEDGE AND MOBILITY

3. Thinking about your current situation, in what ways do you feel you belong and do not belong? Can you describe a moment when you felt confident at work? Can you describe a moment when you weren't confident?

   a. Probes: when, where, what situation, who with, how felt, how felt in body

4. We are interested in learning more about how things are different for people from the way that they grew up and the way things are now.

   a. Some people tell us that they notice differences between how people in their family talk about themselves and present themselves compared to how people do this in their current world. Have you noticed any differences in this area or not so much?

      i. Any differences in how people stand, sit, or present themselves? Some people notice things and others don't.

   b. What about differences between how people talk, curse, or joke around? Are there differences in the people you work with these days and the situation of your folks—people in blue-collar jobs—or not so much?

   c. What about food and drink? Any differences there between how things were with the blue-collar world that you grew up in and your current world?

   d. Are there any things that you felt that you just didn't know that other people knew as you moved from the world of your family to your current world?

5. Do you ever feel like an outsider? Tell me more about that.
   a. Can you describe a moment in your life in which you have felt uncomfortable or out of place when entering a new setting for the first time? At what point did you notice being different from others around you? How did you respond, or what did you do?
6. Have you noticed any changes about yourself?
   a. In what ways? Can you recall an incident when you noticed that?
7. (Optional) Do you find yourself behaving differently in different surroundings? Can you give me an example?
   a. Is there a difference between how you are at work and how you behave with your family and folks from home? How so?

(OPTIONAL) MOBILITY STORIES

8. I'd like to reflect with you on the journey you have been on.
   a. Tell me about high school. What school did you attend, and what was it like? What did you notice, if anything?
   b. Tell me about college. What school did you attend, and what was it like? What did you notice, if anything?
   c. Tell me about your first full-time job. What was it? What did you do? Who did you work for? What was it like? What did you notice?
   d. [Probing for experience of mobility without naming it to the respondent] Did you have significant relationships or friendships during this time period? Can you tell me about them? With whom? What was your experience? How did it end, or if it's still important in your life, what is your relationship like now?
   e. What did you discover about yourself during this time period?
   f. What was your relationship like with your family and people you mentioned from earlier in the interview?
   g. What do you think was key for you in becoming upwardly mobile? Was there a key person?

9. Is there anything else important about this topic which we have not talked about?

10. Participant identity: Race, Gender, Profession/Job History, Ethnic Identity, Educational Background
11. Parent identity: Race, Gender, Profession/Job History, Ethnic Identity, Educational Background (number of years "Tell me about your mother's educational background: did she attend high school?", if went to college, where, if graduated)
12. Do you own or rent? If sold today, what would the house sell for?
13. Do you help any family members? (How much, how often for each person)
14. What is your total combined household income, annually?
    a. Under $10,000
    b. $10-$30,000
    c. $30-$60,000
    d. $60-$100,000
    e. $100-$150,000
    f. $150-$200,000
    g. $200-$250,000
    h. $250-$300,000
    i. $300-$350,000
    j. Over $350,000

In practice, moving through this interview guide took from ninety minutes to two hours and thirty minutes per study participant. Since the goal, as always, was for the respondent to feel comfortable and for the conversation to flow, the order of the questions varied depending on how the interview unfolded.

ASK QUESTIONS THAT ADDRESS YOUR STUDY'S KEY THEMES

Sometimes, in a study, you need to know whether the respondent has experienced any of a variety of different things when they went through a process such as looking for a job, house hunting, or adjusting to college life. You don't want to take the time during an interview to ask whether the respondent had (or had not) experienced each and every possible issue on your list. But, if you don't ask and simply wait for the person to volunteer the information, you cannot be sure that a particular event did not occur; the respondent may have simply forgotten to raise the point. One solution is to hand the respondent a list (backed with cardboard), saying, "Let's look at this list. Did any of these things happen to you?"

For example, during Sherelle Ferguson's dissertation research on how students in a nonselective private college navigate institutional challenges, Ferguson came up with the idea to ask the students the following list of experiences.[14] I thought it was a great idea. When the two of us did another study of 44 white, Black, and Chinese-American first-generation college students in two universities, we handed a copy of the list to respondents about fifteen or twenty minutes into their interviews and asked them to tell us which ones they had experienced.[15]

> Have you experienced any of the following academic issues in your time in college?
> - ☐ I had difficulty with my courses, assignments, or study time
> - ☐ I performed poorly on an important assignment (e.g. essay, midterm)
> - ☐ My grades dropped very quickly in a class
> - ☐ I was unable to meet a deadline for an important assignment
> - ☐ I failed a class/received a low grade
> - ☐ I received an incomplete in a course
> - ☐ I was uncertain when to drop or withdraw from a course
> - ☐ I doubted my major choice
> - ☐ I was not sure which courses to select for a quarter
> - ☐ I had difficulty scheduling courses (e.g., course section full)
> - ☐ I had conflict with an instructor
> - ☐ I had difficulty getting recommendations from professors or advisors
> - ☐ I was accused of cheating or plagiarism
> - ☐ I had difficulty transferring credits
> - ☐ I had difficulty receiving accommodations from the Office of Disability Resources
> - ☐ I got sick and had to miss at least three days of classes
> - ☐ I needed to take a temporary leave of absence
> - ☐ I lost my status in an important program (e.g., honors program, scholarship program)
> - ☐ I was put on academic probation

☐ I considered withdrawing from the university
☐ I was dismissed academically and/or had to appeal my dismissal

After the respondent tells you about one issue, you need to ask, "Anything else?" to the respondent (repeat the question throughout the interview) to ensure you may conclude something did not happen to a respondent. Of course, it can take time to go through this list. As I discuss, more generally, in chapter 5, in every interview you have to make hard choices about which questions to spend time on, probing further to gain as much depth as possible.

INCLUDE QUESTIONS ABOUT RESPONDENTS' DEMOGRAPHIC CHARACTERISTICS

In the social sciences, readers typically want to know basic information about the study participants. Since the respondent's social class background and racial and ethnic membership can shape life experiences, it is common to collect this information. In some cases, the information will surface during the interview, but often not. As a result, it is typical at the end of the interview to briefly ask some demographic questions. All of the major national surveys have their questionnaires available, and you might find it helpful to use their wording as they have conducted extensive research on how to ask "fixed-response" questions in the best fashion.[16]

Here are some sample demographic questions I asked at the end of in-depth interviews in a study I did with Elliot Weininger on how white and African American parents of young children went about deciding where to live and where to send their children to school.

SAMPLE DEMOGRAPHIC QUESTIONS
TO ASK AT THE END OF AN INTERVIEW
Finally, I have some statistical questions that we need to ask everyone in the study.
1. What year were you born? (Or, how old were you on your last birthday?) Are you married? How long have you been married? Have you ever been married previously?

2. Tell me about your educational background. (college attended)
   a. Probe: Highest degree, age at degree, institutions, discipline?
   b. Do you have loans from college? If you had to ballpark them, what ballpark would you be in?
3. Do you work outside the home?
   a. If so, what do you do? Employer, title, tasks, full-time or part-time?
   b. What do you do during the day?
   c. If no, did you before the children were born? Do you think that you will continue in this pattern or do you think about returning to work in a part-time or full-time basis?
4. Where were you born? Where were your parents born?
   a. What racial and ethnic group do you identify with?
   b. How would you describe your gender and sexual orientation?
5. Tell me about the educational background (degree, field of study, school, loans) of your spouse/partner and/or the children's father.
   a. What does s/he do during the day?
   b. What is her/his title? Employer? Responsibilities? Does your partner work outside the home? (If yes: Is the work full-time or part-time?)
   c. Does your partner travel for work?
   d. How old is your partner? Where was your partner born?
   e. What racial or ethnic group does your partner identify with?
6. Did your mother attend high school? (probe: high school graduate? Any college? Graduate?) Does she work outside of the home? (job, kind of job) Ask for other parents or stepparents in the lives of the respondent. Clarify if biological parents.
7. Finally, for statistical purposes I need to know the letter that best describes your total pre-tax family income. I don't need to know the amount, just the letter, "A, B, C, D, E"
8. What letter best describes your savings? I am only asking for the letter, "A, B, C, D" Do you have a retirement plan?

Asking Sensitive Questions: Income and Other Woes

There are many sensitive topics in interviewing such as food shortages at home, infidelity, failed recovery efforts, childhood sexual abuse, unemployment, and so forth. But the one question that almost every researcher asks, and which is difficult for people to answer, is the question of income. Indeed, when I was in graduate school, one of my professors said that it was easier to ask people about sex than income.[17]

In planning sensitive questions, you need to think again about why you need the information and the kind of information you need. If the study is focused on issues like income or unemployment, then you would ask open-ended questions with probes (as discussed above). Most often, however, researchers need income only as a "demographic characteristic" (i.e., description of populations) or "statistical information" in order to describe your sample. If that is the case, then you wait until the end of the interview. The income question is usually the very last question. As you wrap up the open-ended questions, it is good to "signal" to the respondent that there is a change: "Now for statistical purposes, I have some background questions."

There are different ways to ask about income. I type different income levels on a piece of paper. The categories vary depending on the population you are studying—sometimes they are in intervals of $10,000, but for very high-income respondents they are in categories of $50,000. You want to ask categories that fit your population, and also figure out whether it is better to do it by month or by year, by individual or by household (or start with the individual and then move to the household). Once I determine and print the income categories, I secure the income sheet to a sturdier folder or board. Then, with a light, slightly bored voice (as if I am asking something that is completely routine), I calmly hand them the sheet and say:

> Now, for statistical purposes, please tell me what letter of the
> alphabet best describes your combined, pre-tax total household
> income, A, B, C, D or E? Again, I only need to know the letter
> of the alphabet that best describes your total pre-tax household
> income in general terms.

Although you will likely feel anxious and uncertain in asking, you want to act very calm and assured. Be sure that you do not squirm in your chair, run your hands through your hair, or show your anxiety in other ways. You also want to look at the person (not at the floor), speaking clearly and loudly (but not too loudly). And, you are promising to keep it confidential. Without this valuable information, readers will be dubious about or frustrated with your data. Thus, you should practice asking. Ideally, you and a friend can practice it over and over again until it feels more routine.

In general, when you ask about income, there is a pause, and a silence. It is crucial to wait the person out even though you may feel very anxious. Most people will simply answer or ask a clarifying question. At times, people will be uncomfortable because the matter is sensitive. Sometimes it is helpful to reassure people that their name will never be used, and, in social sciences, we are interested in patterns among social groups. But, of course, following established research ethics, you cannot coerce people. So, you need to "read the tea leaves" to see how the person feels. If they are hesitant to reveal their income, I would listen to them very carefully. For example, if they say, "I would prefer not to reveal this," then you must follow their lead. The conversation on that topic must end immediately. If they are less explicit, you might try again, using a different approach. Depending on the dynamic, some interviewers will ask, "Do you feel comfortable telling me if your income is over or under $50,000 (or whatever figure is helpful to you)?" Then, in some instances, researchers push again—"and over or under $100,000?" But others would never do this. It is a highly personal decision. However, most people will tell you their income if you have a matter-of-fact, bored demeanor, treating the topic as if it is "no big deal" and simply a technical matter. They will also tell you whether they have any stocks or bonds (most people don't). Many people, particularly elites, know their net worth off the top of their head and will round it off, "Oh, ten" (by which they mean ten million dollars). How you behave when asking about income makes a big difference in how respondents react.

For questions of wealth, the most important asset of most Americans is their home. You can just ask them casually, "What ballpark would your house value be in if it were sold today?" Almost all homeowners know the answer to this question. (It is also helpful to look it up on a real estate website.) If you need to know the size of their mortgage, I would wait until after you ask income (which is crucial to record while net worth is not). Then I would casually ask, "And, when you got this house, did you get a thirty-year mortgage?" After they answer, I would ask, "Do you know how many more years until it will be paid off?" Usually people will have to stop and think on that one. Finally, you can ask, "And did you put down 10 percent?" (If they put down 20 percent, they will see that as favorable, so you want to start low; even 5 percent is possible.)[18] From these figures, using estimates of interest rates, you can estimate how much they owe and how much equity they have in their house. Or, if you feel that you have sufficient rapport, simply ask them directly.

Asking sensitive questions may make you nervous. You should try it out; you will usually get better with practice. Some researchers do, however, use a laptop or iPad so that the interviewee can simply click on the answer. This can be beneficial. Studies on highly stigmatized health behavior suggests having respondents typing responses into a computer yields somewhat more accurate information compared to verbal replies.[19] (One analysis estimated the benefit to be 4 to 8 percent more accurate information.) Hence, you can create a questionnaire in a laptop, iPad, or other device and at the very end of the interview, ask them to complete the questionnaire, stressing that the information is highly confidential. After they finish, have them close the computer and thank them.

Keep the Recorder On after the Interview Ends

After I ask about income, my interview is officially over. Thus, I normally say, "That is the end of my questions, thank you so much! I learned a great deal." But, I do not turn off the recorder. Rather, I chat with the person for a few minutes. It is extremely common for the respondent to say something interesting and relevant to the interview after you announce the interview has ended. Thus, it is helpful to leave the recorders on. (This is not deceptive since you have announced only that this is the end of your prepared questions, and the respondent can clearly see that you have not turned off the recorders.) Of course, if the respondent asks you to turn the recorder off, you must do so, immediately. But often respondents don't notice or care. It varies, but often this chatting lasts five minutes or so.

In addition, I often want to interview someone else in the family or see whether the respondent can introduce me to other respondents as part of a "snowball" sample. Thus, if there is anything else you want or need from this respondent, the time to ask is after the interview is over but before leaving. Often there is a feeling of warmth after the interview has finished. The two of you have made a connection.

Recruiting Others

If I want to interview a partner or spouse, I will say something like this after concluding the interview:

> I also wanted to sound you out about something. In a number of cases I am interviewing a partner/spouse, and I wondered if it is the sort of thing where it might be possible to talk to [name person here using the first name]. It would be similar to this, and I would come to talk to [name here].

Then I wait to see what the respondent says. I often then add, "Of course, you could tell them what you told me, but I am not able to reveal to anyone what I learned." It is helpful to note the timeframe: "I will be interviewing folks over the next couple of months." If my respondent says, "I can ask them," I then try to confirm that I have permission to follow up with the respondent who just completed the study (rather than wait for the possible future interviewee to remember to contact me, which often increases non-response). What I don't want is for the future interview to be in the hands of the potential new interviewee who, obviously, is busy and less invested in making the interview happen. I want to have an understanding that I may reach out again to the respondent I just finished interviewing.

In other cases, the end of the interview is a great time to try to "snowball" to see whether you can be introduced to other possible respondents. Here, my speech goes something like this:

> I wanted to mention that we are looking for other people. (I describe the characteristics such as "moms of young kids three to six who live in this school district.") You don't know anyone, per chance, do you?

Then I wait, sometimes for quite a few seconds, while the person thinks. It is important not to be impatient here or shift in your chair (which subtly signals to the other person that they should hurry up). I just wait.

Sometimes respondents ask again whom I am looking to interview, and I repeat the type of person we are looking for, sometimes elaborating. If they know someone, then, as above, I express gratitude, and then suggest a pathway. For example, I say, "I wonder if you will cross paths with them in your normal routines in the next couple of weeks or do you not run into them?" If they will see them, I suggest, "It would be great if you might broach it." "People are so busy, that the ideal thing, if you are willing, is to ask them if it is okay to pass along their contact information to me. Then, I will reach out to them. But, by agreeing to talk to me they are not agreeing to be in the study, but only to learn more about it." Then I say thank you.

Often this chatting lasts five minutes or so. At this point, I will slowly pack up my belongings (i.e., the paper I used to take any notes, the consent form, my pen, and so forth) but I will keep the recorders going. Then, I will slowly move the recorders toward me, and when the respondent winds up, I will turn them off, and then swiftly put them in my bag, and stand up to say goodbye.

If the interview has lasted more than an hour, I think it is acceptable to ask to use the bathroom before I leave (since I often have a drive ahead of me). If I see something lovely or charming in the house (which there almost always is), I then volunteer my admiration with the respondent. Then as we walk to the door, I repeat that I learned a great deal, and I thank the respondent. At that point, I might say, "Would it be okay if I touched base with you in a few weeks just to check in?" (i.e., to see if they have referrals for me). Sometimes I make a little comment about people nudging me, and the value I find in nudges. ("Sometimes I ask folks if they mind me looping back in a month or so to touch base and maybe give a little nudge?") At this point, we are walking to the exit.

It is always slightly unclear what to do at the end of an interview. For example, I consider whether I should shake the respondent's hand, pat them on the arm to thank them, or simply leave. In some cases, respondents initiate giving me a hug. You want the respondent to lead the way. Often, I will extend my hand to offer a handshake, look them in the eye, smile, and thank them. If I have brought a gift, sometimes the respondent will thank me for that. Then I leave. At that point, I am often very excited and "jazzed" but also quite tired.

After the Interview

Within 24 hours after the interview (when your memory is most fresh) you want to write a memo. In the memo, describe the person, setting, and key moments in the interview. Ideally you will remember vivid, nonverbal behaviors of the respondent in at least four or five moments of the interview (e.g., "with a frown," "leaning eagerly forward in the chair," "wistfully," or "brushing away the tears with the back of a hand"). If you took notes during the interview, you can then describe for the reader the ways in which the respondent looked or spoke at key moments in the interview. It is crucial that you are completely sure about these actions and, ideally, have notes that you took at the time (if you can take notes without it being disruptive, or, immediately afterwards).

You should upload the interview audio file to your computer. In my current study, I often create a folder for each respondent that has background information, the transcribed interview, the audio file, and other information. (Other people give a respondent an identification number.) But I also have simply stored all of the audio files in one folder and the transcribed interviews in another. Having accurate word-for-word transcription (including the nature of pauses and the kind of laughter) is crucial for conducting data analysis. In an ideal world, you would transcribe each interview yourself. It is slow, and it can be hard to listen to your own voice or the mistakes you make in an interview. ("Why didn't I ask a follow-up?" I think.) Transcription is time-consuming and the automatic transcripts available are often riddled with errors. Some people listen to the interview and then dictate it again using their own voice, as a voice-recording dictation system can transcribe it with fewer errors. Others simply transcribe using a "foot pedal" or other rewinding software to carefully listen; others use a website that allows them to pause the transcript at the push of a button.[20] Some people (those with grants) can afford to have audio files transcribed. If you use a service, put a code name on the file before you upload it to be transcribed. But even the best transcription services make errors. Thus, it is best to listen to it again for corrections (or, if you have a grant, hire work-study students to do so). Transcripts are always labeled with code names. In my current study of very wealthy people, some of whom are well known, I deidentify the transcripts including by substituting code names for all key information such as colleges, addresses, names of businesses, and so forth so that the coders can work with deidentified interviews. (But I still use the original interview [with identifying information] when I read transcripts and write up the results.) Despite these efforts, it is hard to completely deidentify research materials, including the actual recordings. Hence, I always have a long, heartfelt discussion with the research assistants about issues of confidentiality; I ask research assistants to sign a confidentiality agreement. In this discussion, I tell research assistants they may discuss general findings with others if they change the name, city, state, line of work, and other identifying features of the person. But it is extremely important that they never, ever reveal the actual name. We do not want to betray the trust of the respondents.

In addition, you want to write an "analytic memo" where you analyze what you learned from the interview. Many people also find it helpful to do a summary here. Judith Levine, for example, worked with two graduate research assistants to interview graduating seniors about their job search and created an interview profile for each respondent. The interview profile summarized key elements about the interview in about two or three pages (singled-spaced). They also included a reflection of what they learned and, since they had a longitudinal design, questions for the follow-up. In the summary you can also remind yourself that there was a "good quote" on a particular topic.[21]

Most people keep track of the respondents in a spreadsheet, which should be filled out immediately after the interview. One sheet has their real name, code name, and contact information. This sheet, which is of course password protected, is stored in a separate file, away from other data, so you could never get confused and accidentally attach it in an email. Another sheet has their code name, age, race, income, and crucial information that will help to describe your sample. (You can think about what tables you might include to describe the sample; then you can keep track of this information on the summary sheet.) This data summary can be stored on the computer near the rest of your data and shared with others. This tracking sheet helps you summarize your data set. While it can be tedious to fill out, it is also invaluable. (In accordance with my institution's IRB policies, I do not keep the information about my samples in a Google document since employees of Google can see it. Rather, I keep documents in the password protected "Box" on my university server, which has two-step verification and is more secure.)

Summing Up

Interviews allow you to enter someone else's world. When they work well, and they often do, I feel as if there is a bubble where the rest of the world drops away and I focus on what the person is teaching me about their life. Sometimes you can learn the arc of someone's life, their joys, tragedies, and daily challenges. And, you can clearly see pivotal social forces that have transformed their experiences. It is an honor, and usually a pleasure, to do this work.

5

How to Conduct a Good Interview
Dig Deep

In-depth interviews unfold in unexpected ways. As chapter 4 explained, the interview guide you create for an in-depth interview will vary depending on the study. But, often, it may contain only ten or twelve broad, core open-ended questions (plus numerous probes to elicit more details and some short-response questions geared to collecting standard demographic data). During the first fifteen minutes of an interview, your primary goal is to guide the respondent into regularly providing detailed answers. This goal is important. How respondents answer the original, core questions you pose, and how successful you are in formulating your probes (which are the detailed follow-up questions that encourage them to tell you more about their experiences) will directly affect the quality of the data you collect.

Details matter. Asking for more fine-grained information during an interview increases the chances that you will fully understand what your respondent is telling you and you will be able to begin to answer your research question. Unlike quantitative researchers, who use numbers to make claims about their empirical evidence, qualitative researchers who conduct interviews and do participant observation use *words*. When reporting the study's findings, quoting your participants exactly and offering specific, detailed accounts of their experiences give readers a firmer basis for accepting your claims. In addition, these rich details help the reader understand more clearly the lives of the people you are studying. Providing the reader depth and insight helps readers feel as if they are "on your shoulder" and thus with you in the research process. Also, the additional details can give readers the chance to assess the evidence for themselves since then they don't simply have to trust you. They can make up their own minds based on what they have seen. To show readers details, you need to collect this information by digging deep.

Respondents sometimes are surprisingly frank, unpredictably emotional, disarmingly witty, or witheringly sarcastic. Regardless of the tone or length of responses, though, most answers include elements that will offer you an opportunity to probe for more depth in different and unanticipated areas. Having to decide quickly what, when, and how to follow up on something a respondent says can be stressful. At the same time, uncertainty and spontaneity make interviewing both exciting and rewarding. This chapter provides strategies designed to increase the quality of your interview data, reduce anxieties, and increase the pleasures inherent in interviews, for both you and your respondents.

To elicit the kind of vibrant details that will make your findings memorable and persuasive, you need to do a lot of thinking on your feet when conducting interviews. It is helpful to have memorized your interview guide so that you can create a flow of conversation while still including all of the critical questions. No matter what, however, you will have to make instant decisions about what parts of an interviewee's answers to pursue further and what to let stand without follow-up. Furthermore, some participants offer only brief replies; others are too talkative. Both types can lead to problematic interviews and disappointing data. And even though every interviewer makes mistakes, knowledge, practice, resilience—and even luck—all help reduce the frequency and severity of errors. In this chapter, in addition to providing tips and a set of guidelines for high-quality interviews, I take you step by step through parts of two real-life, in-depth interviews.

Both interviews I share here are from a research project I conducted earlier in my career, with the help of research assistants. The study focused on class and race differences in how parents raise children; the findings became the basis for my book *Unequal Childhoods*. The excerpts reproduced in this chapter are from in-depth interviews conducted with two working-class mothers whose nine-year-old sons played youth league football after school (on different teams). I begin by presenting sections of an interview carried out by a novice—a graduate student who was just learning how to interview. (Unfortunately, I don't have a copy of an interview I conducted when I was a novice, but I am certain that I made many similar mistakes.) I accompany the excerpt with boxed comments that draw attention to specific strengths and weaknesses in the interview and, where appropriate, suggest alternative probes that might have yielded richer details. Then I share an interview that I did with a different working-class mother. Here too, I offer commentary, pointing out mistakes I made during the interview and explaining the rationale behind my decisions to follow up on certain aspects of the respondent's answers. The examples provide an opportunity to highlight places where good probes succeed in bringing forth vivid examples and details that lead to a better understanding of the respondent's subjective experience. Before turning to the two sample interviews, I lay out some guidelines for conducting in-depth interviews.

Guidelines for Good Interviews

There is no one right way to interact with interviewees. Every interview is unique. Sometimes respondents volunteer very good answers without the interviewer doing more than token probing. Conversely, even the best techniques don't yield success in every case. Nevertheless, there are some general "rules of the game" for conducting good interviews.

INTERVIEW RESPONDENTS WHO ARE EXPERTS ON THE SUBJECTS OF MOST INTEREST TO YOU

To collect strong data, you need to interview the right people (as discussed in chapters 2 and 3). Respondents can provide excellent information if they are experts on the topic(s) you ask them about. Parents know a lot about raising children. Teachers can discuss their experiences leading a classroom of students. Gang members are experts on being in a gang.

In the interview, keep your respondents focused on the areas in which they are most knowledgeable. Prioritize finding out about their thoughts, feelings, experiences, actions, etc. in as much detail as possible. Try to avoid asking them to talk about how others feel or think or act. For example, normally you wouldn't interview parents about their children's experiences. The children themselves are a better source for that data. Sometimes, however, IRB rules may limit or fully prevent your access to certain categories of respondents (see chapter 3). In the case of children, for instance, you may have to rely on information gained indirectly by interviewing parents, teachers, coaches, and other adults.

LISTEN CAREFULLY AND TALK AS LITTLE AS POSSIBLE

Perhaps the most important rule to keep in mind when you're conducting an interview is to talk as little as possible. You can, fortunately, develop your listening skills as Kate Murphy discusses in the excellent book, *You're Not Listening: What You're Missing and Why It Matters*. Listening closely is especially important in interviewing since, after all, interviews are partnerships in which your main contribution is to listen carefully and hear the respondent accurately. At the start of an interview, however, you do need to talk enough to establish a rapport that encourages your respondent to trust you and thus to feel comfortable providing detailed answers as the interview proceeds.

DO'S AND DON'TS FOR INTERVIEWING

Do ask only one question at a time

Do ask about a specific action, event, or experience

Do use probes to learn many details

Do ask the respondent questions that allow them to draw on their expert knowledge

Do get enough details to create a mental image of a moment

Do show that you are listening closely

Don't give them the possible responses for answering

Don't move too fast

Don't ask them to talk about what other people think

KEEP IN MIND WHAT YOU WANT TO KNOW AND WHY YOU WANT TO KNOW IT

An interview is a zero-sum enterprise. You have limited time. By asking about one thing, you are taking time away from asking about something else. Deciding when to probe for more details and when to move on can be challenging, even for experienced interviewers. Keeping your highest research priorities clearly in mind makes it easier to know what questions you must ask each respondent before the interview ends.

BE A PROACTIVE INTERVIEWER

Even if you are naturally a reserved person, you must be proactive as an interviewer. You have a better understanding than the respondent does of what will be helpful for you to learn. This means that it's up to you to subtly guide the discussion, asking for more details while also helping the respondent stay focused on answering the questions you pose. All the while, you need to try to make it look as though the interview is unfolding smoothly of its own accord.[1] I recommend that you observe, take note of, and, if not too disruptive, jot down brief descriptions: your respondents' body language—including looking tearful, animated, or elated, or using specific hand movements. As mentioned earlier, if I'm taking notes during an interview, I add this information as I go along.

ASSURE RESPONDENTS THAT THERE AREN'T ANY RIGHT OR WRONG ANSWERS

Many people have never participated in a formal interview. It's reasonable for respondents in this category to feel nervous. They may worry that an interview is a test of some kind and that they might not pass. Hence, before the interview starts, you might "chat" with the person to help put them at ease. You might comment on an item you admire in the interview setting or compliment a piece of jewelry; or you might mention something you saw on their work website; or briefly discuss some other aspect of their life. As the interview goes along, you can also smile, joke, and otherwise signal that this is not an interrogation—it is a conversation. You can praise the interviewee for how helpful the answers are for your study. In addition, I think it's a good idea to begin every interview with a statement like this: "Thank you for talking to me. I want to stress that there aren't any right or wrong answers here. It's more like an informal conversation." That kind of reassurance can be helpful in trying to set respondents at ease. Then, to ensure that you are in compliance with IRB rules (see the appendix to chapter 3), you should add something along these lines: "Although I don't expect this, if any question makes you uncomfortable, you can simply not answer it. You can stop the interview at any time." I also often ask, "Do you have any questions for me?" Finally, while the respondent is signing the consent form (see appendix to chapter 3), I say, "I'm going to turn on the recorder now. Is that okay?" You want to get the respondent's explicit permission for each step covered by IRB rules.

USE A PARTICIPANT'S OWN WORDS

When I was new to interviewing, I kept asking probes that put my own spin on what respondents said. For example, I might summarize, "It sounds like you were struggling to keep up." I did this, in part, because it seemed strange to repeat back, word for word, what the person had just said. I thought it was too obvious. Unfortunately, my versions sometimes missed the mark and caused problems. Using a respondent's own words can be very powerful and much better than paraphrasing what you heard. It shows that in addition to listening, you care enough about what the respondent is telling you to reproduce it exactly. One common approach is to take the last few words of a respondent's answer, repeat these word for word, and then simply wait for the respondent to resume talking. For instance, at one point in the novice interview excerpt that appears later in this chapter, the mom says, "Nothing, now that sports is over with." A good probe would be to say, "Sports is over" and nothing more. Good probes aren't always questions. Although it can feel strange for the interviewer to say, usually the words resonate with the respondent, and the words can be a valuable probe.

REUSE EFFECTIVE PROBES

You don't need to invent unique probes for each question on your interview guide. When respondents recognize that you're listening closely to what they're saying, they normally become involved in telling their story and are unlikely to notice the repetition of probes. During some interviews, you may find that it helps to use the same probe over and over again: "Can you tell me more about that?" is a good probe. "Can you think of a recent moment when that happened?" is another good probe. Silence is a good probe, too. When a respondent pauses, wait a few seconds. Often the person will resume talking, adding more details in order to fill the silence.

FOCUS ON LEARNING THE SUBJECTIVE MEANINGS THAT EVENTS OR EXPERIENCES HAVE FOR A RESPONDENT

Qualitative researchers are more interested in finding out what a certain event or experience *means* to a person. In other words, what did the respondent like and not like about the event or experience? What are examples of some of the most meaningful events in the respondent's life? What has been a challenge? The interviewer builds a connection with the respondent, and deep in an interview, it is possible, at times, for the interviewer to ask very personal questions (e.g., "How did that make you feel?" after the respondent shares a great difficulty). Interviews are a valuable tool for exploring subjective meaning.

DON'T BE AFRAID TO ASK A QUESTION THAT
DRAWS ON YOUR OWN KNOWLEDGE

Recently, I interviewed a wealthy, young, Mexican American married mother. She had grown up in a blue-collar home with a traditional, gendered division of labor. Her mother never worked outside the home, even though the family's limited resources sometimes resulted in household food shortages. My respondent also mentioned that her brothers were expected to manage economic shortfalls (e.g., being sent to the grocery store to buy sufficient food with insufficient funds) while she was protected from these economic strains. As she continued talking about her childhood, I sensed that she had faced some difficulty while she was growing up. Just after she told me that she had liked to read when she was young, I decided to take a bit of a chance. I asked, "Did you have to do housework?" This probe was a risk because she hadn't said a thing about housework, and it might seem as if I wasn't listening to her. In addition, my research project was about families and money; housework wasn't a directly relevant topic. Yet, I knew from other research that in some working-class homes, girls are expected to do a great deal of housework. When I asked about housework, her face lit up. With a lot of feeling, she answered, "Yes!" and went on to explain how she hated the many chores of food preparation, washing dishes by hand, and ironing her father's jeans, discussing how she thought it was unfair and so forth. She seemed to interpret my question as a sign that I understood a key part of her childhood. My risky probe ended up creating a turning point in the interview. After that question, my respondent was warmer and even more forthcoming. Sometimes it can be a good idea to take a chance and ask a question based on your own experience or your knowledge of the literature. If the probe doesn't work, just move on. Overall, you generally want your questions to be consistent across interviews, but you also want to be open to being able to dig deep about a unique experience a person has had that sheds light on the issue. Sometimes, these explorations lead you to add a new question to the study to ask your remaining respondents.

KEEP THINKING WHILE YOU ARE LISTENING

During an interview, it's the interviewee who most often leads the way. If your respondent spontaneously begins talking about something you cover in a question that comes later in your interview guide, you have two choices. You can try to redirect the respondent by saying, for example, "Oh, I'll be getting to that later." Or, you can follow the respondent's lead and (without comment) jump to the later question. In my opinion, this second choice is a vastly better decision. Redirection interrupts the flow of a reply and may discourage any further spontaneous sharing of information on the respondent's part. But this kind of pivoting in response to an interviewee's answer means that you must juggle questions as you go on with the interview. You also must continue to listen attentively and look fully engaged even as your mind is rapidly sorting through your options: "Should I keep going with this line of questioning?" "Should I ask a follow-up question?" "Should I pivot to a different line of questioning?" You have to make decisions on the fly, and you must do so without knowing exactly what the respondent has to tell you. (You might find it helpful to jot down some notes while you are listening, so you remember what you need to cover.) The need to manage multiple issues simultaneously can make interviewing nerve-wracking. It is helpful to have a handful of issues that are your highest priorities. In the best-case scenario, you have a clear idea of what you want to know and why you want to know it. But, this also evolves as the study progresses. Ideally, by the time your interviews are about one-half to two-thirds of the way done, you will have found your focus and your priorities will be much clearer than when you started.

RETURN TO A THEME RAISED BY A RESPONDENT IF YOU WANT FURTHER INFORMATION

Typically, even a brief answer opens up several potential lines of questioning. Since you can ask only one question at a time, some paths necessarily go unexplored. Others may resurface naturally later in the interview. But if they don't, it's fine for you to return to them. You might say, "Earlier you mentioned ... What was that like for you?" Or, "Can you tell me more about ... ?" This kind of doubling back also can be beneficial because it shows the respondent that you've been listening closely and that you remember what has been said. In addition, at the end, I always ask, "Is there anything else important on this topic that we have not talked about?" Relatedly, Shamus Khan's final question is this: "In this interview, I was interested in [insert my research question here]. Is there anything you didn't tell me that you wish you did? Is there anything I should have asked that I didn't?"[2]

BE MINDFUL OF POWER INEQUALITIES

There are delicate and complex power dynamics in interviews. The interviewer and the participant arrive at the interview with not only different life experiences, but also social positions that have differential social status—including racial and ethnic background, age, gender, education, and so forth. These factors inevitably shape the interview process. Participants give their consent to be in your study and they decide what they want to share. As the interviewer, you are both powerful (you are asking the questions and guiding the interview) and powerless (the participant decides whether you can talk to them, what to share, and with what depth). You want to be careful that you do not pressure respondents to do something they don't want to do. You want to listen closely and respond sensitively. At the same time, if you don't guide the interview, then you will not get the information you set out to collect, so you need to exert some forms of power in the process so that the interview stays focused. There are no easy answers here, but you want to be alert to these issues and adjust accordingly. Also, information gathering occurs on both sides of the recorder. Participants rarely have a reason to trust you in advance, thus, they are always looking for cues about your agenda. Even if you spent many hours getting one interview, if participants look uncomfortable and signal unease, you want to stop the interview to check in to see how they are doing. You must end the interview if the participant wants to do so. You need to follow the meaning and spirit of informed consent.

TAKE CONTROL WITH OVERLY TALKATIVE RESPONDENTS

Some respondents are "big talkers" and go off on many tangents. Since these individuals are hard to control, you need to intervene in the first few minutes. When respondents' replies are off track, it's important not to fidget while they ramble or pontificate. Your best option is to repeat your question. As you listen to the response, nod and look appreciative, but watch closely for the respondent to draw a breath and then pivot to direct the interview back to what you are interested in finding out. You might say something like, "That is so interesting. Now, tell me [and repeat your question]." One way to gauge whether you're mastering the art of controlling an interview is to examine transcripts. Generally, you want to see replies that are about one (single-spaced) paragraph long. Except in rare cases, if an answer to one question produces a full page of single-spaced text, something is wrong. You need to be asking more questions.

EXPECT OVERLY SUCCINCT RESPONDENTS

Arguably, it's more difficult to interview people who are withdrawn, intimidated, or simply not big talkers. These respondents tend to provide very brief replies. When you ask them to elaborate, some look at you blankly, or worse, they appear to be annoyed. There are several strategies you can try during the first few minutes of an interview to improve your chances of getting the kind of details you need.

Some reticent interviewees respond well to being coaxed: "Thank you so much. It's super helpful to get details so that I can understand your experience a bit more—it varies a lot from person to person." Sometimes making self-deprecating comments boosts the confidence of respondents who feel intimidated: "I am someone who actually doesn't know much about how this works. Can you tell me a bit more? How do you approach it?" Sometimes it helps to stop the interview briefly and talk about something else—an attractive or unusual object in the room, an interesting aspect of the respondent's clothing, or any other topic that seems to matter to the respondent. Shy or withdrawn respondents may relax (sometimes visibly) as they discuss a topic they care about. This lets you get a sense of how they act when they are at ease. It's essential to hide any rising frustration you might feel and to look genuinely and authentically interested in what is being said.

It's also important that you feel entitled to be "nosy" and to ask additional, probing questions. Respondents don't know what kind of information you want. They learn that only if you continue to ask them for more details. If they don't volunteer the information you need, you should simply ask for it, unless you sense that your respondent considers your probing out of bounds. In that case, you should back off immediately. People are unlikely to volunteer information about socially sensitive matters (including sexual practices, anger at their parents, and career failures), but many will do so if they are politely asked. In raising a potentially sensitive topic, you are giving them permission to tell you more. In the end, however, some people are simply more talkative than others. If you have tried all the strategies you know and find that after about one hour, the interview still is not going well, I recommend bringing the interview to a close, thanking the respondent, and leaving. Disappointing interviews happen to everyone.

TRY TO BALANCE DIGGING DEEP AND MOVING ON

There is tension between your goals of depth and breadth in one interview. You want to be sure to have "dug deep" on a couple of issues, especially one topic relatively early in the interview. But, you also want to be mindful that you have more than one question to ask. You might think in advance about what is "nonnegotiable" in the interview. Then, depending on how the interview flows, you can get to other topics. As noted in chapter 4, it can be helpful to give respondents a list of important events for them to review; the list allows you to cover a number of topics more briskly.

DEVELOP A PLAN TO DEFLECT QUESTIONS

You want your time together to be spent on them, not you. But many people are curious about you. You might think about some things you feel comfortable sharing about yourself that are brief and appropriate to the setting, and allow you to pivot back to the focus of the study. For example, as a graduate student, I would share where I was studying and when I hoped to graduate, and I would make a joke about my nervousness about finding a job. Then I would focus on the interview. Or, while visiting families, I would frequently say (in an effort to put a family at ease) that I "grew up with a lot of yelling" in my family, and I would tell a story (described in chapter 6) of how my younger sister and I would "argue all the time" when we shared a room. The goal was to reveal something that would help establish me as a trustworthy, down-to-earth person. If someone persists, you can say, "Gosh, I would love to talk more after our interview is done, but right now I am anxious to hear about your experiences." Judith Levine reports she says, "I'm mindful that I don't want to take up too much of your time, and I want to ensure that we have enough time for the interview." Then, I would chat for a few minutes at the close of the interview, but then plead that I have another deadline and, "I need to run." You might think about why a person is eager to know more about you. Sometimes the person seeks reassurance that you are trustworthy. Sometimes if they say that they are interested in a topic, what they really want to do is to tell you their own perspective on it. Also, remember (as with reporters) you do not have to answer the question you were asked. You can answer a different question instead. In my opinion, as much as possible, you want to be "vague but accurate" in terms of your findings. Maybe there is one, generic (unoffensive) point you can share. Or, you can say "It is simply too early to know" your findings, but you will share a brief overview at the end of the study.

CHECK TO SEE WHETHER YOU HAVE
ASKED ALL OF YOUR QUESTIONS

Since interviews unfold in an unpredictable fashion, it's very common to forget to ask (at least) one of the questions from your interview guide. Since I'm a "go with the flow" type of interviewer, I'm particularly bad at making sure that I ask the same questions of every respondent. Among other problems, this inconsistency makes it hard to use basic tables to summarize the frequency of patterns in the entire sample. One strategy for avoiding incomplete data is to stop for a moment before the end of the interview and say, "Sorry. Let me pause for a second to make sure that I didn't forget to ask you anything important." This helps to ensure that you did cover the core questions contained in your guide. Still, it's inevitable that later you will realize that you failed to ask an important follow-up question. This is both frustrating and normal.

Some researchers feel comfortable asking a follow-up question in an email. I did this once when I forgot to ask a respondent her political affiliation and whether she had voted in a presidential election. She answered the question (saying she was unaffiliated and hadn't voted). But, this kind of follow-up is tricky since it makes the interviewer look slightly incompetent and puts an additional—and potentially unwanted—burden on the respondent (however, some respondents explicitly invite follow-up questions). In my opinion, it's better to have a system that helps you remember to ask each of the key questions. Keep in mind though, forgetting to ask an important question happens to everyone. It's not worth losing sleep over. It happens.

LISTEN FOR GREAT QUOTES BUT KEEP
YOUR EXPECTATIONS REALISTIC

Frequently, there's a moment during an interview when the respondent says something that is especially helpful and, even better, makes a key statement eloquently. (With practice, you will likely find it easy to instantly recognize a great quote.) But it's not realistic to expect more than one or two outstanding quotes per respondent. When I heard this caution as a graduate student, I was shocked. (I thought, "All of that work for only one quote?") Remember, though, that even in a small study, you will conduct multiple interviews. All of the interviews, even those that are not as detailed, will provide a basis for your claims. When you write up your findings, incorporating great quotes from a variety of respondents will make your conclusions more persuasive.

Two Sample Interviews

SAMPLE INTERVIEW 1:
AN INTERVIEW THAT IS NOT VERY DETAILED

The first interview examined here was carried out by a novice—a smart, thoughtful, first-semester white doctoral student named Jenna Harvey (a pseudonym as are all names in this chapter), who was working on the research project for my book *Unequal Childhoods*.[3] The excerpt covers about 15 percent of an interview that runs 40 pages double-spaced; the entire interview probably took around 90 minutes to complete. There are some bright spots. Overall, though, the interview doesn't consistently yield rich, detailed quotes. As I point out in the boxed commentary that accompanies the excerpt, other choices—particularly in the probes—might have been more effective.

The interviewer met the respondent, Ms. Silverman, a white, working-class, married mother, at a fall practice for her nine-year-old son Dougie's football team. Ms. Silverman had already gotten a letter about the project as Dougie was a student in a classroom I was observing as part of my research study. In addition to chatting with Ms. Silverman at the practice, the interviewer called her to set up the interview and contacted her the night before to confirm the December interview in Ms. Silverman's home. The excerpt below begins after Ms. Silverman has signed the consent form and given permission for the use of an audio-recorder.

Starting the Interview

Interviewer: First of all, you told me this at the football practice, but, could you tell me who is in your family? You have an older daughter and son, right?

Ms. Silverman: Right.

Interviewer: I forget their names.

> This isn't an unreasonable probe, but it would be nicer to apologize, "Sorry, I've forgotten their names"; or, even better, "Sorry, can you refresh my memory about their names?" Parents usually consider their kids the most precious thing in their lives. They can be prickly if you forget their kids' names.

Ms. Silverman: Jim and he's twenty-one; Trishie is fourteen; and Dougie, he's nine.

Interviewer: Now, if you were describing Doug to someone who had never met him before, what would you say to give a picture of him?

> Note that when Ms. Silverman refers to her son, she uses "Dougie." The interviewer, starting this sentence, converts this to "Doug" and in doing so inadvertently introduces a small rift between her respondent and herself. The two women now aren't collaborating as closely as they would be if she had repeated her respondent exactly by using "Dougie."

Ms. Silverman: He's a good kid some days and some days he's a bad kid. He's smart. To me, he's very smart. Sometimes I have problems with his behavior. But he's good.

> The mom's answer is a good example of a normal challenge for interviewers: in a single, short answer, the respondent has introduced five distinct points (her son is a "good kid" some days, a "bad kid" other days, "he's smart" (note the hint of defensiveness or maybe awe, "to me he's very smart"), and "sometimes" she has "problems" with his behavior. Being presented with so many

different pathways to explore is stressful. Which one should you choose?

I suggest doing two things: choose a *positive* point and then begin to teach your respondent regarding the data you need by using a probe that calls for specific, concrete detail:

"Tell me of a recent example, in the last few days, when he was a good kid. Did something happen today or yesterday?"

Or, you could say, "Yes, I see in the classroom how smart he is. Tell me what you notice here at home."

The second example is riskier than the first since it emphasizes academics and aligns you with the school. This could have drawbacks if there is tension with the school. I would skip following this path for now.

Of the five paths, I see the positive ones as at the two best choices. As I show below, "bad kid" and "problems with behavior" are negative. They put her son (and her) in a less-than-ideal light. "But he's good" is quite general and thus doesn't provide a good starting point for more detail.

Interviewer: Can you talk more about that, problems with behavior?

This is not an ideal probe because in her reply, the respondent praised her son *four* separate times:

"he's a good kid"
"he's smart"
"to me he's very smart"
"he's good"

Unfortunately, the interviewer's follow-up question doesn't signal that she has heard any of these positive attributes. Instead, she zeroes in on the only negative point ("Can you talk more about that, problems with behavior?") The respondent may conclude that the interviewer isn't listening closely or possibly is more interested in learning information that makes the family look bad.

It's important to always keep in mind the collaborative character of an interview. You and your respondent need to be working together in order to achieve the interview's ultimate goal: bright, detailed data that will strengthen the research. In this interview, focusing the follow-up probe on a positive point ("Tell me of a recent example, in the last few days, when he was a good kid. Did something happen today or yesterday?") would have established more trust. Then, later on in the interview, it might have been possible to return to the behavior problems (or other difficult moments in parenting). But bear in mind that many parents identify deeply with their children; criticizing the child amounts to criticizing the parent.

Ms. Silverman: Like, he'll be tired or in a mood and you'll tell him to do something and he just won't do it, period, you know. He'll like throw a temper tantrum or something, you know. It used to be worse, but now it's getting better where he doesn't do it as often. I guess he's growing up.

Interviewer: Like what kinds of things did he throw a temper tantrum for?

The mom is turning the discussion into a more positive direction — "it's getting better" — and this would be a nice direction to follow. The interviewer's questions, however, is a good effort to get more detail, but she's being overly general when she asks, "Like what kinds of things did he throw a temper tantrum for?" This invites her respondent to summarize a number of different temper tantrums, which in turn is likely to lead to vague and general accounts. It's better to focus on a recent temper tantrum, one that happened in the last week. For instance: "Can you think of a recent example — maybe one that happened in the last week — and tell me more about it?"

Then, as the respondent adds more information, listen for opportunities to probe for even greater detail. The specific follow-up questions you ask depend on what you want to know and why you want to know it. In this interview, useful probes for learning more about tantrums would include, "What happened just before the temper tantrum started?" "Where were you (in the house or outside)?" "Who were you with?" "What was the name of his friend?" "What time of day was it?" "Can you remember exactly what he said?" You should always aim to ask about a specific moment, not a general pattern. Details are key.

Ms. Silverman: If you tell him no, you can't go here with one of his friends, or no, you can't have this. Something like that. It depends on the mood he's in. That always used to happen and I'd just try to ignore him or yell at him. That's about it.

Here the respondent is beginning to set limits on the depth of her replies ("That's about it"). That shift is a bad sign. The goal is to have the respondent provide increasingly detailed answers as the interview proceeds.

In the present case, the interviewer might have asked what it was like for the respondent to "try to ignore" her son:—"Isn't that hard?" She might also have risked asking about the mother's yelling. This would be tricky since the respondent may be embarrassed that she yells. Weaving reassurance into a possibly sensitive probe is helpful: "A lot of moms tell us about yelling, and it varies a lot. What's it like for you?"

Interviewer: Now, do Trishie and Jim both live here?
Ms. Silverman: Trishie yes, Jim no.

It would be better to wait until the end of the interview to ask this question because it doesn't require much more than a yes or no answer. At this early point in the interview, the goal is to coach the respondent to provide long, specific, and detailed answers.

Interviewer: OK. What kind of things is Doug into these days? How does he spend his time?

This is an important question in the study. The interviewer asks it well.

Ms. Silverman: Now that sports is over, he—he'll just find something to do around. Nothing now that sports is over with. He'll sit and watch TV with us, play Nintendo. That's it. Well, if his friends come, he'll go out, but if his friends don't knock, he doesn't go to see them. He'll just stay home and watch TV or play Nintendo.

This is a reasonable answer, but it's still too general. The reply covers a lot of ground, making it hard to get a sense of what Dougie actually does now that "sports" are "over." This is the most interesting part of the answer since for middle-class kids, participation in sports is year-round. In this blue-collar family, the son plays only football. The interviewer has a lot of options here. She could use any of the following probes:

"Sports is over." This would be my first choice of probe. Depending on exactly what followed, the interviewer would follow up by asking how much time the son's involvement with football took, who went to the practices and games, how her son got there, how much work was involved, how she felt about it, how he talked to her about it, and so forth.

"What kinds of programs does he watch on TV with you?" This probe doesn't quote the respondent exactly (Ms. Silverman says, "with us"), but neither does it paraphrase the response. The interviewer could ask where they watch TV, how long they watch, who else is in the group, who chooses the program, and if they have special snacks to understand how Dougie spends leisure time. All of these questions shed light on family dynamics.

"He plays Nintendo." After waiting quietly for her respondent's reply, the interviewer would then probe for any missing details related to where and when the respondent's son plays the Nintendo, how he reacts when he loses, who he plays with, how long he has had the gaming system, etc.

"His friends come by?" This question would let the interviewer get more details about the respondent's son's daily life. She could ask how often friends come to the house, the names of the friends who come, how far from home the kids on the block are allowed to go, whether the respondent's son has a bike, where it is kept, how many hours per day he is outside, if he has to be home by a special time, and so forth.

"Tell me about what happened yesterday after school." This probe doesn't repeat anything the respondent has said, but it creates an opening for the respondent to describe the kinds of daily activities mentioned above and provides opportunities for the interviewer to guide the discussion in ways that will encourage more details.

Any of these probes would have been fine, and any one of them would have resulted in the interviewer getting a lot more detail. But, she chooses not to follow up at all. This signals that she's not especially interested in what her respondent is saying and implies that this answer is completely satisfactory without any further elaboration. Note that after this reply, the respondent's answers begin to get shorter rather than longer and more expansive.

Reaching an Initial Turning Point in an Interview

A primary goal of the study is to learn how children spend their time and how much work it is for parents to get them through the day. Ms. Silverman's previous answer is especially important since it directly addresses a key research question. In a common "rookie" mistake, the interviewer continues too briskly without probing and thus misses a great opportunity to get the respondent to provide much-needed elaboration and details. In addition, by not following up here, the interviewer is inadvertently training the respondent to give shorter answers. At this point, the interview has been going on long enough for expectations of what the interviewer wants, and what the interviewee should provide, to start to solidify. Other options are being foreclosed. The window of opportunity for setting expectations dwindles after about the first fifteen minutes of an interview.

Interviewer: Does he have a lot of friends in the neighborhood?
Ms. Silverman: Yeah.
Interviewer: I mean right on the same block, or how far away?

> This is a reasonable probe because she is asking for more detail.

Ms. Silverman: There are like three or four boys across the street. There's another two here. Then he has one right up the next street. So, in the summertime, they're all together.

> This reply is very interesting. The interviewer should pause to probe for the names of the boys, their ages, whether any are related or all are from separate families, and whether the respondent has a close relationship to the families.
>
> The respondent's last sentence, "So, in the summertime, they're all together," is a rich, quotable line. It suggests a life of childhood autonomy where the kids are hanging out together.
>
> A reasonable probe might be to begin this way: "Wow. How nice. So are the three, four boys across the street in one family? How old are they?"
>
> Additional probes would then seem to flow naturally. "Are the boys all in the same grade?" "Do they go to the same school?" "Do they walk or take the bus together?" Alternatively, the interviewer could begin by focusing on summer. She might say, "Tell me about the summertime. They are all together?" She could ask about the respondent's work schedule and whether she has to make special arrangements during the summer or if the kids do okay on their own during the day. She could repeat, "So in the summertime they're all together," and quietly wait to hear how the respondent fills the silence.

Interviewer: And what kinds of things do they do?

Ms. Silverman: Well, they'll come in and play Nintendo or they'll go outside now since it's football season [on TV] and they'll play football. In the summertime, they'll play baseball.

Interviewer: Where do they go to play football?

Ms. Silverman: Right up here on the street, on the side. They play right there. That's about all they do. Sometimes they agitate each other.

Interviewer: And where do they play baseball?

Ms. Silverman: Right here on the same street.

Interviewer: And so how many afternoons a week would he be out there?

Ms. Silverman: One or two. He's played twice this week.

Interviewer: Does he ever go over to their houses?

Ms. Silverman: Sometimes. Or he'll call and say, "Are you coming out? No, we're gonna go here or there." Or he'll just stay in.

The interviewer could ask here: "Can you tell me about a recent example where he called to see if someone was coming out?" This would help the interview dig deeper.

Interviewer: So he does the football and the baseball and that's in the spring?

Ms. Silverman: Right.

Interviewer: Now, with the football, what kind of costs are involved in signing him up for that?

Ms. Silverman: We pay forty dollars for him for football.

Interviewer: And that includes the uniform?

Ms. Silverman: Yes.

Interviewer: And he has practices how many nights a week?

Ms. Silverman: Well, before school it was like every night of the week. When school started it cut back to three.

Interviewer: And when did the summer practices start?

Ms. Silverman: I think it was August somewhere. It might have been the last week or the last two weeks, somewhere in there.

Interviewer: So, it was every night, Monday through Friday?

Ms. Silverman: Yes.

Interviewer: And what times?

Ms. Silverman: Six to eight.

Interviewer: And when school started?

Ms. Silverman: When school started, it cut down to three nights and that was six to eight, too.

Interviewer: And did you have to remind him often to get ready for the practice?

It's good that the interviewer is asking for more detail here, but note that the way she frames the question, an appropriate answer would be "Yes" or "No." A more open-ended question would be better: "When kids need to get ready for practice, it can vary a lot in terms of how much kids take the lead and what role parents play. How is it with Dougie?"

The use of "take the lead" is likely to frame the answer and thus introduce worries about bias. But the framing also helps the respondent understand what kind of information the interviewer wants.

Ms. Silverman: Sometimes when it was hot out, when they first started the practices—he really didn't want to go because of the laps and the heat and all—he didn't want to go. And he quit once and his coach called him and he went back.

Although the probes are not generating the desired depth, Ms. Silverman begins to tell an extremely interesting story about her son quitting football, and how she and her husband responded.

Here, the respondent reveals that "when they first started the practices," her son "didn't want to go." Given that a key focus of the study is the work parents do to facilitate children's organized activities, this is a revealing moment in the interview, highlighting how parents have to assess how much to push children to participate.

This answer has a lot of potential. It's good that the interviewer pauses to probe it. Again, she has multiple options from which to choose. She could probe with "it was hot," or "he didn't want to go because of the laps," or "he quit once," or "his coach called," or "he went back."

If I were the interviewer, I might say, "Let's go back to when it was hot out and he didn't want to go. Tell me more about that." Then I would probe when the complaints started, exactly what the son said, how hot it was, what the uniform was like, whether she remembered what Dougie's father had said (since interviewers aren't supposed to ask respondents to report on others' thoughts, etc.), what she thought, and so forth. Then after that, I would go back to the day her son quit to ask for details on why it happened on that day, what triggered the decision, who her son told, how she and her husband reacted, how her son told the coach, and so forth. All of this probing would take time, and it would mean that I wouldn't be able to ask other important questions. Whether that kind of trade-off is a good one depends on the nature of your research question. Given the research question in my study, spending more time here would be worth it.

Interviewer: And when he quit, what happened with that ...?

It's good that the interviewer is following up on this story. The probe asks mostly for the outcome (i.e., "what happened"). A more open-ended probe is preferable. There are many options to choose from: "Tell me more about that. How did you feel when you first heard? What did your husband say to you about it? How did you manage it?" This is a better probe because it gets more at the meaning of the event and the details of how it unfolded.

Ms. Silverman: He just didn't want to go because of the heat, and he didn't want to do all them laps, running around at Arrow Field, because it's a long run. He just didn't want to do it. And his coach called him and said he wanted him back, so he decided he would go back.

Here it would have been helpful to learn how hot it was during this time—to get the respondent's estimate of the temperature. "Gosh. It sounds hot. How hot was it exactly—if you had to make a ballpark guess?" Frequently, in reply to this kind of question, respondents say that they have no idea. But if you ask a second time, and give some choices, including one absurd one (Do you think it was 85 degrees, 95, 105, 116?), they will make an estimate. Also it would be great to get more detail around this key line, "He just didn't want to do it." The interviewer could repeat that sentence and wait, "So, he just didn't want to do it." Ideally, when asked, the respondent would be able to recall what her son actually said when he quit. Having his exact words would paint a more vibrant picture of the event.

Interviewer: Did he tell the coach that he quit, or did you have to call him?

The intent behind this quote is excellent (i.e., did the parent or child handle this event), but the wording—"Did you have to call him?"—is not ideal. The mother didn't "have to" take any action, but she would likely have seen informing the coach as something that needed to be done. Her reply shows that she understood the interviewer's intent, however.

Ms. Silverman: He had to do it.

This is interesting. The reply is brief, but it is quotable: "He had to do it."

Interviewer: He did?
Ms. Silverman: Yeah.
Interviewer: Did he do it at one of the practices?
Ms. Silverman: His father took him because I had to go back to work that one night, and his father took him over there, and he turned in his equipment and said he quit.
Interviewer: And then the coach called him?
Ms. Silverman: And I think he went back the next night, and we signed him up again at Arrow.
Interviewer: And was that during a practice that you signed him back up?

Ms. Silverman: Yeah.

Interviewer: And did you have to pay again?

Ms. Silverman: We had to pay twenty dollars because we paid forty dollars and they gave us twenty dollars back [when Dougie quit], so we had to repay the twenty dollars.

Interviewer: And when was that in the season?

Ms. Silverman: About two or three weeks after they started.

Interviewer: And did he talk with you guys about his decision before he did it or about rejoining the team? How did that happen? Was there a fight about it?

> The interviewer is improving here. She makes a nice effort to probe for more details. Each probe is valuable, but it's a better idea to ask only one question and listen carefully to the answer before asking another. The third question would be better to hold in reserve as a probe. Note that when/if the interviewer deploys the third question as a probe, she should use the respondent's own words rather than introducing the word "fight."

Ms. Silverman: No, I just told him that if he wanted to re-sign up, I would sign him up, but I don't want to hear nothing about, "I'm not going to practice, I'm not going to practice." You've got to go to practice. It's a very important part of it. He was just fine. So, we made him go to practice. Some nights he didn't want to go, and I said, "Dougie, you've got to go." Once he got dressed, he was fine.

> This is the best quote of the interview so far because it so clearly conveys the respondent's approach to her son's resistance concerning football (e.g., "Dougie, you've got to go").

Interviewer: So would he put up a fight or throw a tantrum?

It's wonderful that the interviewer is seeking more detail here. But her wording narrows the respondent's options. The question frames two, quasi-fixed choices: put up a fight or throw a tantrum. Although the respondent did use "temper tantrum" earlier in the interview, the interviewer's use of the term here results in too much guidance. It would be better to just say, "Tell me more about it." Or, "Can you think back to a specific day?" Or, "He would say, 'I'm not going to practice.'"

Ms. Silverman: Sometimes. He would say he didn't want to go, but we made him go.

It would be very helpful to learn more about this interesting line. The best way to do that would be for the interviewer to repeat, almost word for word, what the respondent just said, "You made him go." Then she would wait five to ten seconds. Usually that period of silence will nudge a respondent into talking.

It also would be helpful to learn more about what the respondent thought about her son's involvement in football, why she thought it was important for him to go to every practice, game, and so forth, since it highlights a key family practice that she insists on despite the protests of her son. The interviewer could say, "Tell me more about that." Without more detail, it's hard to tell whether the son is moping and whining or raising a full-scale objection to continuing with football. A further probe might be, "Tell me more about how this happened. What was he doing?" The interviewer could also try, "I don't know if this makes sense, but is it possible to describe his tone of voice?" In addition, it would help to clarify the timing of the objections the respondent is referring to. It seems likely that she's talking about behaviors that occurred before her son quit rather than after he rejoined the team, but this isn't completely clear.

Interviewer: And did it ever come down to you actually having to put on his uniform for him?

Ms. Silverman: No, no, no. If it had to come to that I would say, forget it, we won't go then, you'll just have to quit or something.

Interviewer: And when he quit, did he talk to you about his decision to quit?

> "Did he talk to you about his decision to quit?" encourages the respondent to simply answer yes or no. Wording the question differently would yield a more expansive answer. "Tell me more. How did he talk about it?" Or, "Do you remember when you first heard about it? How did he bring it up?"
>
> Despite the way the interviewer framed her question, however, the respondent's answer (below) is a good one.

Ms. Silverman: He kept telling us he wanted to quit, he wanted to quit and finally we just said, OK. There's no sense in forcing him to play. So we let him choose to quit, and we asked him five or six times before we signed him up [again], "Are you sure? You've got to go to practice all the time. You'd better be sure this time." We talked about it before.

> This is a good quote. It has some emotion in it. (The respondent's frustration is palpable.) The interviewer could have followed up here by saying, "So take me back to that moment when you were trying to decide. What were your thoughts?" "What did your husband say?" Alternatively, the interviewer could repeat part of the respondent's answer, "There's no sense in forcing him to play," and then wait.
>
> Ideally, interviewers probe for a variety of details that help paint a compelling picture of the event or experience they are interested in. Here, the interviewer might have asked, "Was there a particular moment when you decided? Do you remember where you were at the time?" The goal of this probe is to find out specifics: Were they

in the car, sitting around in front of the TV, at dinner, or elsewhere? Did Dougie tell his mom only or did he also tell his dad? How exactly did the parents react? Getting as much detail as possible increases the likelihood of correctly understanding what happened.

Interviewer: And then every Saturday they had a game?

Ms. Silverman: Yeah.

Interviewer: And how many times was it away and how many times was it here?

Ms. Silverman: I don't know. I don't even know how many games they played, maybe ten games. So it was like, probably five away and five here I'd say, because it was like every other weekend it was away.

The number of home and away games is useful information. But it's objective data the interviewer could have gathered from a different source (e.g., the league roster), thus leaving her more time during the interview to pursue subjective data by asking questions about the respondent's experiences, values, beliefs, etc.

SUMMING UP: AN INTERVIEW THAT SKIMMED THE SURFACE

The interviewer completed the interview and learned some valuable information. The information she gathered also met the project's goals. The respondent's son had relatively few organized activities, had a vibrant life of play outside of the home, and had parents who were deeply ambivalent about whether he should be forced to play an organized sport after he had changed his mind and wanted to quit.

Yet, the interviewer didn't learn as much as might have been possible. Specifically, she didn't find out the meaning the respondent attached to the experiences associated with her son's involvement with football, the impact of his activities on her own life, her values and priorities, or details about the family's everyday life.[4] Too often, the interviewer asked narrow questions rather than general questions followed by probes on specifics. The interviewer didn't *stay with a question* long enough to get a lot of detail by probing deeply, rephrasing it, or trying different angles. The interviewer also sometimes asked the respondent to summarize several events at once, leading to increasingly general replies. There wasn't much laughter or much praise of the respondent, nor was the interviewer able to create enough warmth to ease the awkwardness that occurs naturally between strangers, especially in the early stages of an interview.

But the interviewer also avoided some common traps. The interviewer did not talk too much. Some interviewers find it very difficult to limit what they say in favor of increasing the time available for the respondent's answers. Although briefly sharing a personal experience can help to foster rapport, an interview isn't a good place to think out loud or to chat about your own experiences or feelings. (But sometimes sharing something personal, particularly early in the interview, can help you build rapport. Some interviewers always say one personal statement early.) The interviewer's goal should be to establish a good rapport and then elicit detailed information from the respondent. Despite being a novice, the interviewer also avoided judging either the respondent or the respondent's son. Also, the interviewer was consistently polite, never becoming rude or curt. Given the interviewer's inexperience, I rate the interview as a reasonable early interview in a project. It yielded a couple of quite good quotes (as noted above, it's not uncommon for an interview to produce only one great quote), but it could have been much richer and deeper. Higher-quality data would have provided a stronger basis for drawing analytical conclusions.

SAMPLE INTERVIEW 2: A MORE DETAILED INTERVIEW

Below is an excerpt from a two-hour interview I conducted with Ms. Celeste Taylor, an African American parent whose family is among those I discuss in *Unequal Childhoods*. She is separated from her husband.[5] At the time of the interview, their son Tyrec was a student in a fourth-grade classroom I was observing as part of my research project. Ms. Taylor has a high school degree, is enrolled in an online, for-profit college, and holds a full-time job as an administrative assistant. Ideally, the interview would have been a one-on-one affair in a private setting. This wasn't the case, in part because I wasn't sufficiently assertive with Ms. Taylor when we set up the interview and in part because this mother's full-time work schedule would have made it difficult to find a time and place to interview her alone. (Circumstances such as these are why Kathryn Edin has developed a pattern of sending two interviewers to one interview; one entertains the children and one interviews the mother.) The interview took place in Ms. Taylor's rented home. I came on a Sunday evening in January, after a week of unusually bad storms and cold weather. Tyrec (who was nine years old) was there for much of the interview, and he was eager to be interviewed. Ms. Taylor's nineteen-year-old son, Malcolm, and thirteen-year-old daughter, Anisha, were in and out. Fortunately, the interview guide didn't focus on deeply intimate questions; it centered mainly on assessing the rhythms of Tyrec's daily life.

The interview excerpt begins after Ms. Taylor has signed the consent form and given me permission to use an audio-recorder. There are several things to pay attention to as you read the excerpt. Note that a great many probes ask for specific detail, that sometimes the same question is asked multiple times in different ways, and that the respondent's answers become more detailed as the interview proceeds. The interview is negotiated between the two people. After getting off to a slow start, I spend about twenty minutes gathering information about Tyrec's participation in organized sports (football) in order to get as clear an understanding as possible of how his involvement affects his mother and the rest of the family.

Starting the Interview
Interviewer: What a cute cup!

> Here I'm trying to build rapport with the respondent. My enthusiasm is genuine, and so I offer this compliment. Often, if I see something that I admire, I say so. This can help ease the awkwardness of the initial moment and soften the interaction.

Ms. Taylor: My Tyrec gave me this for Christmas.
Interviewer: That's a wonderful gift.
Ms. Taylor: I thought so.

Interviewer: Now, imagine that you were describing Tyrec to someone who had never met him—how would you describe him? What kind of child is he?

Ms. Taylor: He's just all boy. He's all boy. I don't know how to describe that. Is it OK to just say that he's all boy? He's full of energy. He's bright.

Interviewer: Imagine that you're describing him to someone who had never met him.

> This is a broad, open-ended question. This respondent knows her son. Her deep love for him is apparent immediately. This is a follow-up probe to help her understand that I'm looking for a lot of detail in her answers. At this early stage in the interview, a probe like this is preferable to accepting the respondent's first answer and moving on.

Ms. Taylor: Oh, he's just lovable. He's just the perfect little kid. He is. He's not bad and he's not good. He's just a kid in every sense of the word, but he's a nice little kid. He's a very lovable little fellow.

Interviewer: He is a nice boy. I've enjoyed him. I've been getting to know him a little bit.

Ms. Taylor: He's a little hyper.

> The mother criticizes her son after I say, "He is a nice boy." She says, "He's a little hyper." I seek to defuse her criticism ("He's only in fourth grade.") In retrospect, I see this as slightly risky. The respondent could have felt that I was criticizing her parenting. It would have been better to say something like, "I've enjoyed getting to know him" and then move to the next question.

Interviewer: He's only in fourth grade. And what kinds of things does he like to do with his time?

Ms. Taylor: Well, his favorite thing is to play video games, of course.

He plays football. This was his first year, last year, that he did football. He loved it. So he's now a football fan and he's all into it.

Interviewer: There's a big football game tomorrow, isn't there?

Ms. Taylor: Yeah. (She turns to one of the kids, "Someone is going to have to go to the store to get some paper towels for our hands.") That's highly embarrassing, to have not one napkin. OK. (Now speaking directly to Tyrec) She wants to talk to me.

Tyrec is hanging around, and he very much wants to be interviewed. His mother is setting limits, so I follow her lead. But I offer to talk to him, with his mother's permission, after my interview with her is over. It's a no-win situation since I want to please both Tyrec, whom I know from school and don't want to disappoint, and his mother, who has set aside time to talk with me. But, I cannot give them both my attention in the same moment. I am worried that Tyrec's presence will constrain the mother's comments, but I am dependent on the mother to decide how to manage it.

If I were to do it again, I would stop the interview with the mom, and interview Tyrec for fifteen minutes. Then, I would go back to interviewing his mother.

Interviewer: (Speaking directly to Tyrec) And maybe after I finish talking to your mom, I can talk to you for a little bit. OK? (Returning to the interview and addressing the respondent) You mentioned football and video games—any other things he enjoys?

Ms. Taylor: What else?

Interviewer: During this last week when he was off from school … (voice trails off)

Ms. Taylor: He video-gamed himself out. That's basically the major number one interest, in-house activity, is playing the video games. He has lots of them and he's very good at it. And that's his thing, so he does that. He has a few programs on TV that he likes to watch. But he's more into the video games. He'll play it for hours.

"He'll play it for hours." This is important. It implies that there are no house rules limiting how long Tyrec plays video games. I want to get a clearer understanding of the situation. I'd like to ask Ms. Taylor how she feels about Tyrec playing "for hours," but I don't want to sound critical. So, for the time being, I focus instead on getting more details.

Interviewer: Where does he play? Does he play downstairs?

Ms. Taylor: Yeah...... (Here I skip eight brief additional questions I asked in order to establish where exactly in the house Tyrec plays video games, the number of video games he owns, and that he received two for Christmas costing around $50 each at the time. Those questions and answers have been omitted.)

Interviewer: Alright. And so, in a typical day, like a day like today [Sunday], how many hours do you think he'll spend doing the video games? Like what time did he get up this morning?

Here I'm trying to get a sense of whether there are any limits to playing video games. I'm trying to get more detail.

Ms. Taylor: He got up this morning about nine-thirty. He slept late today. He usually gets up early, but he did sleep late today.

Interviewer: He usually gets up around when?

Ms. Taylor: He gets up around seven-thirty or eight, even on the weekends. So, I'd say six [hours of video games] throughout the day.

Interviewer: And what about this unusual week, with all this bad weather?

Ms. Taylor: It's been horrible. They've been playing them from the time they get up until (pauses) but, you know, they all get burned out after a while. They'll play them for a few hours and then they have to break from it and start doing something else, I think. But this week, you know, with everyone being at home—we have the nineteen-year-old brother and he has all his friends and they all treat him [Tyrec] as an equal. So he plays with them all the time, you know. He goes to their houses with his brother. He's one of the gang. So when they're all around, like this week, because Malcolm wasn't able to go to work and all, so, yeah, they've been playing an awful lot of video games.

> Two lines in this quote are interesting: "they all get burned out after a while" and "[Tyrec] plays with them [Malcolm and Malcolm's friends] all the time."
>
> I could have lingered longer, but I sensed that there were no rules and that, at a minimum, Tyrec played six hours per day. (Note that his mother says he plays all day but then estimates "six hours throughout the day." But I know from other parts of the interview that he also went to church and did other things.)

Interviewer: And did he go out at all in the snow this week?
Ms. Taylor: No.
Interview: So he didn't have anything like a plastic sled or anything like that?
Ms. Taylor: No. They do that kind of stuff, but I didn't want him out because it's just entirely too cold, and I just didn't want them outside.

> Here I make a small mistake by revealing my surprise at hearing that Tyrec wasn't allowed to play outside. Showing surprise implies criticism (or a view that the respondent is abnormal). In this instance, Ms. Taylor defends her position clearly, "it's just entirely too cold." The day of the interview, it was 31 degrees, which is not that cold for kids, but it was unusually cold that week, and school had been canceled. I could have probed further, but I worried about making her defensive, and I have a lot of ground to cover. I move on.

Interviewer: All right. Tell me about the football. How did it happen that he started playing football?

Ms. Taylor: Well, he wanted to play. I think he went to a practice. He wanted to play last year but we wouldn't let him. We thought he was too young, and he was very upset that he couldn't play last year. And then I think he went to one of the practices with someone around here, one of his friends, and he wanted to sign up. So he told me that he wanted to play football and I said no, I don't think so. He said he wants to play so bad that he dreams about it, and he saw himself running across the football field with a football in his hand, so he talked me into it. He was so good that day telling me this stuff. So I said fine. His father didn't want him to play, but I said, "Well, you're gonna play anyway. I'll let you." And I did. And he loved it. He had a great time.

> This is a rich quote, spoken with a lot of passion, especially with regard to dreaming about playing football. This quote is also good because it reveals the dynamic among the parents and child, showing that social process in some detail.
>
> But the quote also provides many competing possibilities for the next question: Tyrec had wanted to play football last year; his parents wouldn't let him; the pressure he put on his mother; the objections of his (no longer in residence) father; and his mother overruling his father and agreeing to let him play. Any of those five different pathways would be worth pursuing.
>
> I decide to take up the objections his parents had to Tyrec playing the previous year. I ask his mother about her concerns. But, I make a mistake by asking two different questions (see below). I should have only asked one.
>
> In retrospect, it would have been better to ask, "Last year, when you wouldn't let him play, what kinds of concerns did you have?"

Interviewer: And can you tell me about this thing, about what made you change your mind? About last year, what you were worried about with him?

Reaching an Initial Turning Point

Fortunately, the interview is starting to move along well, and the respondent's answers are growing longer and more detailed, even without the guidance of a carefully worded probe.

Ms. Taylor: Well, he was just too small. He's just a little kid. You know, football is a rough game, and I'm not a sports fan, and I don't like rough games either—but he's all boy, so if he wants to do that, I can't hinder him, you know. I can't just stop him from his own development. And I think that he got his little experience in it, so he may not want to play next year and maybe he will. But, you know, it didn't hurt him. He didn't get hurt and it was great. He had a great time. So … [she pauses] But last year he was just too small. I just couldn't think of it.

> I like this quote very much. It's graphic. "He was just too small." "He's just a little kid." "Football is a rough game." She explains her position well.
>
> If it had been important for my research (which it was not), I could have asked more about the day she changed her mind, if she talked to Tyrec's father, and so forth. But that information isn't crucial for my research, and I'm very pleased with the reply I just heard. I move on to ask about the economic costs of football and the demands Tyrec's involvement made on Ms. Taylor's time.

Interviewer: And do you remember how much it cost you for him to be in football?
Ms. Taylor: Fifty bucks. So it only cost fifty dollars, and you had to buy a few things, but it didn't cost a lot of money.

> It's striking that Ms. Taylor, who is a single mother with three kids, describes $50 ($86 in current dollars) as not a lot of money. It implies that she has more wiggle room in her budget than do many other working-class parents.

Interviewer: Do you remember what you had to buy? Did you have to buy the pads?

Ms. Taylor: No, we had to buy the cup and the little strap that holds it, and the spikes, the shoes, and that's it. Everything else was included.

> It often requires a couple of questions to find out the price of any given item. If there's not a lot of variability in costs, you could do internet research rather than spend time querying respondents. Here I ask additional questions because I want to get a better understanding of what parents' obligations are. Also, I know that costs vary a lot across different youth sports activities.

Interviewer: And do you remember how much the extra things cost you, about?

Ms. Taylor: Well, all together I don't think we spent over a hundred dollars on paying the fifty dollars and buying the spikes and the cup—that may have cost about ten dollars—so it just wasn't—it didn't cost anything that, you know. It cost more of your time than anything.

Interviewer: So tell me about that. What time did the practices start?

> This is an unusually specific question. The purpose of the next set of questions is to help me understand the impact of football on the respondent's life and also on the lives of the rest of the family members. But, rather than ask a general question, "What was the impact of football on you?" I ask a series of specific questions so I can understand more of her experience and her life.

Ms. Taylor: Uh, at first six. I think in the beginning—well, between five and six. OK.

Interviewer: And how would he get there?

Ms. Taylor: I took him.

Interviewer: And how would you take him?

Ms. Taylor: I drove him.

Interviewer: OK. And so what time do you normally get home from work?

Ms. Taylor: At five-thirty.

> In these questions, because I'm trying to get the lay of the land for football, I ask several questions but keep them brief. Ms. Taylor's replies indicate a time crunch, even though she doesn't say that explicitly. Below, where I say, "So tell me—it must have been rather hectic," I could have said, "Some moms find it hectic and others don't. What has it been like for you?"

Interviewer: So tell me—it must have been rather hectic.

Ms. Taylor: It was madness.

> This is a wonderful line. It's striking. But it's also too succinct. I ask for more detail which (finally) yields a longer, richer answer. I could have said, "It was madness," and waited for a response. Or, I could have said, "It was madness. Tell me more," or simply, "Tell me more."

Interviewer: Tell me about how it went in your family.

> "Tell me how it went in your family" is a simple, but effective, question that then can be used to dig deeper ("Tell me of a specific day").

Ms. Taylor: He had football practice four nights a week in the beginning because school hadn't started back yet. It started in August, I guess. So it was four nights a week. So I would come home and grab him, and hurry up and find something to eat, and go. Or maybe in the summer—we may not have even eaten first. Maybe we did and maybe we didn't, but they weren't in school, so we could eat afterwards or whatever. So that was better. So I'd just take my work with me if I had something to do, and take the chair [to sit on the sidelines] and just go. And it was great then because it was nice out. I didn't mind sitting out in the park. It was nice out. But then when it started getting cold, we had another problem. I didn't want to sit out and get cold. I won't do it. And I used to feel so guilty because I stopped going to practice, but I was not gonna do it. It was enough—by that time I was really tired. I mean, it had become a lot. And then when school started, it went from four nights to two, so that was a break right there. But, like I said, by the time it got cold—I mean they gave us a half hour because it started at six-thirty—so you just—you come home and you eat, and we did the homework afterwards, you know, after practice we did homework. And you run right out. You get him ready. He was never ready. You know, I would start calling maybe at four, from work. "Get your things together,"—but of course he was always outside playing, having a great time. So that was a problem, too, in the beginning. He wanted to play football and he wanted to go to practice, but he didn't want to stop playing with his friends to go. And then we'd have to go find him to come home so we could get there.

Interviewer: And tell me about him not wanting to stop playing with his friends. Can you think of a day that comes to mind that you remember?

> Here, I ask for more detail ("Can you think of a day?"). I'm rewarded with an outstanding quote-one that's highly detailed and vivid.

Ms. Taylor: Well, sure, plenty of days. He would come running in because, either he just remembered he had practice or [his sister] or one of us went and found him or sent word for him to come home. And they [friends] would all come with him, running in and then it was just hard for him to stop playing with them, to say, "Well, I have to go to practice now." But eventually he got used to it. He'd say, "I have to go to practice now," and he'd go in and get ready. But it was very hard at first, and I would have to say,

"Come on, Tyrec, we're gonna be late." And he'd be saying, "OK, I'm coming," but he'd still be out chatting. So it was like that.

This is an excellent answer, and as I listen, I feel like the interview has reached a turning point. The respondent's answer is longer. It's rich, striking, and detailed. It's directly relevant to the central research question of how much work it is for parents to get their children through the day (including organized activities). I am extremely happy with it. Indeed, a lightly edited version of the previous quote opens the chapter on the Taylor family in *Unequal Childhoods*:

"He would come running in because either he just remembered he had [football] practice or . . . one of us went and found him or sent word for him to come home. And [his friends] would all come with him, running in. Then it was just hard for him to stop playing with them, to say, well, I have to go to practice now . . . I would have to say, "Come on, Tyrec, we're gonna be late!" And he'd be saying, "OK, I'm coming," but he'd still be out chatting."

As is typical, there are multiple lines to probe with my next questions (e.g., impact on mealtime, impact on homework, Ms. Taylor feeling "so guilty" that she didn't want to sit and watch practices [although a lot of parents don't watch practices], that her son is never ready, and that he doesn't want to leave his friends). Partly because it was the last thing she said, and partly because the countervailing pressure of his friends is interesting, I probe that. I state the issue I'm interested in, using some of the respondent's own words, and then ask for a specific example.

Furthermore, Ms. Taylor's reply reveals a tension between organized sports and the ordinary afternoon activity of a bunch of neighborhood kids hanging around playing together. So, I ask for more details. It's not a great probe. I'm asking Ms. Taylor, who is an expert on matters related to her and her own son, to provide information about the schedules of the other boys in the neighborhood, a matter she isn't an expert on. But since she's my best available source, I ask the question anyway.

Interviewer: And none of the other little boys in the neighborhood were into football?

Ms. Taylor: Not most of them. Two of them were, but they weren't in the same weight, so they weren't on the same team. So they went on different days—so they didn't get to see each other and be together like that.

Interviewer: I see. And some families report that there are a lot of— some parents will get upset and spank the children. It can be quite a scene to get them ready to go. Did you find that in your house?

I didn't word this question well. I should have said, "Some parents report that it's very difficult to get kids ready to go, and it can be hard on the parents. How is it here?"

Despite my unfortunate mention of "spanking," which Tyrec's mother dismisses as off base, the reply (see below) includes the memorable line, "He worked me over so good."

Ms. Taylor: No. I would never spank him to go play football. I would spank him more because—well, actually, we never have to go that far, and if I did, if I threatened him, like, "Tyrec, you're gonna get it now," it would be because, let me see, it would be, I guess because he wasn't listening to me more than because, you know, we were gonna be late. But after he started, after maybe the third time, he wanted to quit because, like I said, he was having the problem of not being able to play with his friends because he had to leave them to go to practice. And then, so I just didn't let him. Because he worked me over so good to get him signed up that I refused to let him not continue now. You know, and all the frustration that went along with going, still, it was something that he started, so we were going to go ahead and get through it and pray that we don't have to do it again. But we'll have to do it again (laughter).

The line "pray that we don't have to do it again" reveals what an ordeal her son's involvement in football is for her. This is interesting.

It's also revealing that, as she explains in her next response, "You have to stick to it. You can't just back out."

I'm happy about how the interview is going, but I'm also slightly anxious about how much time I'm spending on the single issue of football. In shifting in her chair, she has signaled that she's in a bit of a hurry. It's a Sunday night and she has to go to work in the morning. But, given the centrality of the issue to the research question, I probe again.

Interviewer: And can you tell me a little bit more about what went through your mind when you told him he couldn't quit after three times, why that would have been bad for him?

Ms. Taylor: Well, because I just thought that he needed to know that if you decide, and you feel so strongly that you want to do something, and you decide that that is what you want to do and you're going to do it, then you have to stick to it. You can't just back out because it's not, you know, especially for the reason that he had—to leave his friends for a few hours. If he was playing and all of a sudden he was afraid that he was going to get hurt, you know, or something like that, then that would be one thing. But it wasn't anything like that. It was only because he didn't want to leave his friends. And, as I said, that got much better. And then he went on.

This is another nice, detailed answer which shows the respondent's subjective experience. Having gotten the specifics I need regarding why her son couldn't quit, I return to the thread of her role and her feelings of guilt. I want to ask her about it, but I don't want to make her feel guilty. I'm concerned that she might interpret my question as signaling that I think she should have stayed. My uncertainty makes me stumble over my words. I end up explicitly referring to her feeling "guilty." A better approach might have been to say, "Tell me how you thought through the issues around staying to watch practice or not?"

On the other hand, the words I use are very similar to my

> respondent's ("And I used to feel so guilty because I stopped going to practice, but I was not gonna do it.") Although I'm not quoting her exactly, neither am I misinterpreting her or putting words in her mouth. My phrasing shows that I'm listening carefully and that I understood what she had said a little earlier. She responds with vigor.

Interviewer: And tell me a little about—when you didn't go to the practices you sometimes felt guilty?

Ms. Taylor: Oh, yes, I felt terrible because, you know, there were some parents that were there every night and you want to do it, too. But, I don't know, maybe I'm selfish in a sense. I did my part, I thought. We sold the chances [raffle tickets]. We did the whole thing, and he was OK that I didn't sit there with him. I cannot stand the cold. I just can't stand the cold. I sat out in the cold for games only because it was a game, but I didn't see why I would have to sit for the practice.

> Sometimes when a respondent is self-critical and the problem is minor, I try to think of a more serious version of the issue and mention that. Ms. Taylor is faulting herself for not going to the practices, and I note that some parents don't go to the games. I'm trying to understand what her attendance means to her. I don't want to criticize her, so I substitute a more extreme version of the behavior she is discussing and then ask what she thinks about it.

Interviewer: Well, some parents don't come to the games.

Ms. Taylor: Right. Some don't go.

Interviewer: And how do you feel about that?

Ms. Taylor: Well, it's unfortunate, but I don't feel anything, actually, about it because you don't know why. You know. You just don't know why. And there are all kinds of things that can cause you not to go. I missed a few. I didn't feel bad about it either because I went to more than I missed. I usually was there. But, uh, you just don't know why someone can't do something, so I don't pass judgment on people.

Interviewer: But if you had never gone to any games at all—I mean, why did you think it was important to go?

Ms. Taylor: Because I had to give him support that I was behind him, that's why I went. And I didn't want him to feel like I didn't care. He didn't want me to come at first. He said, no, I don't want you at the games. And my feelings were hurt that he didn't want me there.

Interviewer: And do you know why he didn't want you there?

This is an example of a missed opportunity. Ms. Taylor says, "And my feelings were hurt that he didn't want me there." I should probe to find out more about what Tyrec's preference means to her. But I feel awkward because Tyrec is within earshot and is likely listening in. I make a mistake and ask Ms. Taylor to report on her son's views. Making this kind of request is usually not a good idea. Tyrec's mother is an excellent expert regarding her own feelings. She isn't an expert regarding Tyrec's feelings. (Still, there are cases where researchers find it revealing to ask respondents about others' feelings.)

Ms. Taylor: I think that he didn't want us there because he wanted to impress us so and maybe he was afraid that he wouldn't or something. I really think that's why. Because he would get so nervous. As soon as he spotted us he would get really nervous. But he got better.

Interviewer: And what do you think he likes about being in football?

Ms. Taylor: Well, like I said, Tyrec is all boy and his motor skills, the coordination and that kind of thing, he's very coordinated like that, so he can do anything like that, I think, very well. And, uh, he knew that he could do it, and I think he wanted to prove it to himself that he could do it, and I think he just liked it. He had all the kids around here playing football every day (laughter).

Interviewer: Where would they play?

Ms. Taylor: Right out here on the street and at the park because they have a little area there.

Interviewer: And like, the time before you agreed to let him play. If you had to guess how many times the two of you talked about it? If you had to just guess.

Here I'm returning to probe the point in the interview when Ms. Taylor refers to Tyrec as having "worked her over" to gain permission to play football. I ask a series of questions designed to get more detail about how Tyrec did this. At first, her answers are quite general.

Ms. Taylor: You mean last year?
Interviewer: Yeah. Let's take last year first—how many times he asked you if he could play.
Ms. Taylor: Oh, a few times last year and, you know, only at the season.

This answer is vague. I ask again, and I offer a range of possible figures. This isn't ideal, since I might be narrowing my respondent's options, but it's better than accepting "a few times" as an answer. I'm also reminding the respondent that I am looking for as much detail as possible.

Interviewer: So if you had to guess if it was one or five, or ten or fifty?
Ms. Taylor: Oh, ten, I'd say.
Interviewer: And what about this year, before you agreed? If you had to guess how many times it came up?

At the risk of being pesky, I'm trying to figure out the true frequency of Tyrec's efforts. The next answer is more concrete.

Ms. Taylor: All week for about a week, he tried to persuade me.
Interviewer: And about how many times a day during that week?

> I probe again (despite feeling that I'm overdoing it). I'm rewarded at last with a nice, clear, specific example.

Ms. Taylor: Oh, in the evenings whenever we would be in a quiet time, then he would talk about it, about how bad he wanted to play.

Interviewer: And the time that he told you that he had that dream—was that in the morning? Or at night?

> Since I'm captivated by the earlier, rich description of Tyrec telling his mother that he had a dream, I return to that issue to ask for more details.

Ms. Taylor: It was in the evening, and we were in the bedroom, and he was telling me about his dreams and how he saw himself running across the field, so I had to (laughter).

> I love this example. It's detailed, has a time and place, and is concrete. It's risky (I might annoy the respondent) and time consuming to ask so many questions about a single issue. But, in this case, I learn a lot. Then I move on to a different football-related topic.

SUMMING UP: AN INTERVIEW THAT DUG DEEP

The purpose of my study was to understand how much work it was for parents to get children through their days, and, ultimately, social class differences in the cultural logic of child rearing displayed in family life.[6] During the two-hour interview with Tyrec's mother, I spent over 20 percent of my time on only one topic: football. This was a huge investment but not an unreasonable one. Other than church, Tyrec participated in only one organized activity (football) and his mother had mixed feelings about his involvement. Investigating the role of organized activities in the lives of children and their families was a central concern of the research project. In addition, during the first fifteen minutes of the interview, Ms. Taylor began to understand that I wanted to know a great deal of detail. We collaborated: I asked her to provide many more details; she grasped my intent; and she was willing and able to oblige. All of this happened subtly, without any explicit discussion. Ms. Taylor was an excellent respondent, and the interview yielded rich details.

Conclusion: Interviewing as Improvisation

As Howard Becker has illuminated, in a jazz ensemble, musicians use the structure of a composition's chord progressions as a starting point and then weave into it new lines of music, sometimes contributed and sometimes in a spontaneous dialogue with other members.[7] In-depth interviewing is similar. People are talking to each other. There's a basic set of questions, but the researcher is frequently improvising in response to the real-time answers provided by the respondent. The interviewer creates the specific probes and controls the pace and flow of the interview but must do so in continuing collaboration with the respondent. Each interview is unique. The experience is often intense and may lead you to feel close to a respondent who has shared private information with you.

USEFUL PROBES

Can you tell me more about that?

Repeating the respondent's words and then waiting.

[Silence]

Can you think of a recent example of that?

What was that like for you?

Some of the people I talk to tell me [x] while others say [y]. What is it like for you?

Can you tell me a bit more about how that unfolded?

That sounds difficult.

The key to becoming a good interviewer is to train yourself to listen carefully and then ask for more detail throughout the interview. Begin probing soon; you don't want to let the respondent settle into a pattern of short, general replies and only then start to probe. Rather, you want to quickly convey to the person you're interviewing what kind of information is most useful to you. As an interview proceeds, I also find that it's beneficial to thank, praise, and reassure respondents that they are doing well and that their answers are helpful. Sometimes you can see them visibly relax in response to your encouraging words.

Interviewing is difficult and can never be done perfectly. It takes practice to get the hang of it, and your self-critique often helps you get better. But it also can be intensely rewarding. Keep in mind that as a researcher, you're engaged in an emergent process. Ideally, as you proceed through the steps of conceiving a study, recruiting a sample, and beginning to collect data (including through in-depth interviews), your focus improves. You begin to see themes. These themes, and the contribution your study makes to an existing body of research, are developed and refined during data analysis. That step is taken up in chapter 8. But first, because in-depth interviews are especially fruitful when they're embedded in a specific context (one where you've been systematically "hanging out" in order to get to know the people in that setting), in the next chapter, I turn to the process of doing participant observation.

6

Learning to Do Participant Observation
A Practical Guide

Unlike interviewing, which is limited to one or two encounters, ethnographic research involves becoming immersed in a social situation.[1] Often, ethnographic research is described as systematically "hanging out" with people on a regular basis. You get to know them, and they get to know you. You write field notes when you go home to help you remember what happened; the notes are your data set. As earlier parts of this book clarify, ethnographic work is valuable in unpacking everyday practices, the formidable gap between formal rules and actual behavior, and the difficulties people face getting through their days—processes that are often not sufficiently revealed in other approaches to research. As you begin a project, you choose a site, see whether you can gain permission to be let in, and then, guided by your emerging priorities, start to collect data. After the fieldwork is over and done, you are left with your memories and a set of highly detailed field notes (which are vastly more accurate than your memories). Since field notes are the lifeblood of a project and any writing you will do comes from them, I devote the next chapter to discussing ways to write high-quality field notes. In this chapter, however, I discuss a host of other issues including managing your entry to the field and figuring out how to meet many of the everyday, practical challenges associated with your role in the field (e.g., note-taking, conversation topics, managing food, and clothing). I also discuss the emotionally intensive nature of the fieldwork, and rituals for managing transitions in and out of the field. In the last section, I discuss frequency of visits and the enormous importance of keeping up with your field notes. Here, I share a serious and painful mistake I made in my first project in falling behind in writing my notes and the importance of scheduling field visits only when you have time to write notes very soon after. Of course, there are other related, pressing topics, including selecting a field site, getting informed consent, and managing safety; these are all taken up in chapters 2 and 3. Your initial research question matters a great deal; see chapters 2 and 8 for your need to "think as you go" and code your completed data set (i.e., reviewing the data in a systematic fashion).[2] Still, there are many important aspects of observational research I cannot take up here; the reference list includes a selection of valuable works.

MANAGING YOUR ENTRY INTO THE FIELD: BE VAGUE BUT ACCURATE

Once you gain access, you want to introduce yourself to everyone more or less saying the same thing with a very brief "elevator speech" (see chapter 3). For example, you might say: "Hi, I am [your name], and I am interested in how much work it takes for parents to get children through the day." What you say should be brief and easy to understand.

It is rare to be introduced to everyone in the setting on the first day. Instead, the longer you are in the field, the more people you will meet. If you are in an organization, and you are in a room with someone you have not been introduced to yet, I would go up to the person, smile, probably extend my hand for a handshake, and introduce myself ("Hi, I am Annette Lareau, and I am a student at Berkeley, and I am visiting Ms. Walters's classroom these days.") It is less awkward to introduce yourself than to lurk around a setting. If the person seems suspicious, you should mention your legitimacy, "I feel lucky

BETTER TO ASK IN ADVANCE
When I started my research, I was approved to obtain passive consent from parents because I was observing "normal classroom activities." Passive consent certainly made things a lot easier as getting written consent forms back from busy parents can be challenging. During the first year of my study, this was not a problem at all. However, during the second year of my study, as I attempted to recruit parents for formal interviews, two parents contacted the school and were confused about the research. I did not get to talk to these parents but, sadly, they ended up withdrawing their children from the study. Next time I will have an informal "informational session" for parents so that we could meet face-to-face, I can tell them about the research, and answer any lingering questions. One thing I learned is that it is better to ask in advance!
Calvin Zimmerman, "Looking for Trouble"

that the superintendent approved the project, and she introduced me to the principal. But, everything is confidential, and the actual name of the school will never be used." If possible, you should ask your sponsor whether you could attend a meeting where many people in the organization will be.

ALWAYS ACCEPT INVITATIONS

Try to never turn down an invitation from a participant (unless you feel threatened) even if it means canceling other plans. Doing serious ethnography means being on their time.

Colin Jerolmack,
Up to Heaven and
Down to Hell

A group meeting helps people learn who you are. You can ask in advance to give a five-minute summary of the project at that meeting (or ask whether your sponsor or someone else might be able to formally introduce you). You might mention to your sponsor that sometimes the sponsor introduces the researcher and other times the researcher gives a quick spiel. You can ask them what they think is better. You can also offer to bring cookies or some other snack to the meeting if that is appropriate.

But many sites are not organizations; they are informal groups (e.g., peer groups, gangs, friends, and so forth). Here, you need guidance about how to proceed, and you should follow what your sponsor tells you to do. You are trying to look innocuous. Thus, it can be helpful to show up, "hang out," and not ask too many pesky questions at first. Gradually, you can ask more questions.

Still, as you are being introduced, sometimes people will misrepresent who you are and what you are doing. Then, you are trapped because you do not want to make the misinformed person look bad. In this example from *Unequal Childhoods*, I am hanging out with a Catholic white working-class family, the Drivers. Their daughter, Wendy, attends a weekly Catholic education program. Wendy was supposed to bring a piece of paper explaining the study the previous week, but the Catholic school principal, who is in charge of the education program, doesn't have the description of the study. The principal, the father, and Wendy discuss this briefly, which I watch.

When the teacher arrives, the father, who has been told multiple times that I am a faculty member with a funded research project "to write a book," wildly misrepresents the goals by suggesting that I am a student getting credit for a class project. I am extremely uncomfortable with the teacher being misled, but no matter how gently I corrected him, I would still be correcting him, and it would make him look bad. I had an ongoing relationship with him, and, in a bind, I privileged my duty not to harm him over my obligation to have the study accurately explained.

> The teacher comes in and the principal comes in too. Dad says, looking at the principal, "We wanted to know if she could be here tonight. She is doing it for school, they are getting credit for school, from Temple." The teacher and the principal look slightly confused. [I feel trapped within this ridiculous story but obligated to sustain it in a general way.] There is a short silence. The teachers look at me curiously. I say, "I am from Temple and I have been visiting children at [her school] and now I have been visiting Wendy's family and I am trying to understand what children's lives are like." The teacher says, "it is alright with me." The principal (again) says, "She didn't get the note." I say, "Thank you very much."

The essence of informed consent is that the respondent must be told that there is a research project as well as what will happen during the data collection, and give permission. In my view, I met the essential elements of informed consent by the way that I explained the purpose of the study without correcting Mr. Driver.

Your Role in the Field
WHO YOU ARE AND WHAT YOU ARE DOING THERE

You have entered a site where you plan to do research, so you must have a good reason for being there. (See chapters 2 and 3 for more on this issue.) You want to remember this reason or, put differently, "who you are and why you are there." Generally, you want to do what the participants do. You want to blend in.[3]

You will need to make a lot of decisions in the site, including what activities you try to follow, whom you get to know, and what you focus on in your notes. As much as possible, you want to be guided by your original research curiosity, with the understanding that your research question will shift as you stay in the field. Even so, you will have moments when you need to choose how to spend your time. Here, it is helpful to think about the big picture. Only you know what your highest priority is given the competing priorities. What is crucial for you to focus on?

There are always multiple pathways. For example, if you are studying how parents manage their children's food allergies, are you interested in doctor-patient interactions (medical sociology), children's autonomy (sociology of childhood), mothers' management of kids' lives (sociology of the family/motherhood), assessments of danger (risk literature), or adherence to medical recommendations in a nonclinical context (sociology of health and illness)?[4] You might consider the books you like to read, and issues that are boring to you. You are trying to find some principles to guide your decision making, and your excitement and interest are important principles for making decisions.

YOUR ROLE IN THE FIELD:
PHYSICALLY PLACING YOURSELF IN THE SPACE

When doing fieldwork, it always seems that the spaces are physically too small or too large. As a result, there often is not an obvious place to stand or sit when you are observing social interactions. In some settings, you have few options, and you may be heavily constrained. In other settings, there are more. Normally you want to follow the suggestion of the respondents, but, if they are treating you as an honored guest, and you want to have to have a less honored position, it is often fine to follow your impulses. My principle here is to take the lowest status seat—ideally where you can see what is going on. For example, in working-class homes, the living rooms are quite small, leaving room enough for only a love seat, a television, and a coffee table. When I was visiting, I would be offered the love seat, but, since the kids typically were sitting on the floor, I would plop myself down on the floor. Similarly, in riding in a car with any of the families, it was typical that the parent would invite me or tell me to sit in the front. But, kids like to sit in the front, especially if they are the only kid in the car with one parent. So, I would make a beeline for the backseat. When the parent told me, "You should sit in the front," I would say, "No, I'm good." Often there would be a pause (as if they were stumped), and then sometimes the parent would shrug their shoulders. On the second car ride there would be a repetition of this exchange, but by the third time no one said anything. Everyone just sat in their places. Sometimes you just get a hunch about what to do, and I would generally follow that hunch. Other times, it might be better to wait until someone tells you what to do. For instance, once when I was visiting Katie Brindle, a child who participated in my *Unequal Childhoods* study, Katie's two uncles were at her grandmother's home, one uncle was sitting (quietly) at the end of the room's two couches watching television. I was unsure where to sit, so I awkwardly stood for a moment, watching:

> We walk into the living room. Grandmom stands near one couch (with the uncle) in front of the coffee table. The girls are in front of the tv and so there literally isn't space to walk to the other couch. [I am uncertain if there should be three people on the couch or if I should walk around the room to the other couch.] Grandmom demonstrates with her hand, "sit down." She sits in the middle; I sit on the end.

Sometimes, kids will want you to play with them, but by doing so, you cannot observe the parts of the setting that you are interested in. If possible, you can persuade the kids to take away the game or toys so that you are closer to where you want to be.[5] In large houses, there are multiple places to stand and people go in different directions. It is confusing, but you should try to be guided by your research priorities.

And, sometimes I didn't have the skills to take part. For example, during the first few visits to an African American low-income family, I noticed that the kids enjoyed playing basketball, but they did not always have a basketball. So, before my next visit, I brought a basketball (and at the advice of the mom, I brought my sneakers too). When I showed up with the ball, the children were visibly happy to see it.[6] But this created a new problem because I had not played since middle school (although I had attended college games and understood the game). I was hopelessly incompetent at shooting. So, I never shot a basket (which was considered by the kids to be very strange), and chose instead to do aggressive guarding:

> I guard kids dramatically (in their face) with arms out and moving back and forth; they smile and drive in and around me and shoot. Jazz says, "Man she guard like a blood." I guard again. Virtually any time I get the ball I pass hard and fast to their chest. It almost always catches them off guard but they catch it and then dribble and shoot. I never see anyone else pass away the ball except a few times in that game but even then not much.[7]

Where you situate yourself in the field depends on the setting, and it also is interwoven with your role in the field. But, it can be good to find ways to be helpful in the space. For example, I also held babies (which I liked to do and there were young children who were fussy), folded laundry, and dried dishes. Chuck Bosk discusses in his book *Forgive and Remember* how he would hold bandages in the hospital and find other ways to be helpful. In her ethnography of a women's prison, Rachel Ellis gained access via the chaplain, and since the chaplain was overly busy, she asked Ellis to open and read the mail, answer the phone, make photocopies, and do other tasks.[8] Although this took a full seven hours per week, and sometimes longer, completing the chaplain's chores was crucial to her being able to stay in the site. Hence, you want to offer to "help out," but you don't want to help out so much that you cannot get your research done.

ROLE IN THE FIELD: USEFUL TOPICS FOR SMALL TALK

Although Hochschild described herself as playing a role akin to the "family dog" in the observational study, *The Second Shift*, I have found the position of a participant observer to be more interactive. When you arrive at a setting, you need to greet people. Often there is chit-chat about the weather, your trip there, and what has happened since they last saw you. In my study of families, I have found (and research assistants I have worked with have similarly reported) that after a few minutes things settle down. You can grab a seat and just hang out, join people watching television, play basketball, or sit around talking. The nature of blending in varies depending on what you are studying. People vary in how much they talk in a setting. Some are much more silent than others. I prefer to be on the quieter side (i.e., more of an observer than a participant), but even so, there are many instances where it would be very awkward to be completely silent. It is better to chime in occasionally. Additionally, people will ask you questions. You can deflect the questions by answering them briefly and then redirecting the conversation to other people (i.e., by asking a question that is likely to produce a lengthy response). Still, sometimes you have to chat.[9]

What are good topics? It depends upon your setting. If you are doing research on musicians, you want to be able to chat about other musicians; if you are studying theater people you want to know something about plays. Since video games are popular with children, it can be helpful to keep up with the latest games. Popular television shows or movies are great. Stupid, funny, or charming videos can be good to share. In general, it is good to keep track of what is going on in the world of sports, since sports can be an excellent, default conversation topic. Even if you have never liked sports, you can easily learn enough to chime in on conversations. In addition, it is helpful to have a repertoire of stories that one can tell, which will vary according to the setting you are studying. When I was studying families, I would often tell the story of how my younger sister, who is only 11 months younger than I am, and I would fight like cats and dogs when we were children. I explained that we shared a bedroom until we were in high school. Thus, there were many spats. We would draw a line down the middle of the room dividing my sister's side from mine. Then, we would sit there and poke our finger across the invisible line taunting each other, "Na, na I am on your side!" "We drove our mother crazy," I would proclaim. This story has elements of what is useful in some kinds of studies about family life: it is universal, it is self-deprecating, and it shows that I understand that families are far from ideal.

Your goal here is to banter or make small talk. You do not want to interrogate people about what they do for a living, for example. In addition, I would stay away from anything that is political unless, after you are there for a while, you have figured out whether you share the views of the people you are studying. If you are doing a research project with people who are low-income, I would also generally avoid any topic that highlights a position of advantage in the social stratification system such as familiarity with expensive restaurants, exotic food, or vacation travel; but these topics might be highly suitable in interviews with wealthy people. I would try to find common ground. This is why sports can be particularly useful, especially if you can root for local teams. Food, traffic, gardening, seasons, weather, snow removal or lack thereof, playoffs, and so forth are good topics. Little jokes are helpful. It is extremely easy to put your foot in your mouth. If you do, just apologize ("Sorry! My mom is always asking me if I make a habit of only 'changing feet' as I am constantly putting my foot in my mouth.") Then I would move on. Missteps happen.

Particularly if you are studying low-income populations, people can be in distress. Hence, it is common for research participants to ask you for help—for rides, small loans, gifts, and so forth. Although this is a common issue researchers face in the field, there is not a consensus on how to respond. Some people help out (just as they would help out a friend); in his book, *Evicted*, Matt Desmond takes this position. Others decline. In my own case, I was studying how families made it through the day, and many did not have cars. I was in the awkward position of driving to the family, parking my car, and then taking the bus with them. Since I was studying how their social position shaped the daily life of children and parents, it was important that I understand the challenges for the family in taking public transportation for children's doctor visits and other activities. When they (inevitably) asked for a ride, I said that the university insurance regulations did not permit it.[10] Another approach is to adopt a strategy of listening closely, "holding up a mirror" to repeat back their concern, and then declining. This is what Blair Sackett, a young, white, female sociology doctoral student, ended up doing, after many long conversations with me and others, about how to proceed while completing an ethnographic study in a refugee camp in Kenya. For people in the study she provided (modest) compensation ranging from small food gifts for people doing interviews to $40 to people in the intensive observational study. But all other requests Sackett declined:

> I was frequently asked to give assistance—from help with money for food or shoes to securing resettlement to the U.S.... I chose a strategy of no intervention.... I had a consistent protocol, which I followed upon each request. First, I made eye contact and actively listened as the request was made. When the request was finished, I would "mirror" that request back, asking, "What I think I heard you say," and then summarizing their request. Then asking, "Is that correct?" Once the request was understood, I would look the person in the eye and tell them, "I am sorry I am not able to help you. I am a student, living here in the camp to do research. I am not an aid worker. I am really sorry that you are having this problem. I hope that you are able to find some way to get the assistance that you need." ... Before beginning the research,

however, I did decide that in the case of a life-threatening problem, such as a serious illness, I would intervene to the best of my ability. Fortunately, this case did not arise.[11]

Listening to people is important (rather than quickly brushing them off), and by listening and repeating back what they have said, you show that you have "heard" them and you are taking it seriously. Whatever you do, you should do it consistently with people in your study because word spreads fast. Sometimes researchers have rules—if the matter is life threatening or if the family will be permanently harmed, they will help; they will help only in small amounts that can be reciprocated; or they will help the people with whom they are closest but not others. Other researchers just make a habit of never carrying cash. How to best respond to requests from participants is a deeply personal decision. In addition, some researchers don't help during data collection but, after the data collection is over, they do help. In my own case, I did not provide additional help to the families during data collection (other than paying them for their participation), but I have sent annual gifts and, in one case, when a boy was threatened with expulsion in middle school, I wrote a letter at the request of his mother. (He was not kicked out then, but he was kicked out a few years later.) Ultimately, the best advice I can offer as you wrestle with settling on your own strategy is to think about what you can live with and what you cannot. Then, share with readers your decision and your rationale.

ROLE IN THE FIELD: SOME GUIDELINES FOR SUCCESSFUL FIELDWORK

ALWAYS EAT BEFORE YOU GO INTO THE FIELD

One of the problems with doing participant observation is you are never quite sure how things will unfold. You are not in control. Since you are intruding on another group or setting, you are beholden to their rules and schedules. Thus, a visit that was supposed to be only two hours sometimes can morph into four. One issue that will surface is meals. Since you are intruding, you do not want to be hungry and ask for food. On the other hand, if they offer food or drink, you should *always* accept unless you have a very, very strong reason for declining, and then you should try to decline only with one item and accept other food or drink with gusto. (It can be offensive to say no.) It is hard to know whether you will be offered something, and you don't want participants to go through any trouble to make food for you when they are not planning to eat. As a result, I have a rule that I always eat something before I go on a field visit. It is hard to concentrate if you are hungry, and I find field-work stressful, so it is good not to be running on empty.[12] Obviously, this means that you sometimes have to eat twice in a short period. It is also helpful to have protein bars that you can eat surreptitiously (even in the bathroom if necessary) if you get hungry and need food. But, under no circumstances should you eat in front of the respondents if they are not eating.

In addition, there are often conflicts over what to eat. For example, certain dietary choices (e.g., vegetarianism) might be seen as strange or even disrespectful in certain contexts, but if they are important to you, then you need to let everyone know right away, ideally with some joking and self-deprecating remarks. Food preferences come into play as well. For example, I do not like to drink soda, but it is a very common drink in some circles. In my study of working-class families, it would have been convenient if I drank soda, but I felt strongly that I really did not want to do so. (I did not let on, of course, that I did not like soda). I simply declined and immediately asked for water. At the time, all of the working-class and poor families thought it was extremely strange that I drank water (and that I drank tea without sugar). It is hard for me to assess whether this practice hurt my rapport with them, but because I wasn't willing to be flexible, we all adjusted.

The bottom line is that it is important to accept some offer of food and eat or drink with thanks and with gusto. If you are going to reject something that someone offers you, it is good to do it immediately, consistently, and apologetically, and to request a reasonable substitute that is not a bother for your host. Once they know what your preferences are, they will adapt.

Role in the Field: Visit Early and Often

Entering a field setting has a set of normal, predictable stressors as you and the participants get accustomed to each other. The more you are there, the easier it will be, so it is a good idea to go as much as possible in the beginning, if you have time to write field notes. Frequency of visits varies from site to site. But one possibility, if suitable, is that you can tell them this: at first, I will come daily and then settle into a routine of x times per week. When you visit often at first, then you meet everyone, and you can learn your way around (e.g., find the bathroom, find where to get coffee, meet people, and learn the rhythm of the day). I find it helpful to go for "only" a few hours so that I have time to write up the notes. (The notes take longer in the beginning since you are describing the setting and the cast of characters.) You should visit only if you have time to write up field notes about the visit. Visits without field notes not only are useless but also cloud your thoughts with things you remember but do not have documentation for in your field notes. Thus, writing notes after fieldwork is a crucial element of participant observation.

As long as you have time to write notes, visit often.

Role in the Field: Who You Are Shapes What You See

In interviews and participant observation, the person doing the data collection is an inextricable part of the process. This role (which some people frame as "bias") cannot be avoided. Rather, it is connected to the issue of "subjectivity," which "is like a garment that cannot be removed."[13] There are multiple elements of it. For example, your own background frames what you "see" as interesting and important. Your training influences how you act. And, your position in the social world—your age, race, gender, and signals of other social positions—shapes how others see you and treat you. How they treat you shapes how you act. And so forth.

Since subjectivity is inevitable, it is helpful to be aware of it, and reflect on these issues regularly, including in memos. For example, working with research assistants closely, I was struck that the most important source of variation in the field notes was the individual fieldworker's own childhood experiences. The research assistants with middle-class origins, who were accustomed to children calling adults by their first names, commented on how the children in the housing project used deferential terms, such as "Hi, Miss LaRonda!" "How you doing, Miss Sally?" By contrast, fieldworkers with working-class origins were shocked by what they considered the rudeness and disrespect middle-class children showed toward their parents and other adults when kids would tell their parents, "I hate you," or whine loudly. Some fieldworkers with middle-class origins were upset by the direct way that parents spoke to children and threatened them. On the other hand, field notes from John Pearson (a pseudonym), an African American research assistant from working-class origins, suggest that he was never upset by threats to "beat" children. Prolonged whining and what he saw as lax parenting, on the other hand, stretched the limits of his patience. His field notes from a twenty-minute car ride with a white middle-class family, the Tallingers, reflect his disgust:

> I was getting a headache [listening to 15 minutes of whining]. I wanted to kick his mother's butt for letting him [the family's youngest child, a four-year-old boy] get away with that whining. And kick his butt for acting like a baby.... I was surprised that the mother said little or nothing. And when she did speak, "Okay, Sam. We have to take this road," she sounded as if she was pleading with him. Who's the parent?

It is common for fieldworkers to be sometimes annoyed by the people they study. In some cases, researchers can feel contempt (most famously expressed in the Malinowski diaries).[14] Of course, fieldworkers undoubtedly annoy the people they study too.

There are no easy answers to this issue, but self-knowledge and self-reflection are extremely helpful. If you know that people of your social position are likely to interpret actions in a particular fashion, you want to "take the position of the other" and try to look at the setting differently. In addition, if you decide what you want to look at, the behavior you record is less susceptible to being influenced by your background than your interpretation of the meaning of the behavior. For example, there is a vehement argument about the status of corporal punishment in the field. Two different fieldworkers are both likely to record examples of corporal punishment, but they may have very different interpretations of the meaning of this form of parenting.[15] In sum, knowing yourself, your assumptions, and your preferences can be helpful so that you can "fight against them."

Finally, it is worth noting that your temperament and general level of sociability may also shape your role in the field. There are many times when participant observation is easier if the researcher is socially skilled and is comfortable being somewhat outgoing (but is still able to listen closely and not dominate social interactions). Introverts and extremely shy people report finding participant observation to be particularly challenging. People who do not want to intrude can find it challenging, and sometimes, because they fear making people uncomfortable, they can be slow to act. There are no easy answers to this challenge, but it is valuable to know your strengths and limits, talk to friends about this issue, listen to advice, and develop strategies. You can do high-quality work, but you might need to push yourself out of your comfort zone a bit or give yourself more time to get the hang of it.

Role in the Field: Keep an Open Mind

As you move through data collection, you need an open mind. As Shirley Brice Heath often tells students in education, "You must not use data collection and analysis to justify your a priori critique of what you do not approve of in classrooms." Similarly, Mitch Duneier insists on the ethnographers making a "humble commitment to being sur-prised."[16] Mental flexibility is a key part of participant observation (and interviewing). What does this mean concretely? You want to be deeply curious about the setting in which you are studying, and you are trying to learn about the experiences of people in that setting. You should not presume that you know how things work. Indeed, you are not an expert but a novice. (This is humbling.) You are there to learn, but usually you don't quite know exactly what you are studying. You need to live with uncertainty. You cannot focus too early, but you need to "live with it" for a while until you get a sense of what is going on. Meeting with friends and colleagues who are skeptical and ask hard questions can be helpful. Also, it is crucial to have tremendous respect for people you are study-ing, to abandon the idea that you know how people should best act (e.g., in child rearing, job hunting). I am also vigilant about looking for opportunities to prove my hunches wrong. For example, if I am drawing a conclusion that women have different experiences than men (for ex-ample in their financial expertise around wealth), I try to imagine that I might be off-base and these patterns are not really tied to gender at all. I look assiduously for other factors that might clarify these patterns (e.g., prior work experiences, educational backgrounds, or childhood experiences). My skepticism leads me to try to dislodge it by seeing whether there is evidence to "blow it apart," thereby revealing that my conclusion was too hasty.[17] In addition to a preponderance of evidence, the quality of evidence matters — especially evidence where the patterns are deeply meaningful to the participants. Sometimes, rare events help to illuminate broader patterns. I am thinking as I am collecting data.

USE DAILY RITUALS TO TRANSITION
IN AND OUT OF FIELDWORK

Participant observation can be emotionally intense.[18]

You will start to feel more comfortable the more you gain gradual acceptance at your research site, which is good, but then you find that your return to your normal life can feel strange. You can begin to see your life with new eyes. Since you are tired from the fieldwork, and home is supposed to offer you a place of solace, this comfort can be tiring even as it is illuminating. As a result, I have ritualized entry and exit with special clothes I primarily use for fieldwork and special food rituals (i.e., getting a cup of tea when I get home). Some people are able to immediately plunge into writing their field notes, but I have never had that skill. I need to decompress by watching television, reading a novel, or taking a nap. Some exercise. Then, in a couple of hours, I can sit down at the computer and begin the process of typing out notes. The point is that I cannot immediately transition to writing notes despite trying to force myself. Just as people have writing rituals, many people have rituals around doing fieldwork. Rather than resist them, it is better to figure them out and work with them. The habits provide a way to organize the process.

> Fieldwork is tiring; you need to schedule time to recuperate from fieldwork.
>
> Vanessa Lopes Muñoz, "Everybody Has to Think"

The exhausting nature of fieldwork means that you need time to rest after you have done your fieldwork. It can be difficult because you are also trying to go to the site as much as possible to gain knowledge and acceptance, and you need to write notes after each visit. Plus, you may be earning a living by doing other tasks such as teaching. You may also have family or other relationships to maintain. Still, schedule short, predictable periods of rest if at all possible.

Reluctance to Go to the Field: It's Normal

Fieldworkers sometimes dread going to the field. They feel awkward and out of place. They do not know what to say. They stick out. Sometimes people feel that when they stop worrying about their research question and just hang out, they have fun. When they have to take field notes, they are exhausted.

You might find yourself wanting to procrastinate and delaying going into the field. It always takes me a lot of energy to get myself out the door to go to a field site. Even though I want to be there, I often procrastinate about departing. I have even had to bribe myself with the promise of a special treat when I got home. (For me it is something sweet, such as a cupcake; others have savory rewards, such as potato chips.) Some days, you may have to drag yourself to your research site.

There is not a lot to say about this, except it is normal to feel this way. If you do not want to go, it does not usually mean anything except that the work is challenging and hard and then it is followed by more challenging work in the form of writing field notes. Some people say it is the hardest work that they do in their careers.

In some instances, these feelings of dread are connected to some problem in the field that you need to work through, such as someone being cold toward you or your access to an important issue being restricted. It is also possible that you don't really know why you are there and wonder whether you are seeing things that will be worthwhile for your project. Trying to think through what is bugging you and then reflecting on options can be helpful. Talking to a friend or writing in a journal is also helpful.

However, my late mother used to tell me that a lot of schoolwork happened only by putting your body in a chair and staying there. A lot of fieldwork happens only by going to the field. It is super-hard work, and you should always give yourself a pat on the back for doing it.

DECISION MAKING IN THE FIELD IS UNAVOIDABLE: INSTANTANEOUS DECISIONS

Because the research processes discussed here are emergent, you have to make instantaneous decisions, and some are going to make you uncomfortable. On the one hand, you are trying to fit in, but on the other hand, you have your own levels of comfort. Sometimes, these factors clash, as in this example from my visits to a low-income white family, the Brindles. The mother has granted her daughter, Katie, permission to hang out at her grandmother's home with her favorite cousin, Amy. I am there too:

> It is Friday evening, and Katie Brindle and I are hanging out at
> her grandmother's house. Her Uncle Ryan, a white, working-class
> man in his 40's who is divorced, has his daughter, Amy visiting

there too; Amy and Katie, who are the same age, are playing. All of a sudden, Ryan announces he is going to go buy a Christmas tree; the girls are excited, and they want to go with him. We all pile in the car, and I am in the front seat. As we get in, he talks about his car having a problem: "Something is wrong with my steering or else my brakes. I don't want to go to no shopping mall or anywhere far away." Normally I wear a safety belt whenever I drive or ride in a car, but no one moves to put on a belt. I later write in my notes: "No safety belt. I desperately want to put one on, but no one else does. I feel unsafe."

I had just met Ryan that evening, I didn't know if he had been drinking, what kind of driver he was, or the state of the car—especially since he openly complained about the car possibly having a problem with the brakes. But, worried about looking pious and implicitly judgmental, I did not put on my safety belt for the short (i.e., 10 minute) trip to buy and then return with the tree. I believe I looked outwardly calm, but I was frightened for myself and the safety of everyone in the car.

Today I would put on my safety belt, and I would make a little joke about it. ("Don't mind me if I pop this on, my mom taught me to be a nervous Nellie.") This is just one tiny example of the countless decisions researchers have to make; many have been extensively discussed.[19] There are no clear rules of thumb except to be safe and avoid doing anything unethical. (As William F. Whyte wrote in his appendix—after describing how he voted four times in one day—in addition to various moral ramifications, illegal activities could jeopardize you and your study.[20]) One practical implication is that you should have a trusted friend to talk to regularly about how your fieldwork is unfolding, and you should talk to advisors or trusted mentors at least every couple of months. You need help sorting these things through, and it is easy to lose perspective.

Gathering and Recording Data
WRITE NOTES FROM THE MOMENT OF CONTACT
The first time you do something you have fresh eyes and insights, which usually fade rapidly as you visit again. For this reason, even if you have not been formally admitted to a field site, you want to write field notes about your contact with it. Records of phone conver-

sations, emails, and visits all should be retained. What do you notice? Write notes as early as possible even if the notes are not as developed as they are later on because you will adjust to the new setting more quickly than you imagine. If you are already part of the setting, "make the familiar strange" by adopting fresh perspectives, asking new questions, and being much more self-conscious.[21]

To Takes Notes or Not Take Notes

Some people like to take notes in the field, pulling out a little paper notebook and writing in it while conducting observations. They like it because it reminds everyone they are being studied. Others, however, reject this kind of note-taking precisely because it frequently reminds the people you are studying that they are being studied. There is no right answer here. But, in your fieldwork, your priority is to listen to people. Especially at the beginning, people taking copious notes will have trouble doing this and truly listening to what people are saying. Some people write notes on their phone or send themselves texts. This is often acceptable. You can also go to the bathroom and write rough notes or make a call and dictate notes (out of earshot). In some settings, it is very acceptable to have a laptop open, and you can then take notes in real time.

But in other settings such as at a family dinner, taking notes would be bizarre and uncomfortable, as Aliya Rao recounted in a coauthored article about the observations she did of professionals who were unemployed:

> In these small-sized families, 3–4 members, an additional person—Rao—stood out in the family. Jotting notes, however discreetly, for example during dinner table conversations where each participant was entirely visible, would have been unfeasible.[22]

Still, Rao was open with the participants that she did write up notes:

> At least one adult in each family she observed asked her about her lack of note-taking—they expected her to take notes. She explained that she made jottings based on her observations on the commute back to her home; then she would develop those jottings into full-fledged field notes within the next 24 hours.[23]

Generally, your notes will get better with time. You can remember more when you train yourself to listen carefully. Often you can remember phrases verbatim if you remind yourself of them word for word. (To test yourself, record an interaction in another space, write notes, and compare.) Remembering emotions or concepts will help your memory. As noted earlier, being rested also improves your memory.

In some cases, researchers routinely carry recorders when they are in the field. Audio recording (or video recording) is increasingly common. Study participants need to be asked if they are comfortable being recorded; it should not be done secretly. For *Unequal Childhoods*, I was worried about the quality of field notes, so all of us audio recorded what we observed. Some research participants ignored the recorders, and some people were always conscious of them. Generally, however, as a seasoned ethnographer once told me, "If they are okay with you, then they are okay with any form of recording, including video." I have found that to be the case. In addition, you can reassure your study participants that if they decide they don't like being recorded, you can bring the recording back and delete it in front of them. They are in control. Video recording can be a nice gift for participants, particularly if you create a polished, edited piece. Some people also play video recordings back to people and ask them to discuss what was happening in these interactions; this strategy can yield additional, fruitful data.

It takes a lot of time to write field notes—easily twice the amount of time you are there, and sometimes up to twelve hours. I usually try to go to the field for two to three hours, and then I budget five to six hours for writing notes. But, when I had research assistants for my project that became *Unequal Childhoods*, they took from five to twelve hours to write notes for one visit lasting two to three hours. In the next chapter, I will focus on the "flashlight" compared to "floodlight" strategies for note writing, and also factors that yield different levels of quality in notes. But, here, the point is the note taking should be immediate while your memory of what happened in the field is fresh.

The rule of thumb is that notes should be written within 24 hours of the visit. Field notes are the lifeblood of a project, and, in many cases, you will be looking at them a long time after crucial details have faded. As I explain below, you should not go into the field again until your notes are written up from your previous visit. Hence, as discussed in more detail in chapters 2 and 3, you might want to schedule field visits every other day, and also work out a schedule that balances your work obligations, writing field notes, and your personal life.

I find that writing field notes for six hours is my limit. If I have an unusually long visit (such as an overnight described in the next chapter), I need to budget my time carefully over *two* days to be sure I didn't take on another visit until my first set of notes was done. As painful as it can be to write up notes, they are an excellent investment of time—even it if means forgoing other important life activities. You might be working with these notes months or years later; your memory is not trustworthy—you can only rely on your notes. So as much as possible, you need to be detailed but succinct. Know that not every single day of notes will be fantastic, and because fieldworkers are human, you will make mistakes. But as much as possible, your visits should generate strong, rich notes on selected issues. If one day your notes are skimpy, don't belabor it, but move on, and write better notes the next visit.

As you write, you want to listen to what you are learning and think. Hence you should write an "analytic memo" at the end of each field visit to highlight key themes of what you have learned, and to link it back to the literature (more on this in chapter 8). You want to meet after every third visit with a friend or advisor. You might talk with them about a variety of points: What are you learning? What is exciting? What is surprising? What are the patterns? Why does this matter? What is this a case of? How does it deepen or add more nuance to the existing literature? By listening to yourself, and listening to their feedback, you can gradually set priorities.

Develop a Second "Elevator Speech" about Your Early Findings

As you start hanging around, people at your research site will ask you what you are learning. (Sometimes they are truly interested, and sometimes they are just being polite.) At some point, after you have been there a while, you will need a revised "elevator speech" about what you have been learning. This is tricky. Since you want them to act as naturally as possible, you don't want to focus them on the key purpose of your study, but you also don't want to be disingenuous. As with your earlier speech, this one should be vague but accurate. I would focus on one point that surprised you but is somewhat innocuous. ("I am surprised by how much parent involvement there is in this school; the

Have you figured out how
you will introduce
yourself and explain
your project to people
you meet?
Have you filed an IRB?
Do you have someone
with whom you can
talk about what you
are learning in your
research?
Do you have time to write
your field notes?
Have you cut back on
family commitments,
competing work
obligations, and
travel?
Have you thought about
what will be your role
in the field? What will
you hope to do and
not do? Do you have a
plan if there are things
that you may need to
decline to do?
Are you listening to the
advice you are being
given?
How can you say thank
you? Are there small
gifts or helpful
gestures that you
could make that feel
authentic to you and
are appropriate in this
setting?

amount of money they raise is surprisingly high."
Or, "The kids are great; it is fun to be here. I am
surprised by how well traveled these kids are."
Or, "I am surprised by how many forms you folks
fill out.") You want something that will make you
look astute, and like you are paying attention,
but nothing too controversial. You should mention a topic you want to learn more about.

Create Successful Strategies
for Managing Your Personal Life

Doing participant observation means in-
serting oneself into a different social world. If you
spend time being there, then you are not spending time in your usual haunts. All work creates
work-family conflict, but the conflict engendered
by this work has a distinctive character. Just as
ethnographers are being intrusive in the lives
of others, so participant observation is intrusive into your daily life. Juggling these competing obligations can be challenging. These issues
are rarely discussed in methodology books, but,
since they are important part of your experience,
I share my personal thoughts here.

Before you begin, it is wise to think about the
unexpected personal challenges that might surface during the study, and whether the study
could still be carried out in the event of such circumstances. For example, the life-threatening
illness of a sibling or an aging parent, the chronic
mental illness of a family member, challenges
of a home renovation, job change of a partner,
or other life events will have an impact on your
study. These experiences are largely unpredictable and out of your control, and yet they also
matter. Although it depends entirely on your
social support, it is hard to do an ethnographic
study when you are caring for a dying parent, are

going through a divorce, or are in the middle of another major life challenge. Even events such as moving, having a car accident, or recovering from knee surgery can throw a wrench into a study. Ethnographies can certainly continue, but they are necessarily delayed. In addition, major life challenges can sap energy and concentration. Researchers who are doing participant observation while they are in the middle of other life challenges will usually need support to find a way to juggle the competing obligations. An ability to compartmentalize is also helpful.

In addition, just as it is helpful to have the blessing of family members before you set off for a six-month backpack trip in Nepal, it is very useful to have the buy-in and support of loved ones before you begin a study using participant observation. Of course, most of our family members have no clue about what we all do in our university lives, let alone understand what it means to carry out a research project involving participant observation. (Why should they? It is a different world.) It can be beneficial to try to explain to them what you are hoping to do and what the research method is. In your explanation, you want to convey your enthusiasm for the project (as well as stress the instrumental benefits of a study for your career future). You might stress how excited (and nervous) you are about it, and you might share that this is very important to you.

Some family members will be excited for you. But other family members will never grasp what you are doing, will be indifferent, or may resist anything that reduces your availability to them. Depending on your relationship with them, you can either decide to ignore their objections or, if necessary, try to defuse the objections. But if a partner is upset that you will need to be away from home for a while, you might think about whether there is something that the partner really wants to do (or has always dreamt about doing) that you can help support. Even if it is expensive, it may be worth it. Or you can make a concrete plan to do something special together before you begin and after the fieldwork is over. If you have a partner, displays of gratitude to your partner are crucial. The key point here, however, is on having the buy-in you need to develop a study.

Summing Up: Beginning the Journey

There are a number of steps in beginning a study using participant observation. As discussed in chapters 2 and 3, you want to think about why you are doing the study and what you hope to learn. You also want to figure out where you will do the study, and you want to make sure that you are able to get there regularly. Some of the tasks in the "Before You Begin" box reveal themselves only as you move through the study, but it is good to think about these issues ahead of time.

Doing participant observation research is special because it involves a set of paradoxes: you are blending in but you are always an outsider, you are participating but you are observing, you are learning but you are often clueless, and you frequently have no idea what you are doing. But, then after a while, things get better. And, it broadens our own horizons to learn, more deeply, about other worlds. You can also share what you learn with others. The Unitarian-Universalist church affirms the principle of "the inherent worth and dignity of every person." This is also a core principle of ethnographic research, and, presuming that you follow the principles of the IRB, the task of doing participant observation is an honorable one. You can take us into worlds we may not know, and you can help all of us understand them more deeply. To do this, however, you need to record, with great precision, what you see. The next chapter takes up the task of writing high-quality field notes.

7

Writing High-Quality Field Notes
Details Matter

In doing participant observation, you are collecting data to use in your social science research project—data that is usually impossible to gain in other ways. When writing your observations, your field notes freeze and preserve your observations. Ultimately, they help persuade your reader by showing them the basis for your assertions (rather than asking readers to trust you). But field notes are always a trade-off between breadth and depth. In some cases, you turn on a "floodlight," providing an overview of a social setting. In other instances, you pinpoint the moment-to-moment interactions with a "flashlight" focus. Hence, you must make decisions about what details to write up. High-quality field notes are characterized by a vivid and precise description of the social process. In their excellent book *Writing Ethnographic Fieldnotes*, Emerson and his coauthors describe this as writing "lushly."

In this chapter, I take up the quest to write high-quality, detailed field notes within the formidable constraints of daily life. I also provide practical tips, including information to include on the first page, key issues to cover in the notes—which I summarize with the acronym WRITE—and common challenges. I use two examples of field notes to provide concrete guidance on how to write high-quality notes. Overall, the point of writing field notes is to create a portrait over time. As a result, your field notes will vary. In particular, your field notes will vary in quality since you will have more time and energy on some days than others. (In addition, more interesting events may happen on some days than others.) This is normal. In addition, the notes will vary in focus. Some visits you will focus only on the "floodlight" and offer an overview. In those notes, you will not capture the emotional and close interactions. Other times, your notes might have a flashlight focus on fifteen minutes of the visit. Here I lay out the ideal goals for high-quality notes. But, as I show, I sometimes have pitiful notes, and you also will likely have days where your notes are a far cry from your goals. Is this ideal? No. Is it reality? Yes. And usually, after the next visit, the notes are much better.

The First Page of Field Notes

By the end of your study, you will have many sets of field notes. On the first page of the notes of each visit, it is helpful to summarize the key points of the visit since each visit often yields ten pages (single-spaced) of notes, and it can mount up quickly. You need a short summary of the key events (what happened) and the analytic themes evoked in these instances. People manage this in different ways. I prefer one long column with three sections. Here is an example from my *Unequal Childhoods* study:

Taylor family
After school (event)
Taylor.AL.15.April 2.afterschool (file name: family, my initials,
    visit number, date, subject)
Lareau (fieldworker name if in a research team)
Month, day, year
2 hours, 13 minutes: 3:47 to 6:00 (time during visit)
5 hours (additional time spent writing notes)
Sunny, nice spring day, 50's (weather)

ANALYTIC THEMES
Child-initiated play
Neighborhood games
Rhythm of daily life
Rule breaking

This information is at the top of the page before the field notes begin, providing a summary of the basic information: who, what, when, where, and how. Note that the field notes are chronologically numbered. I chose to use the pseudonym (what I call the "code name") of the families from the very beginning of the project on all files so that I would get used to using the code names of the families (and so when the book

Table 7.1. *Summary of What Happened*

3:57 Arrived, got drink of water
4:05–5:00 Sat on floor of living room w/ friend, chatting
5:00 Tyrec suggests go outside, gets jacket
5:00–5:30 Outside playing with ball
[Tyrec worrying about mom coming home]
5:30 Mom comes home
5:40–6:00 Go to store to get water ice
6:00 p.m. Say goodbye, arrange tomorrow, leave

would be published the families would still seem like "my families"). I also had the fieldworkers always refer to the code names: "Yanelli family" or "Williams family" to increase confidentiality. In the body of the field notes, I used the first names of the participants.

The analytic themes are not usually clear to me right away. After I have completed my notes and my field note reflection (described below), I go back and fill in the theme slot on the first page.

Others have a different way of summarizing on the first page. The next example is taken from notes written by Peter Harvey, a white doctoral student from England studying an elite private school where he observed a combined fourth- and fifth-grade classroom. He was particularly interested in how the children learned class-based cultural skills.[1] On the first page of his notes, he integrates the events with his time calendar:

Peter Harvey

WEDNESDAY 18TH OCTOBER; 10.55AM–1.16PM
OVERVIEW OF EVENTS

 10.55–11.05 Snack time
 - Girls ransack my bag and steal my stuff
 11.05–11.15 lesson
 - Teacher 1 tells Shawn off and he resists; she talks of empowering him
 - Teacher 2 trying to teach rest of class
 11.15–12.22 lesson on democracy/Greece
 - Kids emphasize MALE citizens more than Teacher 2
 - Rachel expects Teacher 2 to come to her while she calls him

- Several kids interrupting Teacher 2 talking; Aaron taps
  Teacher 2 on shoulder, Gabe refuses to acknowledge others

12.22–1.16 Girls' Science club
- Science Teacher encourages others to do calls
- Girls respond perfectly to chants and apologize for talking
  over Science Teacher
- Do stealth creeps
- Varying power structures in groups, but not dominants
- Girls call each other "guys"

DETAILS
As part of writing "lushly" you want to help the reader see what you saw. That way, the reader can better understand the basis for your claims.

The summary page records the number of hours you spend doing participant observation since it has become fashionable to report the number of hours ethnographers spend in the field. To do so, you need excellent records. (You want to separate out the number of hours you spent doing observation from any other hours such as transportation or writing field notes.) It can be handy to keep a running log of your fieldwork visits with the date, event, time in field, as well as file name and location. Keep a back-up copy of the notes, ideally on a hard drive.

Guidelines for Writing High-Quality Field Notes

Although field notes are the lifeblood of an ethnographic study, there are only so many hours in a day. As discussed in chapters 2 and 3, you need to figure out how much time you can devote to the project. I would budget two to three times as many hours as you spend in the field to write field notes. If you go for two hours, you want to write for around five hours. How much time you can spend in the field depends on how much time you have to write. As noted in the previous chapter, you need to write notes within 24 hours of the visit; you should never, in my opinion, collect more data until you have finished the notes from the previous visit.

Still, there is no one right way to carry out participant observation or to write field notes. And visits to the same site with the same people can vary. Sometimes a lot happens, and sometimes very little happens.

Sometimes you feel that you fit in and sometimes you feel as if you are in the way. As you write field notes, you want to cover some key issues each time. I have coined this as your need to "WRITE" (see box).

W: WHO, WHAT, WHEN, WHERE, HOW

In journalism, rookie reporters are taught that the "five w's": "who, what, when, where, and how" should appear in the first paragraph. In field notes, you want to describe, in varying levels of detail, the action that took place when you were there.

This information will be described in the summary of events and in the content of your notes. Still, you will need to set priorities. Some of these actions you can describe using the flashlight approach, where you slow down the action to provide considerable detail. Here, it could take three pages to discuss 15 minutes of action. Other parts of the visit would be dispensed with in a more cursory manner (the floodlight). In the description, pay special attention to the smells, level of light or darkness, noise levels, textures, colors, and other elements in the setting. You are creating a graphic image for the audience not as a literary device (although it makes the reading more interesting), but so the reader can visualize what you observed and understand the evidentiary basis for your claims. Still, you should be careful to write what you observe or what others explicitly tell you; you want to avoid inferring the feelings of your research participants.

Since there is so much to write, think about your key intellectual goals (especially your theoretical priorities) and, in some instances, turn a flashlight on something that seems important. Of course, since those evolve over time, it is helpful to make your notes as comprehensive as possible in the first half of your visits (when you are still finding your focus). Gradually you will gain clarity, but because you are looking for disconfirming evidence, you want to have a broad vision and an open mind.

WRITE

W: "who, what, when, where, how"

R: reaction—responses to the action in question, and the response to the response

I: inaction—silence or a nonverbal response to an action

T: timing—how slowly or quickly someone is speaking or joking

E: emotions—nonverbal signs of emotion (or stoicism) in the face, arms, and other parts of the body

R: REACTION

There is so much to do in keeping track of who is doing what—the actions—that it can be easy to lose track of how people respond to an action. But, as with a game of ping pong, in ethnographic notes you want to go back and forth documenting the action, the reaction, and the reaction to the reaction. You also want to trace the main players and the witnesses as Elijah Anderson does in his classic work, *A Place on the Corner*:

> On a Friday evening at about six o'clock, approximately twenty-five men were gathered at Jelly's liquor-store room, to celebrate payday with friends.... People joked about their home life, about their jobs, about their wives, about their children; they talked about their good times and bad times.... T. J. and Herman were laughing and playing with each other—both were somewhat high.... Suddenly the sound of a loud slap penetrated the general noise. In their general joking around, T. J. had playfully slapped at Herman, but his hand accidentally landed hard and loud on Herman's face.

Next, Anderson skillfully describes both the reactions of Herman (who was hit), of T. J. (who silently listens to Herman's anger), and, importantly, to the other men who witnessed it (as there is a contrast between "People joked about their home life" and "a hush fell over the room"). As he continues to trace the action, Anderson importantly not only shows Herman's fury, but also how T. J. responds (nonverbally), and how the other men in the room reacted:

> Though T. J. had not meant to slap Herman, those who looked on did not all readily understand that. A hush fell over the room as others waited to see what Herman would do.... Herman held his face and looked at T. J. with a serious expression. He said, "T. J. if you ever do that again, I swear I'll kill you. If you ever do that again." T. J. just stood and looked at the floor as Herman continued to threaten and tongue-lash him ... Soon the men turned back to what they had been doing and the noise level rose, but it never reached the level it was before T. J.'s slap. After a while, Herman eased off for home.[2]

Anderson's portrayal highlights the importance of recording multiple actors around your focal point. Reactions are important.

I: INACTION

In your field notes, you always want to include silences or a *lack* of response when someone says something. Of course, silences vary. Some are comfortable; others are tense. In a field note from a white family below the poverty level from my book *Unequal Childhoods*, ten-year-old Katie is spending the afternoon with her mother, CiCi, her 18-month-old brother, Melmel, her auntie Mary (her mother's ex-sister-in-law), and the fieldworker (a young white woman named Mimi). They are in the living room, and most of the time everyone watches soap operas and Oprah.

> With her mother and aunt only a few feet away, Katie begins to hit herself. There is no mistaking that they have heard and seen her, but there is no reaction on their part.
>
> Katie starts hitting her forehead with her fist. She is sitting on the bed and falls backwards as she beats her forehead. She is hitting with her right hand. She continues for about three minutes, which seems to me like a very long time.
>
> Moreover, Melmel begins to mimic her: Melmel climbs up on the bed between her and myself and imitates Katie. He does this for about a minute. Cici and Mary watch without saying anything. Katie says to me, "That's why I was in the hospital." I ask, "Why?" She says, "For hurting myself." I ask, "What did they do to you?" She says, "They locked me up." I ask, "And then what did they do?" Katie says, "They taught me about self-esteem and told me not to hurt myself." I looked over once and Cici and Mary were watching Oprah.[3]

In this family, Katie was known for having a dramatic flair, which may have contributed to her mother's and aunt's response. Regardless, the key point of the field note is to show that the mother and aunt heard but did not react.

Other times, the examination of inaction develops in an analysis. In his compelling work, *When a Heart Turns Rock Solid*, Timothy Black analyzes the events that led Julio to leave the gang after Julio had "retaliated" for shootings that killed two members of the gang where he was the godfather; he retaliated by shooting "three guys—in the butt, stomach, and arm." None died, and Julio went to Puerto Rico for a few months. When he returned, he left the gang. Timothy Black illuminates the paths not taken:

Less than a year after Julio left La Familia, ten of its members were indicted on drug and firearm charges.... In an eighteen-month span, Julio had been lucky on two occasions—he had shot but not killed three men on Main Street and he had left the gang before the federal investigation..... had he remained godfather of the Warlords ... Julio too might be spending his life behind bars.[4]

Hence, in both field notes and in your analysis, it is helpful to report silences and events that did not transpire that are relevant to your focus.

T: TIMING

Some people rush out their words while others speak at a languid pace. Sometimes in one setting multiple people are bustling about, running into each other, and there is a sense of urgency, while other times, such as a hot, summer day, a group of people barely move. Thus, you want to convey the passage of time: how quickly or slowly something unfolds from speech to action. One way to mark the passage of time is demonstrated in this excerpt from Ashley Mears's book on modeling, *Pricing Beauty*, which shows the training involved in "becoming a look." Here, she has signed up with an agency, and was encouraged to take "walking lessons" before Fashion Week:

At 6:30 p.m. on a Wednesday night, after a day of eight casting [auditions], I arrived at metro to meet another model, Beth, aged twenty-two, and Felix, our runway coach for the evening.

Felix is a forty-something petite [B]lack man..... He is gay, he says, as a "gay dollar bill." He directs us to the back of the agency, where there is a long corridor.... We change into our high heels, and begin our lessons.

First we line up to the water cooler for "hip exercises." ... After a few minutes of this ... it is time now to start walking.... for the next hour, Felix will have Beth and I walk toward him and back again, taking turns. At one point he tells me after I walk: "Don't charge at a man. Come to him. Flirt."

Mears keeps track of time and, indeed, her own experience:

Felix pulls up a chair and sits at the end of our mini-runway, watching. A pizza is ordered.... Felix instructs us to work it better between bites of his cheese slice. It is 8 p.m. and I'm starving and tired, and with each step the leather of my new stiletto digs into my Achilles.... We form a circle to walk in, and we march in sync with each other, and it's a bizarre model military scene and my feet really hurt ... There is Felix, nodding his head, "There you go girl, there you go, yes!"[5]

Here, Mears tells us the time at the beginning (6:30 p.m.), the amount of time they spend on hip exercises ("a few minutes of this"), the ordering of the pizza, and how, by 8:00 p.m., she is starving and her feet are killing her. She is pacing off the event to deepen your understanding, using vivid, precise words ("my new stiletto digs into my Achilles") so that we can visualize her experience.

Timing is part of a more general pattern of describing the setting, including not only the pace but the atmosphere: the light, space, distance, noises, smells, colors, and textures.

E: EMOTION

In participant observation, you want your accounts to reveal the complex bodily interactions that are part of daily life—both the emotions we display on our faces with grimaces, frowns, raised eyebrows, or stern looks, and the tensed shoulders, rigid posture, or brisk walks. You do not want to simply say "he smiled" since there are many different types of smiles: anxious smiles, small smiles, beaming smiles, and broad smiles. As much as possible, emotions and bodily movements should be threaded throughout your descriptions.

It is common for qualitative researchers to be told "show, don't tell." In this instance, Robin Leidner shows the frustration of the first day on the breakfast shift at McDonalds when the crew trainer, Diana, "did not explain the procedures to me carefully." Leidner explains that "I had to ask for directions continually from Diana or another worker." When business picked up, Diana's "help" was even more confounding:

I go on taking orders. Practically every time I start to go get the items, Diana says, "I'll get it; take your money." Worse, when it gets more crowded she takes new orders before I've finished taking the money for the last one. Often while I'm busy making change or something, she's shouting, "Can I help you?" and keeping the new order in her head. She then expects me to hear the second order, remember it, and key it in after I finish with the first order.

(At least I guess that's what she expects.) I often have to ask her what she's gotten or ask the customer to repeat to me what they've told Diana. On top of this, Diana sometimes reaches over and keys an order in on my register. This is tolerable while I'm standing there, but sometimes when I do go to get food items, I come back to find that there's some new order on my register and Diana is shouting, "Take the money." When there are several parties at the counter, I don't even know who ordered what or whose money I should be taking.[6]

When Leidner concludes, "I went through the breakfast shift in a state of suppressed rage" then you understand why. She goes on to say that the experience helped her understand "what happens when McDonald's training procedures are not followed" and why there were "ceaseless efforts" to enforce training.

In sum, there are different elements in the field notes, but WRITE captures the most crucial ones.

The Do's and Don'ts of Writing Field Notes
DO RECORD THE INDIVIDUAL STEPS WITHIN SOCIAL INTERACTION

Interaction is complex, made up of many different steps involving multiple people doing multiple things. In this, you want to know, ideally, what all of the key people in the field note are doing. Here is an excerpt from an excellent field note written by Sherelle Ferguson as part of her dissertation research on class and race variations in college students' interaction with college officials. In her observations at an expensive, nonselective college, she shows how Maya, a Black woman from a working-class family, was anxious about approaching her Anatomy professor with a question. During the lecture on bones, Ferguson reported that Maya "wondered aloud" to her friend Alicia (a Latina middle-class student) whether almond milk had benefits for bone strength. Ferguson, a Black sociology doctoral student in her late 20s, attended the lecture with them, and carefully noted all of the steps where Maya was reluctant to ask the professor and pressured her friend to ask, and the events after Alicia makes the inquiry:

After lecture, we are among the last students in the room. Alicia walks over to the front of the stage to talk to the professor about the final exam and ask a question about the vitamin D content of milk. Maya and I continue gathering our bags and notebooks. When Alicia returns, Maya asks hopefully in a quiet voice, "Did you ask her about almond milk too?" Alicia smiles bashfully and says "No." Maya asks with high-pitched urgency, "Are you going to ask her?" Alicia suggests playfully, "YOU ask her." Alicia leads us into the aisle heading towards the door, but we seem to be moving slowly. Maya is dragging her feet. Maya repeats, "Ask her please." We all take a few more hesitant steps as Alicia hems. They are talking loud enough that is possible their voices are carrying over to the professor. I see the professor look up in our direction. Maya whines again, "Pleeeeaaasssse?" Alicia takes a deep breath, turns, and projects across the room to the professor, "What about almond milk?" Maya does not turn to engage with the professor. The professor answers quickly and matter-of-factly, "Almond milk is fortified with vitamin D and calcium.... Sometimes it's better than regular milk." Maya quietly says, "Yes!" and does a little jig, celebrating that almond milk is part of her diet. As we walk out of the lecture hall, I ask Maya, "Why didn't you want to ask her?" Dismissively, without looking me in the eye, she mumbles, "I dunno. I just don't." I try again, "Is she scary?" She chirps, "No." In a clear effort to change the subject, Maya barely takes a breath before initiating a conversation with Alicia about their plans for the evening.[7]

Ferguson writes, "Maya was clearly uncomfortable approaching her professor and preferred to have her friend serve as a mouthpiece." The notes are exemplary as Ferguson shows the steps in a methodological fashion: packing up bags, Alicia asking a question, Maya pressuring Alicia, Alicia asking the professor, Maya not turning around while Alicia asks, the professor's "matter-of-fact" answer, and Maya's elated response. By including how Alicia, the professor, and Maya reacted to each step, Ferguson anticipates questions readers might have and then answers them.

USE DIALOGUE, BUT A LITTLE CAN GO A LONG WAY

Dialogue enlivens description. But it turns out that in some instances you can construct a moment vividly with only a few phrases relying on your memory (and writing immediately after your visit). Going back to Peter Harvey's school observations, he normally entered the classroom of fourth and fifth graders, but this particular morning, he arrived at the school during snack time and came to the playground. In a published article on methodological challenges of studying children, he describes his liminal status of working to "fit in" with the young people and avoid an authoritarian role, but instead being treated like an older brother, someone to impress and tease, but not subject to the same rules as adults.[8] His patience was tested in this moment:

> I arrived at Truman and see that [my class] is out in the playground having snacktime. As I approach the big grey gates, most of the girls are playing in the area near them, as they often do. Paris sees me through the gates and bounces up and down squealing "Peter! Peter!" and the other girls see this and become similarly excited.... I'm buzzed through the gates. Once halfway through the gate they lay hands on me and haul me through the rest of the way.... One of them takes my backpack from my shoulders and they chatter "What's in your backpack, Peter?" ... I don't resist them taking the backpack as I figure there's nothing really valuable in there. However, the compartments are immediately unzipped and the gang of girls start pulling things out from inside, holding things up for each other to see, gawking at them, and claiming them as their own, like prized booty from a newfound treasure chest.

As Harvey's anxiety rises, he watches the children having fun going through his belongings:

> Paris finds my bike helmet and takes it out, plonking it on her head. Clare pulls out my apartment access card, mistakenly calling "We've got your credit card!" Ava, a bit more timidly but getting in the spirit, chooses which one of my 3 pens she wants to keep; Francesca takes another. Paris and Annabelle then come across the black plastic cover for my bike saddle, which I never use. Paris demands, laughingly, "Why do you have a hair net?!" I explain that it's a saddle cover, and she shrugs, continuing to go through my bag for other treasures. Clare then pulls out my wallet, holding it aloft with wide eyes and a big grin on her face, calling "I've got your wallet!" On this I actually adopt a more serious tone and say "Ah,

I need that back." Clare falters, and actually hands it over. If Paris had found it I may have had a tougher time getting it back.... Paris then finds my reasonable-quality in-ear headphones, and starts trying to tug them out of the bag, but they're caught on something and I can see the wire straining. Worried the earbud will pop off, I take hold of the backpack and actually help free the headphones for Paris, as I'd hate to see them broken. Paris grasps the bundle of wires to her.

The girls abscond with Harvey's belongings:

> Mr. Ryan is not near the girls' playground spot during all this, so doesn't intervene ... he was probably watching the other kids play kickball. He then calls out to everyone, "Line up! Line up!" This causes a scurry of activity. Paris ... moves sharply and my bike helmet topples off her head and lands on the ground, where the (admittedly flimsy) visor falls off. Paris does not even glance at it, let alone offer to, or actually, pick it up. Instead she nips off to the line still holding my headphones. Ava tells me judiciously, "I'm going to keep this one [pen] all day." Clare, one of the more strict, rule-bound girls, has already given back my wallet and card, having seemingly pushed her naughty boundaries far enough for her own comfort.

Although long and written with enough detail to envision the clamor of activity, there are actually few direct quotes involved. Indeed, in this entire, long excerpt, Peter Harvey needed to recall six brief phrases stated by the girls (i.e., "Peter, Peter," "What's in your backpack, Peter," "We've got your credit card," "Why do you have a hair net?" "I've got your wallet," and "I'm going to keep this one all day"). In addition, he recorded the teacher ("Line up! Line up!") and his own statement, "Ah, I need that back." The rest of the long excerpt is based on his description of the event without dialogue. Yet, he effectively evokes the scene. Hence, a few choice phrases enliven an ethnographic moment.

Of course, this was only one incident in the day. That day, he was there 2 hours and 21 minutes (10:55 a.m. to 1:16 p.m.) and wrote around 5,000 words of notes, which (including a couple of photos) totaled 10 single-spaced pages. Often his notes ran 13 to 15 pages single-spaced from a three-hour visit, and, as is common, some notes were more polished than others. Harvey reported that he openly jotted in a small notebook at school (because it was not uncomfortable to do it in the space, to remind them of his role as a researcher, and to make his notes more accurate). But, with only a handful of phrases, you can convey many moments to a reader.

DO DESCRIBE THE SETTING'S SMELLS, LIGHT, NOISE, COLORS

All five senses matter in fieldwork, but the ears, nose, and eyes matter in evoking sound, smell, and light. You also want to pay attention to colors—are they deep-saturated jewel tones or gray and white; is the black and white checkered floor sparklingly clean or dull and worn with broken tiles? You don't want to only describe what people do but convey what it feels like to be in the setting. The mission of social science research is very different than that of a novelist, since social science research uses data to support claims with evidence. Nevertheless, one area of overlap is the use of words to describe settings. As a result, reading novels can improve your writing skills. As you read, you can be attuned to how authors succinctly evoke settings in a detailed and sensory fashion.

Describing a setting is complex, but a few vivid phrases can help the reader envision the space. Here, in her book project, *In This Place Called Prison*, Rachel Ellis describes the community space ("Main Hall") in a woman's prison away from the cellblock, where the women have Bible study, GED classes, and other activities:

> Prisoners and staff enter the Main Hall from the prison courtyard through double-doors. These doors are constantly opening and closing as people stream in and out. The corridors of the Main Hall are usually noisy, with women talking, arguing, or singing, while officers answer ringing phones and beeping walkie-talkies, occasionally yelling loud commands. The building feels sterile: the walls are made of cement blocks slathered in bright white paint, with tan speckled tile floors mopped daily by inmates, and fluorescent lights beaming overhead. The space is bright and squeaky clean, and often smells of Lysol. Around mealtimes, scents of hot meat dishes piping out of the cafeteria are occasionally

pungent enough to elicit complaints, like sauerkraut on hotdog day. Some afternoons, walking down that hallway, a waft of microwave popcorn filters through, recently popped by an officer on duty or an inmate who works in the Main Hall.

Here, Ellis mentions a number of smells: "Lysol," "sauerkraut," "waft of microwave popcorn," as well as the visual factors that make the place feel "sterile" with cement block walls slathered in bright white paint, fluorescent lights, and tile floors. She also describes noises: "beeping walkie-talkies," "yelling loud commands," "women talking, arguing, or singing." In only one paragraph, she helps us envision the prison by using the senses. Also, she uses a number of evocative words: "pungent," "piping," and "waft."

DON'T RECORD EVERY DETAIL: PRIORITIZE OBSERVATIONS THAT ADDRESS YOUR KEY QUESTIONS

Sometimes writing field notes goes smoothly. You get home, you re- lax, you write field notes, and you are done. Other times, it is harder. At times I have found myself in a kind of purgatory where the notes- writing seems to go on and on, without producing satisfactory results. For example, I was the lead fieldworker for the white, middle-class Tal- linger family (who had three boys with Garrett, in fourth grade, being the eldest). I usually went three to four times per week; two other re- search assistants filled in the other days. In addition to visiting three weeks daily, we had one overnight visit. (The overnight visit did not work well because it was rare. Fieldwork turns out better when you go repeatedly and people get used to you.) I spent the night on a late May evening. I arrived at 4:30 p.m.; we had dinner, Garrett got ready for the spring musical performance, and we drove there. We were there 7:45 to 9:35 p.m., and then we drove home. The kids got ready for bed, the mom sat with the two older kids in the dark (and I sat there too) from 10:36 to 10:46 p.m. Then I hung out with the parents until I went to bed (after 11:00 p.m.). I got woken up at 7:20 a.m. (The mom left at 4:30 a.m. for a flight.) The dad got the kids ready for school and made breakfast; the kids fed the animals. Shepherded by a beleaguered dad, we all left at 8:20 a.m. There were interesting moments over the course of the visit. But I was tired, having not slept well in the Tallin- ger's house. I had cleared a lot of time for writing field notes in anticipation of the overnight visits, but it was still not enough. In writing my notes, I got bogged down in simply describing what happened early in the visit. My notes for what I observed the next morning are pitiful:

Dad asks Spencer (8-year-old) about library book
Spencer goes to find library book
Dad goes through Spencer's binder and throws away papers
Dad gets out lunch for Sam (5-year-old) out of his
Sam wants to know what is in lunch; Sam says he doesn't want
    pudding; Dad
says to keep it he might want it later
With a deep sigh he calls the person who responded to the
    childcare ad and
leaves a message on telephone
doublechecks dog food/water
Sam takes pudding out of lunch and hands to father
Dad sighs deeply and puts it in fridge
tells kids we are ready

There were many moments the notes didn't capture, including the brisk way that the dad went through his son's backpack, crumpling up papers and throwing things away (which is rare for fathers to do), and Sam's rebellion in taking the chocolate pudding out of his lunch. But, having been observing this five-member family in multiple settings nonstop since the previous afternoon, I was exhausted by breakfast time. Some of the notes from the night were much better. In fact, a brief, nonverbal moment from that evening was important: as the dad arrives home around 10:00 p.m., the mom is tucking the younger boys into bed, Garrett has gotten a late-night snack, and I am sitting at the kitchen table:

Dad wanders over to phone and stands in front of calendar looking
to see what is on it. Upon seeing the evening is blank except for
the name of the fieldworker, Dad emulates the way weight lifters
celebrate a victory as he lifts both arms above his chest with fists
clenched. (has a slight smile; almost as if he is saying "yes!" but not
audible)

Still, the reality is that sometimes I got bogged down and gave short shrift to events at the end of a long visit. This is not advisable. I should have spent less time doing fieldwork or allowed longer to write notes before I returned to the field.

In setting writing priorities, I find it helpful to reflect on the conceptual priorities of my study. I make a list of all of the moments and phrases from the visit I want to describe; I prioritize the ones that may be most analytically important. Then, as I finish one, I mark it off by striking it out. This strike-out is satisfying. Indeed, studies of job satisfaction find that workers enjoy their jobs more if they can see progress throughout the day. In this instance, I simply wrote chronologically from the beginning to the end of the visit. What I should have done was sit down and assess what I needed to write up, and then try to think about my analytic priorities. (This was hard for me to know at that point.) In addition, since it was my first (and only) overnight stay, there were many new things (as there are on the first few days of a visit). But, as much as possible, you should prioritize writing your most detailed field notes on the key analytic issues.

DO USE A THESAURUS
Writing high-quality field notes often involves the abundant use of adjectives and adverbs. The frequent use of a thesaurus is an invaluable resource. For example, I will quickly check the thesaurus 15 to 20 times in writing up a set of field notes. With practice, the retrieval of more lively words from a thesaurus can be done in a matter of seconds. Rather than writing "says," you might write "mutters, exclaims, murmurs, grumbles, complains, moans, protests, or whines" (if there is a negative tone) or "cheerfully, chirpily, enthusiastically, eagerly, impatiently, animatedly, warmly, excitedly, or earnestly." Presuming the term is accurately capturing what you observed, the lively words add more precision and thus help convey your meaning.

There are many language lists that include words evoking pleasant feelings (e.g., gleeful, ecstatic, jubilant), words expressing interest (e.g., intrigued, absorbed, engrossed, concerned), words about fear (e.g., afraid, suspicious, anxious, alarmed, scared, worried, timid, shaky, or menaced), indifference (e.g., nonchalant, neutral, reserved, or disinterested), and words about good feelings (e.g., calm, peaceful, at ease, comfortable, pleased, encouraged, surprised, content, quiet, certain, relaxed, serene, free and easy, bright, blessed, and reassured).[9] These synonyms add precision to your notes. Word processing programs such as Word have a built-in thesaurus function, and a real thesaurus is even better. You should use it.

WRITE A FIELDWORK REFLECTIVE MEMO AFTER EACH VISIT

At the same time I write my field notes, I write a reflective memo. The purpose of the memo is to process the visit and take a step back. Field visits are intense and can leave you preoccupied by what you saw and heard. Sometimes, as I show below, it can be a space to vent an emotional response to what you see in the visit. In addition, it is a chance to reflect on the big picture. Fieldwork is so absorbing that it can be hard, in this moment, to even recall the general research questions that drew you to the study. In a reflective memo, I ask, "What did I learn today?" "How does this advance my thinking?" "How does this information fit with the studies I have read?" Sometimes, of course, I draw a complete blank at first. However, I force myself to stay on this task for fifteen minutes or so. Gradually I can start thinking about the analytic themes. Since I make a list of things to look for in the future, reflective memos can help focus future data collection. While writing the memo, I may remember an article I have read, and this may help me advance the conceptual contribution of the work. The process of writing the reflection also gives me additional insight into the role I am playing in the field. A reflective memo is a chance to take stock of whom you have been with in your field site; you can consider whether hanging out with others might shed new insight. As I explain in the next chapter on data analysis, two or three times per month, I write a more detailed analytic memo that is related to, but still different from, a reflective memo. An analytic memo covers issues over a set of field notes, engages seriously with the literature, and develops a possible argument. I also show the analytic memo to others and get feedback on it; reflective memos usually are seen only by the researcher or, in some cases, the research team.

Two Sets of Sample Field Notes

The field notes I share here are from family observations the research assistants and I carried out as research for the study ultimately published as *Unequal Childhoods*. As noted in an earlier chapter, this book examined child rearing in white and Black families with children around ten years of age; we found middle-class families have different approaches to child rearing than working-class and poor families.[10] This method of "intensive family observation" used in my study is different than a classic ethnography where someone hangs out in a setting. After conducting interviews, each researcher on the team entered the family as a quasi-stranger to visit daily for a fixed period (in this case three weeks).[11] We worked in teams of three, and visits usually lasted around two hours but sometimes went longer. Crucially, I spoke on the phone with the fieldworkers after every visit to guide them in the writing of the field notes.[12]

The excerpts reproduced in this chapter are a visit with a family early in the study, including a family dinner where we were all still getting acquainted. I accompany the excerpts with boxed comments that draw attention to specific strengths and weaknesses in the field notes and, where appropriate, suggest alternative language that might have offered up a richer portrait.

AN UNEVEN SET OF FIELD NOTES

The first set of field notes examined here were carried out by a novice— a hard-working, intelligent, caring second-year doctoral student (Megan Williams, a pseudonym as are all of names in the field notes shared in this chapter). The excerpt is from an early visit Megan made with a low-income, deeply religious African American family that included Tara (10), her older brother Dwayne (12), her grandmother, Ms. Carroll, and her uncle. Tara's mother, Tabitha, worked full-time, and visited frequently, but Ms. Carroll had custody of the children. (Tara's mother had recovered from a difficult period in her life—a period that included a drug addiction.) On this particular Sunday, Megan met the grandmother, Ms. Carroll, before church (as everyone else had gotten a ride to church earlier). Megan and Ms. Carroll waited at the bus stop together, caught a ride, went to the service, and had dinner with the family afterwards. She was with them over seven hours, meeting some of the family members for the first time. Megan, a Black/white biracial woman, whose family was not religious, was gregarious and unusually socially skilled; she made people feel comfortable. Her outstanding skills in building rapport with family members were extremely valuable to the study, but her notes are uneven. Some are excellent. Others need more detail.

In this visit to an African American church with Ms. Carroll, the description of catching a ride is excellent, both vivid and detailed:

At about 11:00, we hear a horn across the street, and I look and see a large old blue car coming out of the housing development, stopped now at the light, and Ms. Carroll says, "Come on, Meg! We got a ride!" I ask who it is, and she says, "That's my neighbor, Sister Wanda." We begin to run across the street, trying to avoid the puddles, toward the car; I am ahead of her. Ms. Carroll tells me to go ahead and get in. I stop, faltering, and ask if she thinks it's okay since her friend doesn't know me. She guffaws and says to go ahead. I open the door and sheepishly say hello to the woman and wait for her to say to get in. The woman pauses, but is smiling, and as Ms. Carroll catches up, says to get in the car.

> In this section of notes there are details (i.e., puddles to avoid and the excitement of catching a ride). She takes us through each step (e.g., hearing the horn, running across the street, arriving at the car, and getting in the car). The notes have important strengths.

The notes from the one-hour-and-forty-five-minute Pentecostal church service, however, are much more general, making the interaction difficult to visualize:

From the time we enter the church, about 11:15, until a few minutes after 1:00, the church program involves singing, chanting and prayer, and announcements.... Singing is overwhelmingly the greatest focus. At one point, one woman from the choir comes to the center of the platform, to use the microphone, and sings a solo, a hymn that eventually (after maybe five minutes) is transformed to include first the general choir and then the entire congregation and ends with her spinning around the platform for a few minutes, apparently overcome emotionally by the "spirit" of the song.

> Ideally, we would want to know much more about the woman, her affect, the content of the song, the source of music, the response of the congregation, and the way that "spirit" showed in her singing. The notes are overly general.

Two weeks later, she was at church again with the entire family (including Tara's aunts and several cousins). The fieldworker, Megan, thoughtfully comments on the misery of the children:

> Throughout the service (both the music and the sermon), the children are mostly incredibly bored looking: the girls alternately stare, look tired, talk to each other, and fill out Christmas cards. As time goes on, Tara and [her cousin] Tia start drawing pictures on the church program and look as though they are playing some kind of game.... Several times during the service, Aunt Jody specifically tells Tara to be quiet. Tabitha [Tara's mother] never does this.... During the sermon Tara makes faces at and waves to a toddler [nearby].

This is valuable, but it would be helpful to know more about the emotion on their faces and the movement of their bodies. What do they look like when they stare? Is it a blank look or do they look annoyed? Do they wiggle their bodies and stifle a yawn? For nine-year-old children, a one-hour-and-forty-five-minute church service is taxing.

The fieldworker draws an interesting contrast between the emotion of the adults as the service draws to a close:

> Then there is a culminating hymn that goes on for a few minutes, getting wilder and wilder, with the choir moving and dancing and the kids on the drums really going (Tabitha is fully dancing in her seat now, though she has put her coat on).... Many people dance their way out of the sanctuary.

Here, it is excellent detail to know that Tara's mother has her coat on and is dancing in the seat and that people dance their way out of the sanctuary. But key details elude us. What is Tara's mother's facial expression? Is she radiant in her smile or is she somber?

In her reflective memo, the fieldworker provides a valuable analysis of the contrast:

I am really struck by how unmoved the children are at church. Even during the music, they don't respond. Looking around, however, it seems to me that most of the children in the congregation have the same blank look on their faces, like they are simply waiting for it to be over with. The contrast is remarkably great, then, between the adults, who are oftentimes ecstatically moved, and the children.

> The field notes provide support for this interesting claim that children are in a different social world than adults, but there is not as much support as would be ideal. The notes are skimming along the surface.

To enter a family as a virtual stranger is extremely challenging, and the fieldworker excelled in making people feel comfortable and integrating herself into the setting. At times she is unsure what to do, as when she was told to sit down (but none of the other adults were sitting) at the Sunday dinner after church:

I sit down in the chair placed at the table against the back wall. Carolyn (Tara's aunt) tells me first to serve myself, even before she serves all of the children (which she does alone, asking each what they want).
I am hesitant to begin serving my plate, uncomfortable that it seems to be protocol for the guest to go first, by herself. Carolyn sees this and says, "Take a little of everything if you want." So I begin to serve my plate with a bite of everything and a small piece of chicken (rice and gravy, stuffing, broccoli, candied yams, baked macaroni and cheese, corn, roast beef, chicken and Cornish hens cut up, rolls).

These details are helpful in understanding the family culture. It looks as if the children continue to be in a different social world, but the field worker is in a bind since she was invited to sit with the adults. She must talk to the adults, and she cannot see very well what is happening with the kids. However, there is nothing she can do about this.

I hear the children talking amongst themselves a little and to Carolyn, but can't really get into it since Ms. Carroll sits to my right and Jody (another aunt) sits to my left and they engage me in conversation. Jody first asks me what religion I am, and we talk a good deal about different kinds of churches and levels of expression and "praising the Lord."

The fieldworker is caught here; she is a grown-up and hence invited to sit at the table with adults, but then, as she notes, "I hear the children talking amongst themselves a little" but "can't really get into it" since she is being asked questions. Still, she is struck by the speed of the dinner ("how fast it goes") and how the children "disappear."

Serving the food becomes much more comfortable after a couple of minutes, when the others have sat down at the table and began to ask for things to be passed to them as well as reach for them. Ms. Carroll and Dawn (a third aunt) move to seconds easily, and I do too, with the macaroni (of which there is a lot). I am astonished, however, at how fast dinner goes. None of the children want second servings, and they are all finished after about ten minutes, disappearing again from the dining room as quickly as they came in.

The notes have some very interesting findings, and she was heavily constrained, but still, it would be ideal to have additional details of what she could see from across the room. Did the kids bow their heads at the prayer? Did the kids ask questions of the adults? Did the adults look over at them or tell them to mind their manners?

> What was the prayer? Did they giggle together? Was the TV on? Did they argue loudly? Was there a clanking of forks on the plate? Where did they go when they disappeared? The fact that the children are at a separate table, that the adults are not talking to them, and the parents are not cultivating their interests is all very interesting for the research project, but it is hard to get a picture.

SUMMING UP: A SET OF FIELD NOTES THAT RAISED UNANSWERED QUESTIONS

At an early visit, the fieldworker excelled, moving with the family through a number of different settings, able to integrate into a Sunday dinner with many people she had never met, and being well liked by the family. This is a considerable achievement. She also provided valuable insight into the family, particularly the separate worlds of the children and the adults in this family—an issue that was central to the research focus of this study. She observed that the children were completely disengaged in the long church service while the adults were animated and noted there was little discussion with the children at dinner, where they came, ate, and disappeared quickly. Given that middle-class families (not discussed here) interrogated their children with questions and constantly interacted with them, this finding was striking.

Yet the notes don't capture as much of the social dynamics as would be ideal. In particular, it was hard to get a striking visual image of Tara in church, and, in the family dinner, it is difficult to know what the children were actually doing. Nor did we learn much about the grimaces, grins, or heavy sighs as people heaved themselves out of a chair, the exasperation in the voices of mothers when they talk to their daughters, and the general display of emotions and the body (especially the face) in social action. Specifically, although tension was evident between the grandmother and the mother (which the fieldworker mentioned in weekly meetings), this tension doesn't surface in the notes. Too often the notes were very focused on the action—providing a chronology of what happened—without looking at the reaction—how others reacted to what someone said, or the inaction—when someone's speech was met by silence. The timing of events, the setting, and the actual scene at the dining room table is hard to imagine. The family dynamics don't quite consistently come into focus.

A FRUITFUL SET OF FIELD NOTES

The following field notes, written by a research assistant, are richer and more detailed. The research assistant, Ashleigh Tyler, was a white third-year doctoral student with a slightly reserved manner, although she also liked to joke around. She had a knack for writing exceptional notes that were vivid and succinct. Here, Ashleigh is visiting the white middle-class Handlon family; the focal child, Melanie, is in fourth grade, her brother Tommy is in sixth grade while Harry is in eighth, and her father is an accountant. Her mother (who has a community college degree) is a church secretary. They live in a four-bedroom suburban home with a homey, relaxed feel, with clutter scattered about in piles, such as the unfolded, clean laundry resting in a bundle atop the dining room table. We visit the family in December, and for many days the project of decorating the Christmas tree is stalled, as Ashleigh's notes show:

> The Christmas tree is in the corner of the room and is decorated with lights and ornaments. The room is a mess. There are boxes of ornaments stacked on the floor and on the chair. There are pine needles on the floor around the tree. Most of the boxes are opened and half empty.

Ashleigh drove to the house, and at 3:15 Ashleigh and Ms. Handlon leave to pick up Melanie from school. During the trip, Ms. Handlon complains that she wants to make more cookies with Melanie today, but it depends on homework:

> "Hopefully if Melanie gets her homework done today early, we can make some more." She added, "She worked on her homework yesterday for 4 hours with her father. From three until seven. I can't believe that the teachers assign so much on the weekends. Don't they have a life?"

Melanie has many woes with homework, which turns into a daily battle. Here we see Ms. Handlon trying to help her daughter with multiplication. Melanie and Ashleigh sit at the dining room table while Melanie huddles over her math homework:

Melanie has her pencil clenched in her hand and she alternately looks at the book and the composition book in which she is to be writing the answers. Melanie jumps up from the table and walks into the kitchen with her composition book. I hear Ms. H say, "Now come on Melanie, what is eight times four?" Melanie gave the wrong answer and Ms. H said, "No that's not it. You need to think what it is and then you need to see if you can take something bigger into that. Is seven as high as you can go?" I heard Melanie say, "OOOOH, I just don't know how to do this. This is so hard." Ms. H asked her to try it again. Melanie returned to the dining room.

> These notes are high quality. There is dialogue. The stretched out "ooooooh" conveys emotion. Saying Melanie "jumped up" shows action. It would be ideal to know the tone of Ms. H. when she said, "No, that's not it." Also, I suspect that Melanie had a whining tone of voice when she said, "I just don't know how to do this." One step is skipped; after Melanie walks into the kitchen she must have shown her mother the book; it is unclear if Melanie said anything.

After about 5 minutes, Ms. H returns with a mug [of warm milk and honey] and gives it to Melanie. Melanie asks if she can help her and Ms. H suggests she give it a try by herself. Melanie says, "I try them by myself, but I can't do it." Harry (Melanie's brother) comes in then and runs into the dining room. He walks to the cookie container, which is behind Melanie's head, and selects a cookie. He then asks disgustedly, "What is that we're listening to?" and heads to the family room where he switches the setting to FM radio.

> It is good how she is keeping track of multiple people. Harry's disgust at the music is interesting. Again, Melanie asks for help (although we don't quite know the tone of voice) nor is it clear how impatient Ms. Handlon is. But the field note captures action and reaction.

The notes continue:

Harry is standing up next to Melanie and he is batting at the hanging reindeer on the chandelier. Melanie is watching him. She begins to sing the Spanish song and Harry begins to ask Melanie her name in Spanish. He spends maybe 5 minutes bantering with Melanie about Spanish and Melanie brags that she knows how to count to ten. She correctly counts out the numbers. Ms. H sits down next to Melanie and Harry goes into the living room. She asks Melanie how it's coming and then quickly says, "Oh Melanie, look. You're still doing the same thing. Now you know that's not going to work. Go through it again. What is x times x?" Ms. H was grasping a pencil in her hands and when Melanie began to write down an answer, Ms. H began to impatiently and forcefully tap the point into the composition book. When Melanie incorrectly wrote down something, Ms. H would tap heavily and say, "Do it again. Now check your work." Melanie finished the question, and then triumphantly said, "I got it right." Ms. H said, "Good. Now do 2 more without me." Melanie mumbles something about, "But I can't do them by myself."

This field note captures the frustration Ms. Handlon has with Melanie. The fieldworker captures verbal and nonverbal signals: "You know that's not going to work" or "impatiently and forcefully tap" with a pencil. It is excellent detail that could never be captured in an interview. In retrospect, it would have been ideal to have looked in the composition book to share the exact math problem as well as the incorrect answers. When she gets it right, the field worker uses the term "triumphantly," which also helpfully conveys emotion. She might have told us a bit about how Melanie looked too.

[At the same time as the math drama, the fieldworker elaborates a scene where Tommy goes off to watch television (which was not permitted in this house in the afternoon), and the mother impatiently cut it off. She sent Tommy off to find out about his homework; Tommy calls a friend and finds out he has no homework today.]

Ms. H returns to the kitchen and I hear the sound of an electric mixer. It is 5:30.

> The fieldworker later complained, privately, that it was hard for her to concentrate, and she wondered how Melanie could do her homework in all of that racket. Here, she details the noise.

Tommy moves into the living room and begins to play the piano. The playing is loud and dramatic-sounding. The mixer in the kitchen is whirring too. The country music is still playing. This continues for about 5 minutes. Then Harry walks into the family room, comes back into the living room and I notice that the country music is much louder. The competing sounds of mixer, piano, and music continue unabated for 8 minutes. Melanie is still poised with pencil over her books.

> This note highlights the noise, which is good. It would be ideal to know what Tommy was attempting to play as well as the country music song playing at the same time. Also, it is not clear why it stopped.

Mr. H then asked if I had any plans for dinner because, "We have more than enough here, and we'd like you to stay." I agreed and at 6:05 we sat down at the kitchen table. Melanie asked me to sit next to her although Harry had grabbed her seat. When Melanie weakly protested, he said, "Why can't I sit there. That's where I always sit." Ms. H said, "She wants Ashleigh next to her. Let's indulge her." The kitchen table was cramped with food and people. There was a long glass baking dish filled with skinless chicken breasts and a clear sauce. Another clear casserole dish had pasta shells, and a smaller blue casserole dish had peas in it.

Tommy was serving himself the chicken and Mr. H said, "Just help yourself Tom." Tommy then immediately moved the serving spoon to my plate and said charmingly, "You see, I was going to serve Ashleigh first." He then places chicken on each plate. The pasta bowl was passed and so were the peas. Melanie's plate was filled with food and her mother had just finished slicing the chicken when the doorbell rang. Ms. H said, "Well that's for you, we'll save this for you. Why don't you put it in the microwave?" Melanie followed the instructions and then you could hear the warm-up sounds of the piano lesson.

Everyone's plate was full, and Tommy had taken a bite of his chicken. Mr. H said, "Why don't you say grace for us Tommy." Tommy then prayed for "the nourishing meal before us." Everyone ate. The dinnertime banter mainly consisted of Tommy's announcement that he would need to type his mother's chocolate mousse recipe so that he could take it to school for his class. He then said, "Oh yeah, we need to make that [chocolate] mousse for 32 kids, mom." Mr. and Ms. H both looked startled and they inquired about the logistics of the activity and how long Tommy had known about it. Ms. H said she would not make it because of the expense and the threat of salmonella. Both parents seemed bemused by his request and only chided him for not giving them enough notice when he had a week to do so. They settled on a cool-whip/pudding compromise.

After about 40 minutes, Melanie bopped into the kitchen and said cheerily to Tommy, "It's your turn."

The field notes show how much work school activities create for parents. But, it is unclear from the notes when Tommy needed to bring in mousse for 32 kids. It is also unclear what Harry is doing during the dinner. It would be ideal to have even a few words around Ms. Handlon's complaint of the expense of the dessert. This is an example of a "floodlight" while the homework scene is a "flashlight" approach to writing notes.

The notes continue to describe Melanie heating up her food, her parents praising her playing, and her eating dinner before Melanie abruptly announces she needs a chorus outfit the next day, before finishing her dinner and "rifling through her backpack" to pull out another school paper for her mother to sign. After a few more minutes, the fieldworker thanks them for dinner, arranges the next visit, and leaves. The fieldworker was there an unusually long time, over four hours, while most visits were only about three. In her reflective memo, she expressed her great frustration with what she calls "bullying" as well as the chaotic family environment:

This visit was excessively long and troubling because my senses were over-stimulated. In recounting the chronology of events, I used the loud music playing as a guidepost. In terms of watching Melanie's homework session, I was troubled because in the 50-minute period in which she was "working," I think she only completed 2 problems. Her slow work pace was abetted clearly by the multiple distractions of the house ... and I did not hear a correct times table answer even once during my visit.

I was surprised that her study area was so cramped...... I was also stunned by Ms. H's often bullying and frustrated interventions. She seemed bent on hammering in the times tables.... Something seems hopelessly misguided here. From Ms. H's comments in the car to the rapid-firing of times tables, the efforts to help Melanie seem off target and only skew the problem more. Melanie clearly relies on the phrase, "I can't do it," even if it is a simple task. No one intervenes and says, "Yes you can." There seems to be a pervasive lackadaisical quality to the Handlon household's activities.

> The fieldworker is frustrated, and the reflection memo provides a space for her to vent. But there are also intellectual points. She highlights how Melanie's study space is not centered around her needs, the mother's frustration and ineffective badgering of her daughter, and the "go with the flow" nature of the household. These themes are valuable and helpful to illuminate. Still, although researchers often feel frustrated with their respondents, you want to acknowledge these feelings and try to diffuse them. You also should try to understand the situation from their point of view. As much as possible, we want to deeply respect the actions of the people we study. We don't want to view them with disrespect.

At a different point, in weekly meetings, I shared an analytic memo I wrote using field notes to suggest the labor-intensive pattern of middle-class child rearing could create misery for children. These thoughts eventually merged into an analysis of how parents worked with institutions. In the book, I show how middle-class parents often gain advantages but, in the case of the Handlon family, there were many tensions and difficulties in the family-school relationship. The analytic memo focused on putting the data in conversation with the previous literature to highlight the new contribution of the study to answer the question "so what?" The fieldwork reflection, by contrast, is a chance to blow off steam, reflect on what you saw (particularly your reactions to and potential judgments of what you saw so as to reflect on your positionality), and muse on valuable next steps in data collection.

Conclusion: Rigor, Determination, and the Creation of High-Quality Field Notes

It is a skill to write detailed, vivid field notes, and it is a skill that you can learn. Field notes that are general or vague may often have outstanding sections in them. Hence, the goal is to consistently write the kind of detail that makes for high-quality notes. Put differently, the ability to produce outstanding field notes does not require a rare, innate talent. I have seen many people learn how to do it. Usually, if novice fieldworkers get consistent, detailed feedback, their field notes improve over a handful of sessions. Hence, the first lesson is that you want to seek out critical feedback right away when you start doing participant observation. The first visits are when you have a fresh perspective, seeing situations that you will take for granted later. Ask for help; show your notes to more experienced ethnographers. Then, write more notes and show the new notes to others for feedback. Just as the first fifteen minutes of an interview are an important time, the early visits to a research site are a special time, offering you valuable insights.

Writing field notes is different from the excitement and stress of participant observation. You need to write them even if you are tired, are in a bad mood, or simply don't feel like it. You must write them instead of having fun with others, relaxing, or going out with friends. Notes are tedious to write, since it takes hours to recount what you have experienced. It is also a formidable challenge to bring complex social events to life on the page. Indeed, it takes a great deal of "strength of the soul" to write field notes day in and day out and to not skip steps, but it is a rigorous commitment you need to make. The longer you stay in the field, the more used to things you become and there is a strong temptation to say, for example, "Melanie and her mother had a homework battle again." But that would be a mistake, as vivid detail brings depth throughout your study. Your perspective changes as you learn more, talk with people more, read more, and focus more. The goal of writing field notes is to convey, using words, your experience so that others may experience it too, albeit in a different fashion, as you show them your data. Thinking through your data is an ongoing task, but once you have all of your data at hand, you will be able to reflect upon your data in new and original ways. This is the topic we address in the next chapter.

8

Data Analysis

Thinking as You Go

In research using numbers, researchers have to wait to carry out the data analysis until data entry, data cleaning, and other related tasks are complete. Similarly, with interview and participant observation data, there will be a distinct period after you have the entire data set in place where you scrutinize your data set, look for holes in the data, refine your argument, and consider whether your argument is sound. Formal coding is an important part of that process—with or without a software program (as I discuss below).

But data analysis in qualitative research also occurs *throughout* the entire process. After all, as noted in chapter 1, you have an emergent, and evolving, focus. Throughout data collection you refine your initial question, assess emerging results, consider competing explanations, and deepen your focus. As you read transcripts and field notes, and even as you are writing, you are thinking. It is "iterative"—which means that there is a repetition of tasks, a cycle of repetition that helps you look at the data, reflect, look again, and so forth; this process will help you to gain insight.[1] Indeed, this is a strength of this method— you can address new questions as they emerge, and you can discover things that are fresh and original. If you reflect on your research goals after you have done a few interviews or done observation for a few weeks, then you help set priorities for the "zero-sum" nature of data collection. You simply cannot collect everything that might be interesting. You can also ask yourself hard questions about whether your emerging conclusions are plausible interpretations that are robustly supported by the data and whether there might be other ways of interpreting what you are seeing. This will, in turn, trigger more data collection with more of a focus and more reflection. The specificity of a research question before the study begins varies enormously, and the goals of a study vary, as noted in chapter 2, from providing a rich description of social processes to addressing a specific theoretical question.

Remember, the journey will be moving, broadly conceived, from a research topic to a research question. A research topic is a subject. It is an area of investigation (e.g., studying women in prison, the homeless, food scarcity, children's activities, or racial discrimination by the police).

Your research topic can be exciting, but you do not have a question nor are you suggesting possible answers. By contrast, when you have a research question, you are asking a question to which you do not know the answer (e.g., how does parents' social class shape child rearing, what is the experience of mothers in prison separated from their children, how does the threat of violence shape the experience of homelessness, or how does organizational culture influence excessive force by police officers?). Generally, a research question has multiple possible answers or, put differently, competing explanations. Over time, the research question and the concepts become clearer to you and more refined. Here, a theoretical concept in your discipline that you admire can be a guiding light. This theoretical debate, and your effort to improve the terms of the debate, can guide and narrow data collection, data analysis, and writing. Always, it helps if you remember your concerns about the limitations of the literature, the data you have, and the concepts you find exciting and interesting. Your goal of answering the question "so what?" guides the process.

As we have seen, data collection is challenging and tiring, and it is difficult to keep up with data management, transcription, and field notes. With so much going on, it is not surprising that researchers sometimes become singularly focused on data collection. But this preoccupation with data collection has a cost: you can forget to think.

In this chapter, I discuss key steps and techniques in figuring out your research focus.[2] These techniques are valuable during data collection. In addition, once your data collection is complete, you want to do a formal coding phase by both "going deep" and "stepping back." As the data analysis process progresses, the line between writing and data analysis blurs, as editing quotes is inextricably interwoven with your analytic goals in each stage of the writing process. Throughout, you want to be "listening" to your data rather than imposing your own ideas on it. The final section of the chapter highlights the steps in transforming a raw interview transcript into an edited quote. Although arguably this section could have been part of the next chapter on writing, there is quite a lot of data analysis and thinking in editing a quote, which is why I include it here.

This chapter does not take up the relationship between theory and data, which is extensively discussed by others and varies significantly by discipline.[3] Theory-focused ethnographers, such as Michael Burawoy, claim "we need some set of presuppositions, questions, concepts, coding schemes—*theory*, in the most general meaning of the word, to make sense of it. Theory tells us what to look for. . . . A *good* theory makes predictions and fosters surprises. As social scientists, our final goal is . . . to learn from the case in order to expand scientific knowledge."[4] Other social scientists, of course, have different approaches. Regardless of the role of theory, qualitative researchers face a number of practical challenges, including how to manage the data collected.

What to Do with All of These Data?

Normally you will be swimming in data by the end of a study (but still, ironically, panic at times that you might have missed something and need more data). Each field visit usually yields at least ten single-spaced pages of notes. In addition, most people collect a variety of documents to analyze. Many doctoral students have between 1,000 and 4,000 pages of field notes and interview transcripts when they sit down for a formal stage of coding.

Thus, I'll say it again: you have to think as you go. By the time you are between the one-half to two-thirds mark, you want your study to come into focus. The last one-third of data collection, you should ideally have a relatively clear sense of the purpose of the study, a research question, the key concept(s) you are using in your study, and the kinds of evidence you consider to be very strong in supporting your claims.

Projects, as we have seen, vary in size. My undergraduate students are often overwhelmed by the amount of data they collect in eight to ten sets of field notes and four interviews over the course of just one semester. In a class, you might do five interviews or a visit once per week for an undergraduate thesis, and maybe 25 or 30 interviews or one semester of observations in a master's paper. For a bigger study, you will do more. But let's imagine you are visiting twice a week for eight months or so, but sometimes you go three times per week, aiming for 65 to 75 visits in total. It is too soon to move to a research question after a single visit, but after ten visits (over three weeks) and five interviews (depending on what comes first), you want to start finding a focus. It will take a while to center your project, but you want to work at it. Part of the focus depends on what literature you care about (discussed more below). Your focus should be based on what is surprising you in your ethnographic research, what you are excited about, and what you are learning that you think is important. Record your developing ideas as you go.

As noted in earlier chapters, you will have written "analytic memos" regularly during your data collection in which you reflect on what you have learned, why it is potentially important, how it acts in "conversation" with other research, and what you need to do next. These memos are hard, even painful, to write, since they wrench you out of your focus on empirical detail and force you to reflect on the big picture. (Or, put differently, they shift your focus from the leaf in your hand to consider the broader forest.) Go back and read all of your analytic memos from time to time during the data collection process; after each of these reviews, write a new memo on your emerging thoughts about what you are doing in your study.

REFINING YOUR RESEARCH QUESTION
AND YOUR EMERGING ARGUMENT

How do you decide?

One exercise is to take a blank piece of paper and write down all of the research questions that occur to you. Don't judge. Just write question after question after question. Set it aside for a bit, and then come back to it. Organize the questions according to broader questions or themes. Thus, you might start with 10 to 20 different questions and narrow them down to around 3–5 different, broad research questions.[5] You will continue along and ultimately settle upon one question that is *the* most important question, along with a few subordinate questions. The choice of the most interesting question depends on many factors: what is interesting to you, what is new, what literature you know, what you care about, what other people think is interesting, and where you have the most data. Most studies can go in multiple directions (just as you could enjoy being on vacation in different places, have a number of different hobbies, or even be content with very different careers). There is not one perfect choice.

It can be difficult to figure out what you are doing in a project. Why are you doing it? What do you hope to learn? What have other scholars found? Sometimes you might feel that you don't see anything. You might think that nothing is interesting. As the box indicates, talking to and listening to others' feedback is helpful, since researchers get blinded when they get too deep in the data. It can be helpful to create a writing group to get regular, constructive feedback, offer to give a presentation to a nearby department, give a guest lecture on the topic for a class, or start a "half-baked ideas" workshop to create settings for regular feedback. While self-criticism can be helpful at other points in the study, this is not the time to be self-critical. Develop your ideas, and then get feedback from colleagues, friends, or other people who are willing to spend time helping you find your focus. You do not want to stomp out an idea before it is given a chance to develop.

Ultimately, you want to arrive at a research focus with an intellectual position (or "thesis") that both is well supported by your data and adds something new to the field. In the process, it is easy to hop wildly among different research questions. The journey to this final goal is inevitably filled with dead-ends and frustrations. For example, I find that at first some of my possible answers are too broad. Some are too narrow. Some questions are interesting, original, and important, but unfortunately the questions cannot be answered with the data I have collected. False starts are the norm. For some people, particularly those who are used to getting good grades in school and controlling key aspects of their lives, the chaos and uncertainty of fieldwork is anxiety provoking. If this is the case, you want to recognize the process as time limited and remain confident that you *will* find a focus. At some point, as you keep collecting data, reflecting, and talking with others, you can usually find a research question that works for you. In order to gain perspective, step back and consider the big picture of the study's path. Why is it important to gain perspective, to be able to get a close-up and a more distant view?

First, you are trying to find ways to reflect on what you have learned from your field visits. Look for key themes in what can seem like a jumble. *You are trying to figure out what you have learned so far.*

Second, remember what the literature has said and focus on your top priorities. *In other words, you are trying to settle on your conversation partners.* For example, one body of data—say participant observation of coworking spaces—could be of interest to people who study social networks, workers and their labor process, community activities, time use, identity, work-family balance, or other topics.[6]

Third, attempt to demonstrate, using your data, that the current conception in the literature is inadequate and incomplete. Find your way to a "so what" contribution. *You are aiming to identify what problem with the literature you want to fix.*

An Example of Choosing One Research Question from Many Possibilities

One body of data could make a contribution in many different subfields and answer many different questions. As Howard Becker puts it: there is "no one right way."[7]

Only you can decide what you want to do here. Rather than being a strictly rational choice, your decision is a "heart" connection as you discern what topics you are drawn to investigating. In addition, it is common to go into a project expecting to find one thing but to end up finding something else. Ideas before entering a site are often incomplete or not quite right.

To give an example, in my undergraduate ethnographic methods course, I got to know Rob Lyons (a pseudonym), a white man in his 20s auditing my class to learn more about sociology. Since he was working full-time in a homeless shelter after graduating college, his time to do fieldwork was limited. While Rob and I met to discuss potential studies he could conduct while working full-time, I happened to mention I was interested in whether social class determines pet owners' differential treatment of their dogs. Since the publication of my book on social class and child rearing, people kept telling me that they see middle-class dog owners reasoning and pleading with their dogs, "Now, Fido, let's be patient. After I finish this chore then we will go out, okay?" similar to how they raise their children. Working-class dog owners, by contrast, would give directives to dogs, "Cut it out." Also, while family sociologists have not fully considered the inclusion of dogs in the definition of family, for many children and parents, dogs are integral to the family unit. Rob was interested in the idea and decided to do observations of dogs in a public park. He also filed an IRB application and was approved to do interviews with and to shadow dog owners.

After he had done four interviews, agreed to foster a pit bull with his fiancée, noted interactions with the foster dog, and conducted participant observation in a local park, he and I took stock of what he had learned. He found that in some households, dog "parents" who were raised in different social class backgrounds had conflicts about how to raise the dog. Some were more indulgent. Others were not. These differences did not seem to be tied to the type of dog in the family or other family-related factors (such as whether the owner worked at home or instead the house was empty during the day). He also discovered, as had been explicated by Elijah Anderson in earlier work, there was racial tension between Blacks and whites around dogs in his mixed-class/mixed race neighborhood.[8] He and his fiancée spent time walking and playing with their "foster dog," and as he walked and drove with his pit bull, he (a white man) experienced more racial tension (i.e., stares, avoidance on the street, and drivers yelling "cool it, white boy") than he had experienced living in the neighborhood for many years. (Here he was referring to the literature, although he couldn't think of anything different than what Anderson had demonstrated.) As he collected more data, he also became increasingly interested in the idea of personhood and "citizenship." In his daily trips to the homeless shelter, he noticed that the children were corralled into small rooms without permission to wander the halls of the shelter. Nor was there much of an imperative for the children to exercise or breathe fresh air. By contrast, among the dog owners, there was great attention to the pets' needs for fresh air and exercise. There was a growing movement for dogs to have legal rights; in some recent court cases, dogs have had lawyers after their owner dies.[9] He also interviewed a dog owner who said that her dog was the most important "person" in her life.

In short, Rob's project shot off in different directions: how pets exacerbate class-conflict among marital partners from different class origins (a point not discussed by research on class-conflict in marriage), how managing pets can become a flash point for racial tension in a heterogeneous neighborhood, and how pet ownership can be used to examine ideas of personhood and citizenship (e.g., social construction of dogs as persons, rights and privileges granted to dogs, comparison of privileges given to dogs and children). There was also the question of "how to define a family" and suggestion that pets should fall within the definition. Each of these analytic questions engaged different prior research studies (i.e., class and daily life, race and urban life, animals in society, childhood, and political conceptions of citizenship). They were all interesting, but different. Furthermore, there was no logical reason for choosing one over the other. Still, he was particularly intrigued with the notion of citizenship, frustrated that studies of citizenship had not fully captured the limits on the rights and needs of children and the robust (and growing) sense of entitlement of rights for dogs. This approach, however, took him both into a historical analysis of changes in legal status and into ethnographic work regarding dogs and children.

In the end, Rob focused on issues of citizenship, and his study took him into the political sociology literature, leaving behind the sociology of the family literature. His question came into focus, asking, "What rights are given to dogs and children in terms of their rights for freedom of movement, social interaction, and outdoor experiences?" He thereafter shaped his data collection to be able to address the question.

The process of explicating these questions and laying out the choices was not easy for Rob, as he was often confused by the multitude of different ideas and questions. Through writing reflective and analytic memos, giving a class presentation, and discussing the conundrum with me, he found that the various pathways gradually became clearer. In some cases, researchers can feel unmoored and confused when they are not seeing what they expected. As you adjust to the new topic, it is a mistake to be "pennywise and dollar foolish" by choosing a topic because you have read 10 or 20 articles in one field and you have less familiarity with another field.

What might you do if you are discouraged by your data, or if it doesn't seem interesting at first? Talking to other people—people who are positive, knowledgeable, and constructively critical—is helpful. For one of my students, I articulated my understanding of the emerging findings in the study, and shared that I felt that the literature had not addressed one element of the question. Put differently, I picked out a couple elements of what I thought was exciting, helping the student to focus.

What else? You should be interested, curious, excited, and open minded about the topic; you should *not know the answer* to your research question when you begin your study. It is fine to have an inkling, but it is a mistake to start a project because you "know" something to be true and you want to prove it. Ideally the answer is unclear, and you will be learning something that might challenge your deepest beliefs. You should admire some work in this area that can be a role model (even if the work is based on research done by someone in a field wildly different from your own) with an approach to research that you would like to emulate. Remember, however, that this is not the only project that you will do in your life. It should be reasonably interesting, but it does not need to be perfect.

Parallels in Other Fields

Making choices about focus, argument, and analysis is not unique to academic research. This kind of decision making occurs in other situations, including art. Many forms of art—architecture, dance, opera, rap, and movies—tell a story. Stories are more satisfying when they have focus. Still, that focus can be hard to achieve. In a radio interview, the movie director Francis Ford Coppola recounted in a radio interview his decision to end *The Godfather* with the door shutting on Michael's wife as Michael goes into a gathering where he will be crowned the new Godfather.[10] Coppola's explanation reveals that some of the key decisions in ethnographic research are similar in artistic creation.

> When I make a movie, I always have to have a theme, preferably in one word that I can—when I made *The Conversation* the theme was privacy. When I made *The Godfather* the theme was succession.

Here, Coppola indicates he has a one-word theme to guide his making of the movies. Knowing the theme helps him in making countless decisions:

> [As a film director you] have to answer so many questions every day, like should she have long hair or short hair? Should she wear a dress or a skirt? Should he have a car or should it be a bicycle? And you know the answer so you just fire them off. But once in a while you don't know the answer. And that's when you say, "Well, what is the theme?"

The theme would help him know what he was doing:

> So your theme, in the case of *Godfather* being succession, I would always know that as long as I was telling a story of the succession of—there was a king and he had three sons.... I knew ... what I was doing.

> When I make a movie, I always have to have a theme.... [In] The Godfather the theme was succession.
>
> Francis Ford Coppola, movie director

In interviewing and participant observation, if you know what you are doing, having a one-word theme for your study helps you make decisions both large and small—what to observe, read, and probe, and, ultimately, how to tell your story. Slowly and gradually through the data collection process, you compile the essence of your study. By arriving at the central focus, you are turning your back on other possibilities. (You potentially can take up those studies in the future.) But you are trying to figure out what is wrong with prior studies, focusing on your highest priorities, and clarifying the importance of your work. (See also table 2.2 on the steps in an intellectual journey.) In sum, you are looking for self-knowledge: who you are and what you are aiming to do in this study. Once you figure this out, making other decisions will be easier.

Aligning Your Research Question and Your Data Collection

As you figure out your focus, make sure that you can answer your key research question, and the subordinate questions, with the data you are collecting. If there is a mismatch, *it is easier to change your research question than to change your research site.* (Although some people may be disconcerted by learning that you made changes as you went along, they probably don't understand the reality of qualitative research.) It is a strength of the method to be able to adjust your data collection. Furthermore, the goal of the study is not to summarize the frequency of behavior in your sample; instead, the goal is to build new knowledge. You want to ground your claim. Sometimes, you can demonstrate a pattern by using several different approaches—multiple people and different forms of evidence (i.e., observations, interviews, documents, or policies). You should also, as I discuss below, seriously think about the possibility that you have gotten it wrong; you should consider alternative explanations, and search for evidence to overturn your emerging thoughts.

For example, I had an undergraduate student interested in studying the attitudes of legal immigrants towards immigrants who lacked documents. To answer this question, he started to volunteer at a nonprofit providing services to immigrants. He also attended meetings of a group of undocumented immigrants planning rallies to protest anti-immigrant legislation. There were a few immigrants with legal documents involved in this group, but most were undocumented immigrants. Hence, his desire to compare immigrants with and without papers was hampered by the composition of the group he was studying. He immediately learned many interesting things in this group, including how undocumented immigrants were trying to figure out who could take care of their native-born children (whose status as US citizens is protected by the 14th Amendment) in case the parents were unexpectedly deported. But the project had problems (including ethical issues).[11] One challenge was that he was not learning about the attitudes of documented immigrants towards undocumented immigrants via his data collection. He needed to change the research question or change the data collection. For example, he could have sought to understand factors facilitating or impeding political activism. He might have looked at the experience of nonprofit workers in trying to serve people in need with low pay, insufficient legal support, and turbulence in the organizational dynamics. Since he was worried about gaining access to these new groups and there was limited time remaining for finishing his project, he resisted changing the research question or his data collection. His paper ended up having inadequate data to support his claims.

Aligning Your Research Question and the Literature: Who Are "Your People"?

The literature that is going to help frame your research question in a precise fashion is almost always literature that uses a similar method. To be sure, quantitative studies can show a relationship between a factor and an outcome, but, without a clear explanation of the mechanisms involved, they leave a "black box" about why a given relationship exists. By contrast, qualitative studies can provide results that highlight the need to know more about the processes or mechanisms. This hole is important, but it is only a beginning step in your research. A more developed statement of the weakness in the literature is created by looking at how researchers in your field have *conceptualized* the existing mechanisms. And that means looking at other work done using interviews and participant observation.

Take, for example, the literature on class and child rearing. There is debate about the degree to which the social class gap in parenting (variously defined by mothers' education, a socioeconomic status index, or income) has widened, stayed the same, or narrowed in recent years. Many studies have shown a correlation between parents' education and children's educational outcomes. Other studies have shown various aspects of class-based child rearing methods, including time with children, reading to children, enrolling children in extracurricular activities, restricting television, and engaging in other developmental activities. The frequency with which parents perform various behaviors is an excellent question for survey researchers, although these behaviors are subject to social desirability.[12] It is, frankly, a lousy question for qualitative researchers, since summarizing how frequently something happens in a small, nonrandom sample doesn't tell us much. Furthermore, in many quantitative studies, it is difficult to unpack conceptually why there is a relationship between two factors. Quantitative researchers are left to call simply for a study of the processes, which doesn't help much in conceptualizing these precise processes.

Qualitative studies can often help us overcome conceptual weaknesses in the literature. For example, in the field of child rearing, we can learn about the gaps between normative ideals (e.g., parents have authority in the home) and reality (e.g., children resist, sabotage, and humiliate parents in different moments). Or, many families espouse ideals of treating children equally, but, in some families, some children have favored status. Qualitative studies can teach us about authority relationships, alienation, powerlessness, identity, and other key processes in daily life. For example, Dawn Dow showed variations among Black middle-class mothers in child rearing in the strategies they adopted to protect their children from racial discrimination.[13] She challenged models of class and child rearing by showing there is more variation than previously acknowledged. Hence, before beginning a study, you ought to be able to look at other qualitative studies (or experimental and quantitative studies) and understand how the two factors (i.e., variables) are related. How do parents understand what their kids need? For example, does the concept of aspirations make sense? Does it capture daily life? Do parents promote a sense of entitlement in middle-class kids as some have suggested? Here, you want to read other qualitative studies of motherhood, child rearing, or children's daily lives and focus your critique on other studies of the same processes. Your critique is a "set up" to show that there is a hole in our understanding of the topic, and your study seeks to fill this hole. At times, studying the same process might take you into a different substantive field. For example, to understand relationships between prison guards and prisoners, you might look at other "total institutions" such as the military and relationships between officers and soldiers. Military and prison are different settings, but military studies can also reveal power dynamics. In short, you want to look at the explicit and implicit conceptualization of behaviors embedded in a study. Sometimes key issues are discussed in a superficial fashion or ignored. These under-conceptualizations of key mechanisms in the literature are a good start for thinking about a new study. A good question grows out, in part, of your understanding of the literature.

The problem is that it is easy to get overwhelmed when you do a review of the literature. There are dozens and dozens of studies.

It can seem, at first glance, to take months to read them. If you spend all of this time reading studies, how will you ever do the work and finish the project? Howard Becker calls this being "terrorized by the literature." But keep reading, writing memos, and listening to yourself to discern which topics you find to be the most interesting. (Notice that the focus is on *you* and not others, including your professor, your parents, your partner, and so forth.) Think about the fields that you know the most about but are curious to learn more. You might consider whether there are any professional advantages (such as greater opportunities down the road) to choosing one question rather than another. And even after you have thought about all of those factors, there are always trade-offs. I'll say it again: there is no one right way.

SEEK FEEDBACK

Even though it seems as if it is way too early, it is good to get feedback and other's perspectives when you are in the middle of data analysis and seeking to build an emergent argument. Why? You want to make sure that you are framing a research question that is important, is a real question that others care about, and is based on a true hole in the literature. You also want feedback that your tentative claims—your emerging argument—is sound. You need to be prepared for negative as well as positive feedback. One of my students received the following journal review on a paper:

> The author takes aim at sort of a phantom target here.... Other than maybe a few dogmatic types, I don't think anyone really believes that.

Similarly, another student received this critique: "The theoretical contribution the author is pursuing is less theoretically novel than it is presented in this paper." Or this review that I received on a coauthored paper: "The argument is rather thin. Essentially the paper argues that middle class parents can and do engage in collective efforts on their children's behalf. This is not surprising or quite as innovative as they propose. It is narrow both in terms of the literature reviewed and the conceptual reach."[14] Thus, not unlike Goldilocks and the Three Bears, you don't want a conceptual argument that is too narrowly framed, you don't want an argument that is too broad, rather, you want a conceptual framing and contribution that is "just right." Your friends, and then your critics, can help you figure out when you have reached this point. But I assure you, you usually will not achieve success on your first, second, or even third try. Finding a "better, stronger, more interesting, and more important" question and framing is a process that evolves over time.[15] When you stop getting criticism (from teachers, peers, and reviewers) that your "contribution needs to be more developed," then you are doing well. But it is good to frame questions while you are collecting data so you can add more data, search for disconfirming evidence, and "test out" your ideas in real time. As Luker points out, she has known people where "the single piece of information (or the body of data) which they need to really nail the point beyond quibbles is back in the field and they didn't know they needed it, or it's disappeared, or they can't afford to go back."[16] She also emphasizes the importance of thinking through the process, noting that some researchers collect vastly more data than is likely to be needed if they had thought more deeply earlier in the process.

Thus, your intellectual journey (highlighted in chapter 2) involves thinking, taking stock, figuring out a number of possible pathways, and settling on one that is a good fit for you. A solid critique is behind most great studies. Once you have this critique and focus, then you adjust your data collection accordingly.

A Formal Coding Phase: Going Deep and Stepping Back

After you have your data set in hand, it is helpful to analyze the data systematically by "taking it from the top" and starting again. Data analysis has multiple, and, at times contradictory goals. On the one hand, in data analysis, you want to really *go deep* in your data. You want to be extremely familiar with all of your notes, what everyone said in interviews, and the nuances and shades of meaning in what you have learned. The best way to learn this is to read the notes and transcripts and listen to the audio files multiple times (for example when you ride your bike or do the dishes). On the other hand, you want to gain perspective by stepping *back* to reflect. Look for the big picture in part by looking for common themes, disconfirming evidence, and trends. Reflect on how your study connects or challenges an idea, or set of ideas, in the literature (which you are seeking to modify and challenge).

Coding your data set helps you take stock of your evidence, to see where you have plenty of evidence and where the evidence is thin; it also helps you look for disconfirming evidence.[17]

AN EXAMPLE OF A CODING SCHEME

It is often unclear how many coding categories you should have, and it is easy to feel as if you have too few or too many. Each study is unique, but to give you a sense of the size and scope of a coding scheme that worked well, I share (with permission) the coding system created by Benjamin Shestakofsky in the ethnographic study for his book project, "Venture Capitalism: Startups, Technology, and the Future of Work." This book focuses on organizational change in a software firm called "AllDone," which is a digital marketplace bringing together services such as photographers and plumbers with clients in their local community. Over the course of nineteen months, Shestakofsky did participant observation in three sites. He was primarily based in the headquarters in San Francisco (where software development took place), but he also visited and, in his organizational role, worked closely with workers in the Philippines (where behind-the-scenes information processing tasks were done), and Las Vegas (where workers provided customer service). Shestakofsky had five main categories for his codes: ACROSS, to denote occasions when workers across different sites interacted with one another, ME (for his own thoughts and reflections), and one for each site, SF (San Francisco), P (Philippines), and LV (Las Vegas). Then, within each main category, he had subcategories as in the ACROSS code.

> ACROSS: Culture Clash, ACROSS: Emotion, ACROSS:
> Emotion:Excitement, ACROSS: Emotion: Relational Work,
> ACROSS: Gifts, ACROSS: Meetings, ACROSS: Physicality,
> ACROSS: Privilege, ACROSS: Speculation

In addition, he had additional codes for each of the three sites (presented in table 8.1). A key point in his book is that venture capitalists' desire to get a speedy return on their investment created an incentive for innovation. These continuous innovations had consequences for workers in San Francisco, the Philippines, and Las Vegas. Since the impact of these constant innovations were not the same in each site, he tailored his coding scheme to reflect the unique evidence in each

Table 8.1. *Codes for each of the three sites (San Francisco, Philippines, and Las Vegas) in the Company Studied by Shestakofsky*

○ SF:Biography	○ P:Biography	○ LV:Anxiety
○ SF:Contractors and Local Outsourcing	○ P:Comparisons to Other Jobs	○ LV:Biography
○ SF:Costs	○ P:Conflict	○ LV:Charismatic Leadership
○ SF:Culture of Experimentation	○ P:Consequences of Org Dynamics	○ LV:Conflict
○ SF:Description of People	○ P:Cost	○ LV:Food
○ SF:Excitement	○ P:Culture	○ LV:Gender
○ SF:Fun	○ P:Downstream	○ LV:Hardship
○ SF:Gender	○ P:Emotion	○ LV:Lacks Org Knowledge
○ SF:Gifts	○ P:Emotion:Relational Work	○ LV:Morale
○ SF:Goals and Future and VC (venture capital)	○ P:Family:Tension	○ LV:Organizational Structure
○ SF:Growth	○ P:Gender	○ LV:Resistant to Change
○ SF:Hiring	○ P:Gratitude	○ LV:SF:Visibility
○ SF:Ignores P and LV	○ P:Ignored by SF	○ LV:Speculation
○ SF:Innovation	○ P:Invisibility	○ LV:Team Members: Description
○ SF:Innovation:Automation	○ P:Lacks Org Knowledge	○ LV:Technophobes
○ SF:Innovation:Routinization	○ P:Love	○ LV:Views of SF
○ SF:LV:Invisibility	○ P:LV:Gifts	○ LV:Work Hours
○ SF:Motivation	○ P:Meetings	○ LV:Work Spaces
○ SF:Networking	○ P:Narratives of Transformation	○ LV:Workforce Stats
○ SF:Office Environment	○ P:Organizational Structure	
○ SF:Optimism	○ P:Performance	
○ SF:P:Costs	○ P:Priorities	
○ SF:P:Gender	○ P:Recruiting	

Table 8.1. *Continued*

○ SF:P:Relational Work	○ P:Reverse Substitution
○ SF:Party	○ P:SF:Gifts
○ SF:Politics	○ P:SF:Relational Work
○ SF:Privilege	○ P:Writing Team
○ SF:Recruiting	○ P:Survey Team
○ SF:Relational Work	○ P:Matching Team
○ SF:Scene	○ P:Training
○ SF:Speculation	○ P:Unstable Self
○ SF:View of Capitalism	○ P:Visibility of SF
○ SF:Views of LV	○ P:Work from Home
○ SF:Views of Me	○ P:Work Hours
○ SF:Views of P	
○ SF:Work Hours	

site (allowing him to dig deep) while also having the "across" codes to reflect on patterns that arose when members of each group interacted with one another. Finally, Shestakofsky had codes to allow him to reflect on his role in the field (e.g., "belonging") and his reactions to events (e.g., "emotion," "discomfort: privilege," and "work:confusion"). In all of these cases, he put the term "ME" as the main category (e.g., "ME:Belonging"). This coding scheme helped him make sense of his thousands of pages of field notes and his notes from his informal interviews. As he explains in his methodological appendix, these ideas took shape only gradually through his regular creation of analytic memos as well as reflections and conversations with others. The codes for each of the three sites are in the table.

Note that the number of codes is not perfectly equal, and some of the codes, Shestakofsky discovered over time, could have been consolidated.

Shestakofsky used a software program (Atlas.ti) to code the data, but he also could have done the coding by printing out the field notes, cutting them up, and putting them in file folders or highlighting the notes in different colors on his computer. Or, he could put them in a spreadsheet such as Excel. Qualitative coding programs are becoming pervasive, and for large data sets they can be invaluable, but there is also considerable value in poring over transcripts, looking for themes, and considering disconfirming evidence. Some scholars, even in large studies, do not use qualitative software programs.[18]

One type of coding that I find helpful is the creation of data matrices.[19] Here you take a large piece of paper and create a table. (You can also use an Excel file, but being able to tape it to the wall can be helpful in gaining perspective.) You put your respondents down the column and key ideas or concepts across the top of a row. Then you put a few words, snippets of quote, or a summary of evidence inside the cell. It is easy to be overly influenced by vivid statements or dramatic moments in fieldwork that linger in your mind. You want to listen for silence as well as speech. Hence, the people who did not have a concern are important to "hear."

A blank cell in this table is meaningful because it can show that there is variation in the sample on an issue. The people in the blank cells—who didn't have anything to say about a question—need to be given voice, and they need to be given the same amount of weight as more articulate respondents. A data matrix can help with the "listening" process as you think through your data. Once again, the data analysis process is about being completely curious and completely honest. You are seeking the answer to a research question (not presuming that you know the answer). The data immersion and coding process are intended to help you slice the data in different ways to consider alternatives as you work "to make the familiar strange."[20] The essential point is this: there are many different ways to go about coding, and they often involve going deep (to really "see" your data) and stepping back (to gain perspective).

PRE-WRITING ACTIVITIES: TAKING STOCK OF YOUR QUOTES, INCLUDING DISCONFIRMING ONES

As you make progress on your emerging argument, look again at your field notes and interviews for support of your ideas. This activity is both data analysis and the early stages of writing or, at the very least, prewriting. Here, first make sure that you have a solid amount of data to support your claim. For example, you should have multiple pieces of evidence from the fieldwork, and you usually should have evidence from multiple people. Normally, qualitative studies highlight routine interactions in daily life: that is why you keep going and going until you stop learning new things. The pattern need not apply throughout the entire data set. After all, usually studies are designed to show variation in how people respond to a situation—and people in your study often have differing responses because the real world is often messy. In addition, it is unrealistic to expect that every single person in the data set will report the same experience. In families, brothers and sisters often have different experiences in family life, as do students within the same academic course. Hence, not unlike course evaluations, you are looking for patterns experienced by a clear portion of people in your study. It is hard to put a number on it; the claim should be "solid" in that many people have expressed this point. In an interview study it is harder, and sometimes you have only a few people making a crucial conceptual point. In these cases, a fellow ethnographer I admire told me that for a small subpoint, she likes to have at least three people who make the same point (ideally three people from different points in the organization). For a main point, you want a clear preponderance of data. You need to be sure that you are not overly persuaded by particularly eloquent speakers. But you also want to be attuned to discrepant cases and to disconfirming evidence. You cannot ignore cases or evidence that don't seem to fit; you need to acknowledge their existence in the data, but you can and should evaluate their importance in context.

As I am fumbling toward figuring out a point, I start to copy quotes into a new document. I often carry some identifying data with the quotes I choose (e.g., African American middle-class mom with the code name Carter). Sometimes I carry over two or three quotes/field note excerpts per person. I don't edit the quotes at this point, instead I dump them into a file under "Quotes: Idea" (with the emerging idea named). Then I look for disconfirming evidence or challenges to the idea, and I put those at the bottom of the document under a subheading: "Challenges" or, more simply, "Doesn't Fit." I keep looking for quotes by reading the field notes and interview transcripts (sometimes highlighted through post-its or word searches—but word searches are a very crude way to do it; or else drawing on codes if I have used a software program). I keep moving quotes into the document. This raggedy document can, depending on the data set, be very long (10 to 20 pages single-spaced for one idea). Then, I pause, go back and read more literature or reread the existing literature, think about my argument, and try to figure out the main idea as well as how these three or so ideas fit into an overall thesis. I try to be skeptical about my emerging finding. In addition, by considering challenges to my emerging thesis, my final account is likely to be more credible to dubious readers.

At some point I will have accumulated more quotes than I can possibly discuss. A 30-page double-spaced manuscript (such as a conference paper, book chapter, senior thesis, or article) will usually have only about 25 or so quotes. This means I display only a limited number of quotes per point in my published work, and often there are only two to four quotes per claim. (Sometimes there is only one.) Vivid quotes — ones that are lively, precise, image filled, emotionally tinged, and attention grabbing — are ideal, but it is crucial that the quotes remain consistent with other results in the data set (or be highlighted as a piece of disconfirming evidence for a general theme). The quotes, more or less, capture an important theme in the data set — they are less about capturing the person than about capturing a key social process. I always have favorite quotes or moments in the field that I see as illuminating — they are dramatic or funny, or zero in on the key issue.

Still, as I am getting clearer, I go back, "taking it from the top," and review the field notes and the interview transcripts. I press myself, again, to make sure that I have a nuanced view of the data — that in my eagerness to make a claim, I am not steamrolling over disconfirming evidence. I try to imagine this: "What if you got it wrong?" So, in my study for *Unequal Childhoods*, I imagined, "What if social class does NOT matter in child rearing? What is the evidence?" I also thought, "Maybe it is all about race and not fundamentally about class?" I then looked for evidence. Of course, as social actors, each of us has a particular position in the social world — not only a race, social class position, gender, and age, but a set of political beliefs, theoretical orientations, preferences, and tastes. We bring all of these to the research process. To give one example, if you have strong views on the existence of climate change or on abortion, it can be harder to understand and empathize with research participants who vehemently reject these pathways. Throughout, you want to be extremely conscious of your biases and ways of looking at the world. (Writing memos and self-reflective essays can be helpful here, as can showing your work to others, including those whose views are different from your own.) You want to challenge yourself not to simply impose your world view on the data but to *learn* from the data you have collected. There are practical and ethical reasons behind this tenet of data collection. For example, it is inefficient, or even a waste of time, to go to the trouble of collecting data and then report what you believed before you began. It is also not ethical to assure your reader that your claims are based on the evidence you collected, but then ignore the disconfirming evidence. (As I explain in chapter 9, it also makes your account more credible to readers when you consider challenges to your thesis.) Since data are private, most people won't know the degree to which you scoured your data for alternative accounts, but it is important to do a slow, thorough, and careful analysis of alternative explanations.

Guideline for Editing Quotes to Make the Analytic Point Clear

The crafting of raw interview transcripts and field notes into finished quotes is necessarily a highly interpretative, analytic act. The editing process involves helping the reader focus on your key intellectual contribution—your argument. Hence, as you edit quotes, there are numerous judgment calls without clear guidelines. Yet, little has been published on this moment in the writing process.[21] To be sure, researchers often provide basic guidelines such as, "Original names have been changed." Or, as I often write:

> Some of the normal stumbling in verbal speech has been removed for readability, including false starts and "uh, um, you know, and, like, so," and repetition of a word such as "I-I." If a longer swath of words is removed, then three dots appear "..." to signify a break in speech. In some instances, the strict chronological order of speech is altered. For example, if a respondent spoke of the same issue at two different points in the interview, these examples may be put together (always separated by a ... marking) but the later example may appear first in the quotation.

Still, this summary of steps, while essential, does not reveal the hidden clockwork of the multiple decisions researchers make in editing quotes that support their intellectual claims. Nor, as with quantitative data, is it possible to check the work of the researcher, for example, by ordering up the data set and running the analyses. Yet, some works give me a lurking sense of unease. I have read books, for example, where the participants seemed to me to be amazingly fluid, intellectually sophisticated speakers. As a result, I did not fully trust the quotes, feeling that the hand of the author had been too heavy. On the other hand, I have read books where I longed for more intervention by the author to help the point of the respondents' words shine through more clearly. Instead, in a sea of "ums," "uhs," and "you knows," I felt the point was buried. Finding the proper balance is not easy.

Here, as part of my overview of the data analysis process, I provide concrete guidelines on the quote editing process. But editing quotes is a highly personal decision, and I do not believe that my approach is necessarily the right one. (Of course, as I edit quotes, I am also writing, and this next section could also have been included in chapter 9.) The example I use draws on interview data and, to a lesser extent, field note data from a family in my book *Unequal Childhoods*. The Marshalls (a pseudonym), a Black middle-class family, lived in a suburb of a major city. Both parents graduated from college; the mother worked in the computer field; the father worked in a civil service position. The two girls, Stacey (10) and Fern (11½), were involved in a number of activities.

FINDING VIVID PHRASES

The goal of the study was to understand the child rearing process, particularly in terms of how parents from differing classes and racial and ethnic groups acted. I was interested in what they wanted for their children and the varying ways they went about trying to bring their own hopes and dreams for their children to life. In this case, I am taking up an interview with a mother as she explains her daughter's experiences in organized activities, but the process would be similar if I were using a field note from observation. In reading the data, I am listening to what the respondent says as well as listening to how it is being expressed in terms of tone of voice and nonverbal cues. In writing, I am conveying what I learned to the reader. Vivid phrases in transcripts and field notes are prime candidates for quotation. But colorful phrases are usually buried. Original transcripts are far too lengthy, wandering, and cumbersome for direct quotation. In this original transcript (below), however, there are some promising phrases that immediately catch my eye, including "free night," "void," "dirt cheap," "she was having a ball," and, most importantly for a discussion of social class and networks, "just listening to some of the parents I started putting my ear to the grapevine." Some of these phrases, especially "free night" and "grapevine" became quotes I wanted to use. In a few lively words, they help bring to life key aspects of my argument (e.g., of middle-class children being kept exceptionally busy and the mother using her class-based social networks to scout out information). But these quotes have to be "set up"; the reader needs sufficient detail to understand what is going on. Some of the context can be sketched out in the writing process as you set the scene for the reader. But, in the editing process, you refine the quote, balancing readability, accuracy, and succinctness; you also want the point of the quote to emphasize your analytic point.

Original interview transcription:

I: And how did it happen that you started her [in gymnastics]?
R: She had um ... I guess in her third grade year, um ... when she was starting in third grade I couldn't find a Girl Scout troop for her to be in. She had been a Brownie I think four years so ... And um ... Fern was in a Girl Scout troop. Stacey wasn't old enough to be a Girl Scout so we went to this free night [laughs]. So Stacey, I-I kind'a needed her to ... I wanted her to do something and she ... it was a void. You know. Um ... and I didn't want her sittin' in front of the TV and-and that kind'a thing so ... Sylvan township, which was where we live, runs these programs in the evening. Uh ... recreational programs ... among them was gymnastics. And it was conducted at, actually the school Fern is going to next year, Springfield School. Uh, I called, all thing considered it was cheap, it was dirt cheap. I think it may have been twenty-five, thirty dollars for twelve weeks. You know. Uh ... I asked, "Stacey, would you be interested." She said sure. Um ... I enrolled her in the fall and it was, tumbling and-and uh ... I don't think they had a beam. They did have unevens. Um ... I forget what other apparatus, I think some rings. And she was havin' a ball. She was really, it was just very obvious that she was, you know, catching on quickly and uh ... so ... And so I enrolled- that was the fall session. I re-enrolled her in the spring. Again it was just very obvious that she was, she was mastering the things that the instructor there was showing her. And the instructors of the township were, were uh ...

the first one was a um ... I think she taught phys. ed. at one of
the parochial schools. You know, and the second one was actually
a- a high school girl who-who was on a gymnastics team, I think
at [a Catholic high school], which isn't really far. She-she had been
very good. She had earned her-her rights to teach a class. Uh ...
she even said, she says, "You know Stacey's good." You know.
And I didn't even answer her. I said, "Well, do you think I should
enroll her in a program?" She said, "Oh yeah." She told me about
the-the Y really. She said, "You know, the Y has good programs."
And she, she said, "Of course," she said, "there're private clubs ...
but they're more expensive." And she was right, you know. Um and
just listening to some of the parents I started putting my ear to
the grapevine um ... and ... I heard a number of parents mention,
"Well I, if the kid really likes gymnastics, you send um to Wright's."
You know. I called Wright's I guess in the spring of Stacey's third
grade year and they told me that um ... typically summer would
be a good time to bring a child into one of their programs. The
summer sessions were ... somewhat laid back and they typically
had openings because people were on vacation ... blah, blah,
blah, whole nine yards. So, um ... mentioned it to Stacey, she
was excited, and that's-that's how we got there.

The first thing I did was try to break this long stretch into a more
readable form. When I had read and reread the transcript, there were
a number of analytic points that struck me. First, she kept Stacey so
busy that she didn't want her to have "a free night." Second, essentially
it was an accident that Stacey started taking gymnastics. Third, that
Ms. Marshall drew on social networks in making numerous decisions,
including the advice of the gymnastics instructor. Fourth, that the role
of social networks was so powerful that Ms. Marshall had a phrase for
it: "put my ear to the grapevine." These key ideas were linked to the
broader conceptual argument that I was developing in the book about
concerted cultivation, which was an argument that middle-class parents engage in a set of strategies to develop their children in a systematic fashion. One key aspect of concerted cultivation was an effort by
mothers to expose children to a variety of leisure experiences organized
and controlled by adults. (By contrast, working-class and poor children

had more control over their leisure time; their mothers and fathers felt it was crucial to take good care of them, but exposing them to numerous organized activities was not part of their definition of good parent.) Within the broad rubric that argued middle-class mothers took systematic steps to expose children to activities, and that a mother's activities were a form of labor, I began to look for quotes from the Marshall family. The transcript provided a number of possibilities. For example, for this family, leisure life is so busy that even when one "free night" opens up during the week, the mother does not define it as a time to relax but as a "void." She seeks to fill the time, avoiding the child's engagement in activities that the child might prefer (e.g., watching television), but that the mother does not define to be useful. When I begin editing a quote, however, I often have only a vague notion of the idea that I am trying to bring out. Instead, I try, within limits, to clarify what the respondent is saying. Then, I reflect on what the quote says in light of my broader ideas. Thus the analytic (i.e., thinking) part and the technical (i.e., editing) part are interwoven.

GUIDELINES FOR EDITING QUOTES TO MAKE THE ANALYTIC POINT CLEAR: AN ANATOMY OF A DECISION PROCESS

How do you decide where to break up a transcript? In general, there are breaking points in a transcript that seem to "flow." I break the long quotes into "chunks" that reflect stages/ideas/steps in the process. Roughly speaking, it is a) how the issue of gymnastics came up, b) where she investigated, and c) what happened after she got there. These chunks do not, obviously, mirror the analytic points.

At this point, I do not eliminate any words. Occasionally, if I am having trouble separating the material into "chunks" because there are some sentences that do not fit, then I will block it and move it to a footnote temporarily to "get it out of the way" but keep it accessible.

Once I have the quote in manageable chunks, I start "cleaning it up." The first thing I do is try to get a strong beginning and a strong ending for a quotation without distorting the meaning. In verbal speech, it is rare for individuals to speak as concisely as we expect text to read. People often warm up to a topic, repeating key phrases several times. In this unedited quote (with a blurry beginning), note that Ms. Marshall says the same idea (that Stacey was in third grade) twice:

I: And how did it happen that you started her?

R: She had um ... I guess in her third grade year, um ... when she was starting in third grade I couldn't find a Girl Scout troop for her to be in. She had been a Brownie I think four years so ... And um ... Fern was in a Girl Scout troop. Stacey wasn't old enough to be a Girl Scout so we went to this free night [laughs]. So Stacey, I-I kind'a needed her to ... I wanted her to do something and she ... it was a void. You know. Um ... and I didn't want her sittin' in front of the TV and-and that kind'a thing so ... Sylvan township, which was where we live, runs these programs in the evening. Uh ... recreational programs ... among them was gymnastics. And it was conducted at, actually the school Fern is going to next year, Springfield School.

To clean it up, I strike "She has um. .I guess in her third grade year, um." I begin the quote with, "When she was starting in third grade I couldn't find a Girl Scout troop for her to be in." I think the words I have taken out are repeated by the words I have kept. I have eliminated some hesitancy, "I guess in her third grade year." But this hesitancy is about something that is not heavily consequential to the research question. In other words, in this particular study, if it was her second, third, or fourth grade year is not strikingly important. (If the study was on age of children, development, and enrollment in activities, I would have kept the "I guess.") I presume the reader will understand that the quote was lifted from a longer transcript. Some people always begin a quote with an ellipsis mark (this mark of three periods can be found as a symbol in Word—using the symbol prevents it from being auto-corrected in a spelling check). I use the ellipsis mark only when I feel that I am literally breaking into a thought of the respondent or when I am eliminating words other than um, uh, and so forth. I think this is a reasonable breaking point to begin.

Turning to the ending, the last few words in a sentence are very important. The power of these words is that they linger in the mind of the reader; the end of the sentence rings in your ear. When possible, I want my most important words at the end of the paragraph. I end the quote with the "didn't want her sittin' in front of the TV and that kind'a thing." In a later version, I slice off "and-and that kind'a thing." It doesn't seem to distort the meaning. It makes the point clearer and ultimately more powerful:

> When she was starting in third grade I couldn't find a Girl Scout troop for her to be in. She had been a Brownie I think four years so ... And um ... Fern was in a Girl Scout troop. Stacey wasn't old enough to be a Girl Scout so we went to this free night [laughs]. So Stacey, I-I kind'a needed her to ... I wanted her to do something and she ... it was a void. You know. Um ... and I didn't want her sittin' in front of the TV.

Having set the "bookends" for the quote, I now make a number of editing decisions. In the sentence, "She had been a Brownie I think four years so." I delete the word "so" without making a notation of an ellipsis mark since it is on my list of free words to take out. I also eliminate the "And um." I break the sentence "Stacey wasn't old enough to be a Girl Scout so we had this free night" into two sentences without putting a signal to the reader in the text. The sentence is really two different ideas. It is easier to read and understand if it is two sentences rather than one. Nevertheless, when I take out the phrase "I-I kind'a needed her to. ." I marked the omission with an ellipsis mark since it is an elimination of words. The phrase I took out was not simply a false start. It has different words (i.e., "I *needed* her to") than the phrase that follows it (i.e., "I wanted her to do something"). As I make these decisions to try to highlight the intent of the quote, I am doing two things. On the one hand, I am improving readability. But on the other hand, I am in the process of figuring out the idea that the quote illuminates. As the quotes become edited and then lined up in a data file, they provide a roadmap to the argument that I will make. Thus, the argument and the editing of quotes are inextricably linked.

There are other decisions in this process of editing. Most are made quickly. For example, where Ms. Marshall says "she—it was a void" I struck "she." It is arguable that I should have put in an ellipsis mark, but these clutter up the text. It makes it harder to follow the words. In this instance, I thought, in a judgment call, that her sentence was a reasonably straightforward false start. By switching from "she" to "it" she substitutes a grammatically correct pronoun; there was no change in meaning.

But, in the next sentence, in a mark of caution, I eliminate "You know and Um" but I mark it with an ellipsis mark. I could have struck it without marking it since the words are, technically speaking, on my list of words I can take out without telling the reader. But in this instance Ms. Marshall seems slightly hesitant. She seems to be getting warmed up to say something difficult for her to articulate. (She has three marks of hesitation: "you know," "um," and "and.") The ellipsis mark "slows down" the pace of the reading. Without it, it makes her seem firmer and more decisive than she seems in the interview. This is how it would read without the marking of an ellipsis mark:

> So Stacey, I wanted her to do something and it was a void. And I didn't want her sittin' in front of the TV.

I reject the above option as too much of a shift in meaning. Now I need to decide what to do. Of course, I could have left it alone and had it read:

> So Stacey ... I wanted her to do something and it was a void. You know. Um. And I didn't want her sittin' in front of the TV.

I almost, in fact, took out the "um" and left in the "you know" so it would read as follows:

> So Stacey ... I wanted her to do something and it was a void. You know. And I didn't want her sittin' in front of the TV.

The problem with this approach is that it is making the reader read extra words—"you know"—without much payoff. The ellipsis mark indicates there is a break in speech without requiring extra effort of the reader. In the end, I settle on:

> So Stacey ... I wanted her to do something and it was a void ... And I didn't want her sittin' in front of the TV.

Here is the final version:

> *When she was starting third grade I couldn't find a Girl Scout troop for her to be in. She had been a Brownie I think four years. Fern was in a Girl Scout troop. Stacey wasn't old enough to be a Girl Scout. So we went to this free night [laughs]. So Stacey ... I wanted her to do something and it was a void.... And I didn't want her sittin' in front of the TV.*[22]

There are other stylistic decisions I could have made but chose not to do. I could have eliminated the "So Stacey" before the "I wanted her to do something and it was a void." But Ms. Marshall did include these words. In addition, her daughter's name is what I consider to be a "vivid" word that helps a quote. It might help the reader remember the quote. It is different than "you know," which is flat. I could have taken out the sentence "She had been a Brownie I think four years." But I like it because it suggests that there was a long duration of being a Brownie. The "free night" makes more sense if you understand she had been doing something on that night a long time. I could have taken out the "Fern was in a Girl Scout troop" since, strictly speaking, it wasn't relevant to the point of the quote. But the mother had said it, there wasn't any compelling reason to take it out, and it adds a more natural flavor to the quote especially since the reader knows well who Fern is. But if the quote had been too long, I would have eliminated the "Fern was in a Girl Scout troop" and marked the omission with an ellipsis mark.[23] I also could have used the word "sitting" rather than "sittin'" (which is more colloquial). This is a tricky matter of how much you formalize prose. I prefer to leave, as much as possible, the words in the tone of the speaker unless it impedes the reader's comprehension. Mostly, it doesn't matter what you do as long as you do it consistently. In sum, in editing a quote I usually check and double-check every word to see if it is necessary. As a writer, I want to keep as much detail as possible. But as a reader, I appreciate every word that I do not have to read.

Although this sounds cumbersome, I made all of the editing changes in around ten to fifteen minutes. Still, since there are many quotes in a piece of writing—the time adds up. And, sometimes I will find a quote, edit it, decide it changes the meaning too much, backtrack to the original data, try again, drop the quote, or put the shorter phrase in the subheading or text. It is better to use a duller quote than change the respondent's meaning. Sometimes you spend time editing a quote and then don't use it. Sometimes I let a quote "rest" and then go back to it and see how it reads. In addition, if you cannot work with a quote, then there are other options for highlighting a key phrase. You can put it in a subheading, repeat it in the beginning of a chapter, or even italicize it in the quote. These approaches seem more straightforward than heavy editing of quotes. More to the point, the reader knows that you wrote the subheadings and introduced italics in a chapter. The reader is less aware of the numerous, but invisible steps, taken in editing.

Summary: The Importance of Thinking Your Way through Data Analysis

Sometimes in ethnographic research it seems like everything happens at once. Within the same week, you can go to a field site for the umpteenth time, persuade a new person to do an interview, work on transcribing a tape, and try to write a paper. This is in addition to doing your laundry, being in touch with your family, earning money, and running your life. With so many different things going on at the same time, it is easy to feel overwhelmed. And it can be hard to find time to reflect. Nonetheless, thinking while you are collecting data is crucial. It helps you to figure out where you have been, what you have learned and how it fits in with the scholarship written by others, and what you should do next. As I discuss in the next chapter, some people put off making important decisions because it raises anxiety (that you will never figure this out) or reveals chaos (you have no idea what you are doing) or makes you scared (none of what you are learning seems that different than other studies you have read). These are all normal, common, and predictable experiences. It gets better. Finally, some people will be shocked that you are changing your study in certain ways as you go. But those people don't really understand the nature of qualitative research. You have to make changes—add questions, collect additional data, while, at the same time, trying to keep some core features consistent through the entire study. But, even if you have invested time into one feature of data collection, if the emerging data analysis suggests that another pathway is more promising, take this seriously. When I was a doctoral student in Michael Burawoy's class, he stressed that the "journey of discovery is different than the journey of presentation." When you turn to writing up your results, most of your journey of learning new insights in your study is not that relevant to the reader. Instead, the story that you are trying to tell becomes the focus. How to go about writing up that story in a way that clearly conveys what you learned is the subject of the next chapter.

Writing

Becoming Clearer about Your Contribution

"Writing," Tracy Kidder and Richard Todd assert in their book, *Good Prose*, "remains the best route we know towards clarity of thought and feeling."[1] Although nearly all qualitative researchers would agree that the written word is indeed a powerful form for conveying our findings, for most of us, writing is hard.

Partly, writing exposes our thinking. And, while we like to consider ourselves clear thinkers, in the early stages our thinking is often muddled. So, it is *appropriate* to have jumbled thinking at the initial stage of a writing project. Remember, the writing process is an excellent way to clarify your argument.

In this chapter, I have simply chosen to present the issues in the sequence that is common in published work: introduction, literature review, methodology section, findings, and discussion. There are special challenges in writing up a study where the data are words rather than numbers. For example, the written products from a study vary (e.g., classroom papers, theses, journal articles, and books), yet almost all include a methodology section. Here, readers will want to know how you "selected" your site of study. But the reality is that you may have been begging to get into any site. This messy process can make writing a methodology section daunting, but since this is a common problem, as I show in this chapter, there are standard approaches to navigating it. Relatedly, the term "literature review" may lead you to think that you should summarize the key studies, but really what you want to do is to *guide* the reader to see the weaknesses in the literature and thus the need for your study. There are also writing challenges in developing your argument with your data. For example, you do not want to introduce the argument in the beginning and revisit it only at the end of your piece (which is a common rookie mistake). You want to weave the argument through your analysis. You are trying to convince the reader that your argument is supported by your data, that you are doing something new, and that it is important. In addition, it is always wise to present quotes that provide disconfirming evidence for your argument. Then you show the reader why this disconfirming evidence is not a fatal flaw. Throughout the writing, you try to be vivid, detailed, and clear. You want readers to imagine the scene. I will take up all of these writing challenges in this chapter.[2]

Writing is also hard because the process can trigger anxiety. For example, as a young person, I suffered as I sought to transform the data I had collected into publishable papers. A key obstacle was that I found my early drafts hopelessly inadequate, and my feelings of failure were sometimes overwhelming. I have subsequently learned that a more helpful approach is for me to expect the first drafts to be incomplete.[3] Like a little, frail green shoot of a tomato plant that breaks through the earth, early ideas need to be coaxed along with the intellectual equivalent of sunshine, air, light, and water. They should not be stomped on as being insufficient. Nor should they be seen as deficient since they are not immediately springing into shape as a strong, glistening plant.

Hence, writing includes both the process of learning how to present qualitative data in an effective fashion—by thinking through the connections between the data and the literature, selecting vivid quotes that represent the data set, and connecting the data to the argument—as well as the process of learning how to cope with the uncertainty inevitably tied to writing (i.e., uncertainty about what you are saying, and about how it will be received). Most of this chapter will focus on the logistics of presenting data in a compelling fashion, but I will have a few words to say about managing the uncertainty of the writing process.

Before I proceed, however, I want to emphasize that there is no right sequence in which to write various sections of a piece. Some people begin by writing the conclusion; others always start with the literature review. I always begin by editing quotes and writing "around them" (as I explain below), but I also switch back and forth among tasks, including reading the literature and taking a stab at the literature review as well as writing the introduction and conclusion. As noted in the last chapter, the fancy word for it is "iterative" (i.e., "repetition of a cycle of operations").[4] In these iterative cycles, I try to figure out what I am saying by looking at the data, think about which works I will highlight in the literature review, read more, hone the concepts that I believe the data support, and develop the language to show the reader the ways in which the data offer a friendly amendment to the existing literature. It is slightly chaotic to be moving back and forth across various sections in different ways, but it works for me. My collaborator Elliot Weininger, however, is the opposite. He writes a detailed outline, and then he follows it exactly. Shamus Khan suggests beginning by picking a paper you admire on a related topic to your work and looking closely at how the paper is organized; it could be a role model. All of these strategies, however, can make writing seem more orderly than it is. Writing is iterative since the formulation of the argument begins in data collection, continues in data analysis, and develops in the writing process. Some people say that by the time you sit down to write, you have done 80 percent of your thinking. (Others believe they are only halfway through the process when they start to write.) On the one hand, this point highlights the tremendous amount of thinking you have done at every stage. On the other hand, a lot of thinking takes place during the writing process.

Getting Ready to Write

Before you can begin writing, you need to have collected some data, and thought carefully about what you learned from it (i.e., analyzed it) as discussed in chapter 8. But the line between data collection, data analysis, editing, and writing is a blurry one, and the discussion of data analysis and editing of quotes (chapter 8) could easily have been included in this chapter since thinking is pre-writing activity.

Overall, the heart of the writing process involves figuring out what you want to say and then marshaling data to buttress your claims. It involves taking the position of the reader to think about what the reader needs to know. It means assuming less and explaining more. "Show, don't tell" is a mantra for qualitative researchers so that you share the actual quotes or field notes that led you to draw a conclusion. Then the reader can, effectively, look over your shoulder to see what you see. Showing is vastly better than asserting that a pattern exists. But, space is almost always tight. For example, in an classroom paper or journal article, you can usually show evidence for only three or four points (particularly since you often want to show more than one quote per point, and you want to acknowledge disconfirming evidence that adds com-

plexity but does not undermine your conclusion).
A book is longer, but here you have more ground
to cover. You will need to *focus*. A lack of focus
(along with the related problem of trying to do
too much) is the most common problem qualitative researchers face early in the writing process.

The overly ambitious nature of writing is
understandable. You were immersed in a setting,
and you learned a great deal. You want to share
it. Put differently, it can be painful to prune the
argument to focus on one central element. Some
people describe the process as involving grief—
there are so many interesting things to say, and
it is frustrating not to be able to include them
all. You can mourn the loss of an example, just as
artists mourn when a song they wrote is cut from
the final production. Still, as a reader, it is confusing when one piece of writing has many different lines of thought. It is also hard for a reader
if the purpose of the work is unclear. Ideally, as
noted earlier in this book, you want to improve
our understanding of an issue by overcoming
a problem in the literature. After reading your
piece, your readers should be able to answer the
question: "So what?"

The specifics of writing will vary a great deal
across disciplines and subdisciplines, so having a
role model is a good idea. Particularly for younger
scholars, the process of writing seems bewilder-
ing. When I was in graduate school, and I was at
the very beginning of my dissertation project, I
found an article that I admired.[5] It was absorbing to read, and it was extremely interesting; it
also made an important and original conceptual
argument. I showed it to Charles Benson, who
was one of the members of my dissertation committee, and I asked him what he thought. He
very graciously said something like this, "I think

WRITING WOES

- presenting too many different arguments
- telling the results rather than showing the results through quotes
- not showing enough data
- quoting a large number of different points in an unclear fashion
- having a mismatch between claims and evidence
- discussing different levels of analysis in a haphazard fashion
- unexpectedly taking up, in the middle of a work, a new idea or literature not previously introduced
- changing the argument as the piece unfolds so that the introduction and conclusion discuss different ideas
- including too many words, and ideas, in one sentence
- not being sufficiently systematic
- including jargon

it is good. But I think that you can do an even better job." Armed with this boost of confidence, I used the article as my guiding light, and my goal was to do a similar study in a different setting. Of course, each study is unique, but it can be helpful to choose a "sister piece of writing" that captures key elements of what you are hoping to do. Before you write, you might think about the audience for the piece. I often write to an intelligent sophomore in college or a "general reader." People in the academic world who hope to publish their piece might, as Belcher suggests, choose a journal—and write to its audience—before they begin.[6]

Normally a piece represents a finding that you are convinced surfaced in your data, and you want to begin with one of the strongest findings. Although you will undoubtedly have qualifications, you want to get the main story across first before you start to alert the reader to exceptions to the main thesis. As in the famous "rule of three," you want to state the overarching point first: "say what you are going to say, say it, and say what you said."

As you write, you want to be as clear as possible—which is not the same thing as being simple—since, after all, sophisticated ideas can be conveyed clearly. Writing clearly often involves striking unnecessary words and limiting one sentence to one thought. Unclear sentences are weighed down with multiple clauses, parenthetical phrases, and numerous ideas. Also, it is helpful to briefly define key terms the very first time you introduce them and, as much as possible, to avoid jargon. Acronyms can also be off-putting to the reader. By contrast, headings and subheadings generally are the equivalent of highway signs that point the way through the narrative. Likewise, readers usually appreciate occasional, brief summaries of key points you have already covered and where you are heading next. You might look at your prose through the eyes of an undergraduate and see whether you can figure out the main point. As I explain in the last section of this chapter, listening to people by asking for feedback (and social support) is an essential element of the writing process.

Writing the Introduction

Since it is often only about 5 percent of the finished piece, the introduction for a paper needs to be succinct. You want to say why your project is important and why people should care about it. It is helpful to begin with a vivid example. (Since there are so many, it can be hard to choose.) But very quickly, after a few sentences of your example, you want to pivot to show the reader how this example illuminates a broader, important social process. Tell the reader that you will show below how the current literature has some limitations. In a few sentences also convey to the reader how you did the study. (Again, this will be elaborated in the methodology section.) And, you want to highlight the main points of your study. To wrap it up, you tell the reader the implications that you will lay out in the discussion section.

In his helpful book *Writing for Social Scientists*, Howard Becker writes about the importance of an introduction *not* being a series of "I.O.U's" where you list the topics you will discuss (e.g., "I will summarize the literature, describe my methods, and summarize my findings"). Instead, it should be a "road map" where you state the actual ideas or findings you will include in the piece of writing:

> That introduction, laying out the map of the trip the author is going to take them on, lets readers connect ... the argument with the.... [contents]. Readers with such a map seldom get confused or lost. [7]

Many people write the introduction last. (As the late Everett Hughes reportedly said, "How can you introduce something that you haven't written yet?"[8]) Still, it is common for me to draft an introduction after I have drafted part of the findings section—still relatively early in the writing process—as well as a conclusion. Then I make the conclusion my introduction (since it is clearer) and write another conclusion. The second conclusion becomes the new introduction. It is a cycle. As Becker suggests, in the process, my sentences become less "evasive" and "vacuous."

To give you an example, here is an early introduction that I wrote for a paper coauthored with Aliya Rao, on the methodological elements in doing family observations. The first introduction is verbose, vague, and overly ambitious:

> Although we have many fine pieces of family sociology, there remain important gaps in the character of research results and the dynamics within families in daily life. First, in daily life, it is undeniable that families are composed of multiple people who have multiple perspectives.... Yet, most family studies only capture

the perspective of one person (e.g., a mother). This is unfortunate because ...

Second, despite the fact that family members are embedded in many other social worlds, families also remain a powerful, and arguably unique, space where family members retreat for privacy, replenishment, and renewal from the challenges of daily life, and enjoyment. Families have expectations of privacy not found elsewhere; families also can develop special family rituals or family culture.

Third, families function in a broader context. The government has the power to intervene if families are not in compliance with (historically-specific) norms for raising children. Family members go to work, childcare centers, school, church, prison, and community activities. Each of these institutions require skills and knowledge as families negotiate with them. ... Yet, many studies remain focused within the home in part because there are formidable methodological challenges in studying families as well as their institutional experiences.

In this paper, drawing on data from two studies of family life which used participant observation, we argue that participant observation is a useful methodological approach for studying family life. We see participant observation as particularly valuable in helping to address these enduring gaps between research results and family life. Nonetheless, participant observation within families has key challenges. For example, that expectation of privacy makes participant observation more intrusive than participant observation in other spheres.

The final, revised introduction is narrower, sharper, and clearer. It also gets to the point more quickly.

Using observational methods with families, especially within their homes, presents significant challenges for ethnographers—ones not found in other spaces where participant observations are more commonly conducted. Families are frequently set apart as a distinctive grouping because members often have a strong expectation of being assured of respite within their own home. Employees expect to be observed at the workplace. ...

But families—and the home—are idealized as somewhat more private … [and] sociologists have often been reluctant to collect observational data from families.

Some studies of family life have used observational data; but systematic strategies for managing this methodological challenge have not been sufficiently discussed in the literature. Methodological appendices of some observational studies of family life catalog specific concerns arising from family observations. … Yet, beyond these methodological appendices, guidelines to minimize these challenges have not yet been developed.

In this article we explicate elements of the method of "intensive family observations."

In the second introduction the ambitions are reduced, and the scope of the study is specified more clearly and succinctly. In sum, the introduction is a road map to the intellectual journey the reader will experience when they read your piece of writing. In this road map, you want to avoid the approach of a mystery writer who shares the most important finding only at the end of the work. After all, as a reader, you don't have the benefit of the speaker's facial expression, tone of voice, and body language to convey the speaker's point. Writing is much more constrained, and readers need all the help they can get. You want to spoil the ending and share your main point right away.

Writing the Literature Review

The literature review is usually the first stop in this journey and you are the tour guide for the reader. Your purpose is to show that your study has not been previously done and that it fills an important gap in the literature. Your study is needed. Another author could review the identical articles with a different point in mind and a different research agenda. To give a simple analogy, in Chicago, and in many cities, guided tours help visitors journey the city. These tours range from a tour of the architecture to a tour of the history of "gangsters, mobs, and criminals."[9] In some instances, people on these different tours traverse the same blocks of Chicago but, guided by different leaders, they look for different things. So too with a literature review. A key purpose of a literature review is for you to help the reader understand that there is a limitation to the literature and hence a need for your study. I'll say it again: your study is a friendly amendment to the literature. But, as Kristin Luker aptly notes, "you don't need to write about every book and/or article ever written that is remotely relevant to your question." Instead, you "give readers an intellectual road map of the existing literature in a smart and critical way, and show us that ... [the] literature doesn't really answer the question" you are pursuing.[10]

This purpose means that you need to introduce an idea (or a topic sentence) in each of the paragraphs in the literature review. Rather than plunging in to describe a relevant work, you want to tell the reader what they should be looking to learn from your analysis of prior work. You might point out, for example, that the literature has offered one conceptualization of a process, but this conceptualization emphasizes one aspect of the process too much, and it doesn't pay sufficient attention to other aspects of the process. After you state this idea, then you briefly summarize the prior studies to show the reader what you mean. You then state your point: you just have shown the reader that the conceptualization in prior studies has particular flaws, and there is a need to be attuned to a particular element of the process. Put differently, the literature review has an argument.[11]

One danger in the literature review is for you to slide into summarizing your results. Avoid it. In an article, you want to wait until the findings section, and in a book, you want to separate the literature review and your summary of the plan of the work. It is tricky, however, for you to offer a critique of the literature. You are trying to show the need for your study, but, there have not been any studies of the topic of your study. So, how do you show the need for it?

First, you have to figure out your critique. As you read the existing studies, what troubles you about them? Is there something that nags at you, like having a little pebble in your shoe? Can you articulate the flaws? As discussed earlier, the problems can vary in size, and the scope of your writing varies too between a class paper, article, or book. Regardless, normally you want to go beyond saying that the studies have not addressed a particular social group (i.e., a particular racial or ethnic group, gender, sexual orientation, or age group). Instead, you want to focus on the social process. You are saying that the current studies are incomplete, hint at a somewhat different process, have been imbalanced in their focus, are dated in a time of important social change, or have some other flaw. Of course, including a group not previously studied may enable us to see the process differently.

Once you have your critique in hand, you need to present it to the reader. There are various strategies. Sometimes you can quote others who call for the kind of study you have done. Sometimes there are in-depth articles by journalists (for example in the *New York Times*) that highlight a key pattern, but this pattern has not been taken up by social scientists. Sometimes the pattern you are examining is hinted at or discussed as a side issue in other studies, but an in-depth analysis is lacking. Sometimes researchers have been preoccupied with a particular flawed approach, and have not given sufficient attention to a promising approach that has been found in only a very few settings. You can point to those patterns. As you gather your thoughts for a critique, it is imperative that you provide an accurate view of other studies. Sometimes, in trying to make a point, researchers provide an incomplete summary or even a caricature of the work they are criticizing. Indeed, the late philosopher John Rawls, author of the renowned book *Theory of Justice*, wrote, "I always assumed that the writers we were studying were much smarter than I was." His approach was "to present each writer's thought in what I took to be its strongest form."[12] It is good advice.

Although tempting, you do not need to discuss all possibly related literature, but only the literature that is centrally and directly related to your research question. There are surely other related literatures, and it is important to let readers know that you are aware of them. But since these other studies are peripheral, not central, to your main argument, you can acknowledge them in a footnote (e.g., "A full discussion of xxx is beyond the scope of this piece, but see a, b, and c," where "a" is a review essay, "b" is a classic work in this area, and "c" is a recent empirical piece).

In sum, you want to remember that while some readers are new to a topic, other readers are deeply familiar with the pieces you are discussing in the literature review. For well-read readers, it is a waste of time to read a summary of works they already know well. (The ones who are unfamiliar with the studies you are discussing can look them up.) Instead, you are building an argument that these studies have limitations. Your challenge is to be clear in your critique, but to not overstate it. If you submit your article for publication, the reviewers are likely to include people you are critiquing. As in intimate relationships, how you state a criticism matters. You want to write your critique in a way that is respectful but persuasive. That approach makes it easier for people who do the kind of work you are discussing to "hear" your criticisms.

Writing the Methodology Section

Readers are curious about the details of data collection and the rationale behind decisions. The purpose of the methodology section is to answer these questions. In a longer piece of writing, such as a dissertation or book, it is common to provide a methodological appendix that elaborates on the key challenges the researcher(s) faced. In almost all qualitative studies, however, you want to provide certain crucial details in the main body of the text.

The trick here is to be honest while acknowledging the reality of the situation. Methodology sections were originally designed for quantitative researchers, and it is awkward, and at times crazy, to try to squish the "yeasty" nature of building rapport and gaining access into the constraints of a conventional methods section. For example, the reality is you generally gain access to a site through an informal social tie, and, since it is incredibly hard to gain access, you study whomever you are able to study. In this context, the question "how did you select your site?" makes no sense. Since you were virtually begging to get into a site—any site—you did not make a "selection."

Nevertheless, there is still a method here. When you were asking around to gain access for a site, you probably had an idea of whom or what you wanted to study. And, you had a reason for this decision. These criteria for selection that guided your request to conduct the research need to be described to the reader. These were crucial decisions. For example, in my study *Unequal Childhoods*, I ruled out preschoolers and middle school or high school students. Instead, I sought children in third grade since they were old enough to have some activities outside the home but were young enough to not be drawn away from family by peer groups. (This decision felt momentous although, in retrospect, second graders or fourth graders would have been fine too.) I did the research in the Midwest and in a large Northeastern city. Both times, I started asking people I know whether they knew someone who worked in schools who might give me permission to study a school. There were numerous other bureaucratic steps, including the approval of the IRB, the letters that the principals sent to the parents, and so forth, but the key moment was the introduction to a school official through an informal social tie. Although I was focused on how desperate I was to gain access to the schools, the reality is that I had made a number of key design decisions that guided where I tried to gain access: I wanted public schools with catchment areas, I wanted middle-class and working-class kids in the study, and so forth. Similarly, you settle on a specific age range (e.g., children in preschool, or elementary school, or middle school, or high school, or college). Or, you might select a business with certain criteria. If you do this, you want to share with the reader the factors you considered in making the decision. It helps them understand your rationale. And, if your rationale shifted significantly over time, you might share that information with the reader (particularly in a methodological appendix). Since it is always sensitive to be admitted to study a research site, sponsorship is often crucial. In methodology sections, people rarely indicate how desperate they were to get into any site; but these experiences are often conveyed in a methodological appendix. Even in your most difficult moments, however, you would probably skip some proposed sites because they are not what you wanted to study. This is the information you can convey to the reader.

Sometimes you do not have wonderful reasons for choosing one site over another. Or, you have not-perfect decisions or a significant weakness in your study. If any of these situations are true, you need to tell the reader. Similarly, in a methods section, don't hide these woes, but remind the reader that many qualitative researchers have faced difficulty finding a site and recruiting participants, and simply explain to the reader why this happened. For example, I have interviewed people from very wealthy families, but the number of people who decline is extremely high, so, at this moment, my "response rate" is about 20 percent. I find this worrisome. Yet, there are many researchers who have also struggled.[13] So, all I can do is to say it is not as high as I wished, share the steps I took to recruit a broad sample, and note there is a comparable response rate for other studies. If I believe that my respondents are unusual in some fashion, I need to share that information. Put differently, I need to "say it loud" and not try to hide it. Similarly, in your study, there are undoubtedly flaws. Explain your rationale, and explain why any potential problems did not distort the study. Rather, you can tell the reader how your sample gave you a chance to learn unexpected insights. It is usually the best you can do.

Here are some of the pieces of information that are very commonly included in a methods section. They roughly follow the "five W's" of journalism, by reporting "who, what, when, where, and why" you did the work. Once again, your goal here is to share with the reader your thinking in making the decisions in a challenging situation.

- Why did you select this site? (Did you consider other sites?)
- How did you gain access? Did you have IRB approval?
- What was your role in recruitment? For example, how did you explain the study to others? Did you do small favors?
- How long were you there?
- Did you write field notes? Did you ever record people?
- How many interviews did you complete, who were they with, and what were the interviewees' characteristics (e.g., according to race and ethnicity, age, social class, and so forth)?
- Did you ask people to participate who declined to do so?
- How long were the interviews and where were they held?
- Were people paid or given a thank you gift (including food or flowers)?
- How did you analyze the data? Did you transcribe the interviews? Did you develop a coding scheme? Did you use any kind of coding software? If so, which one?

You want to deliver this information succinctly and non-defensively. Look at methodology sections of pieces you admire, and at other finished products similar to the one you hope to produce, to see how others have handled these issues. Finding a good role model is helpful. But, each situation is unique.

HOW TYPICAL IS YOUR SITE?

It is generally difficult, if not impossible, to tell the reader how your study might have been different if it had been done elsewhere. The reality is that you just don't know. Yet, readers are inevitably curious about this issue, so often you have to assess it in some fashion. If you know anything about how your site is similar to or different from other sites, you can share that information with the reader. For example, in discussing the 12 families who agreed to have researchers follow them around for about three weeks on a daily basis, readers (reasonably enough) worried that anyone who might agree was truly weird. Of course, I had worried about this too, but I conveyed my thinking about this issue. I noted that I had gotten to know the families and the children in the school, and over a number of months, had interviewed them, confirmed the interview the night before with a phone call, sent thank you notes, and built a rapport. I reported that 12 out of 17 agreed, the ones who declined seemed to be worried that they were "not the perfect family," and that families below the poverty level also declined (although I worried that the payment of $550 in current dollars would be seen as potentially coercive). I also noted that I did not base the decision to ask families on an expectation that they might agree; I asked one family where the original interview had gone badly. They agreed. In other words, I acknowledged the worry, and then I shared what I knew about the situation that led me to see the sample as a reasonable one. Once you have taken these steps, try not to worry about it. You cannot change it, and all qualitative researchers face these worries. See how others deal with these issues in a methodology section, and follow their lead. (You can also read book reviews to see how prominent books were assessed.) Some criticisms are inevitable, and this is a "garden variety" critique of qualitative work. Furthermore, with the plunging of response rates in quantitative work, many studies have a very difficult time gaining respondents.[14] It is hard for everyone. Further research can discern whether your study is different from other ones.

Writing the Findings Section

The findings are the heart of your writing, and usually the most interesting part to write and to read. Here is where you can share what you have learned — and you can share the voices of the people you studied as you bring them to life in the reader's mind. Since the findings are the core of the paper, it is here that the contribution of your paper becomes particularly important to highlight.

THE "SOUL" OF A PIECE OF WRITING: THE "SO WHAT?"

Finding your theoretical contribution means making some hard choices about what you are not doing as well as what you are doing. (Some people end up being sad about this stage of the process.) Thus, rather than being centered on why you need to write a paper, you want to switch to focusing on what the paper is actually going to say. John "Rob" Warren wrote an essay as he stepped down from editing the journal *Sociology of Education*, sharing his surprise at how few of the submissions made it through the review process:

> *Most papers lacked a soul—a compelling and well-articulated reason to exist. The world (including the world of education) faces an extraordinary number of problems, challenges, dilemmas, and even mysteries. Yet most papers failed to make a good case for why they were necessary. Many analyses were not well motivated or informed by existing theory, evidence, or debates. Many authors took for granted that readers would see the importance of their chosen topic, and failed to connect their work to related issues, ideas, or discussions. Over and over again, I kept asking myself (and reviewers often asked): So what?*

This is your challenge. I believe that, realistically, readers will not find your topic as fascinating as you do. You want to "go bigger" in your ideas and show how your study can contribute toward answering broader questions. You can also help us understand why those broader questions need to be answered. (What will we miss if we don't ask these questions?) Here, you want to remember that you can leave the specific subfield you are in to suggest a conceptual argument that might illuminate processes in an entirely different subfield. If you are studying power and coercion, for example, how prison guards treat prisoners might be relevant to how military officers treat solders. It is almost always possible to think of another conceptual application for your idea. You should. Your conceptual contribution is your answer to the "so what?" question; it is included when you summarize your key findings for your work. Put differently, you want to ask: "What do we misunderstand if we don't explore this research question?" As noted earlier, in the "famous rule of three" you say what you are going to say, say it, and say what you said. Your conceptual contribution should be highlighted in each of these three points.

A WRITING TIP
Read a lot. You take in a great deal of knowledge without intending to. Familiarity and pleasure breed ease. When you read other [books], you get models of what to do and what not to do.

Jane Smiley, novelist

HOW TO WRITE A FINDINGS SECTION: ONE APPROACH

As I noted earlier, I spend hours reading and rereading the data I have collected to look for themes, print out and read quotes in subcodes if I have used a program, and gradually move potential quotes into a file. Then I edit the quotes to help eliminate false starts and so forth, and to focus on the germ of the idea. As I detailed in chapter 8, in the book *Unequal Childhoods*, I include the quote about Girl Scouts and gymnastics from an interview with Ms. Marshall, an African American middle-class mother. As the project unfolded, I gradually decided to make three main points in the book: social class shaped language use, use of organized activities, and intervention in institutions. While the various families could have been used for different points, in the end, the Marshalls exemplified institutional intervention. After looking at the quotes, I wanted to show how much work it was for the mothers to raise children.

Hence, in my book *Unequal Childhoods*, I take this quote, and write that it is through the work of the mothers that children end up in organized activities. (In working-class and poor families, by contrast, the children often initiated the activities.) Then, I state the idea (Ms. Marshall does the labor) in the text first in my own words:

> It is overwhelmingly Ms. Marshall who handles the girls' lives and their activities, as well as any complaints about Fern's or Stacey's institutional experiences. Ms. Marshall's efforts on behalf of her daughters are not unusual.... Most middle-class mothers undertake similar labor with respect to organized activities. The way in which Stacey came to be involved in gymnastics, for example, is typical in that it takes effort by the mother.

Then, by presenting Ms. Marshall's own words in a quote, I don't ask the reader to trust me, but instead I *show* the reader the basis for my claim:

> When she was starting third grade I couldn't find a Girl Scout troop for her to be in. She had been a Brownie I think four years. Fern was in a Girl Scout troop. Stacey wasn't old enough to be a Girl Scout. So we went to this free night [laughs]. So Stacey ... I wanted her to do something and it was a void ... And I didn't want her sittin' in front of the TV.

I also wanted to show that moms learned information from their social network, so the second part of the quote was used to make that point. I explain that the gymnastics instructor recommended a program, but that was not enough:

> Not content to rely only on the instructor's recommendation, Stacey's mother also taps into her own social network:
> "And just listening to some of the parents. I started putting my ear to the grapevine, and I heard a number of parents mention, 'Well, if the kid really likes gymnastics, you send them to Wright's.'"

Note that I don't simply assert that Ms. Marshall talked to other parents. Instead, I show the evidence by presenting a quote where Ms. Marshall explains how she was "putting her ear to the grapevine" to learn where to go for a gymnastic program. I then follow the quote with a discussion of Ms. Marshall's class-based networks:

> While in this instance Ms. Marshall was gathering information on a recreational program, in other instances she was looking to solve educational problems (as when Stacey did not qualify for her school's gifted program). As with middle-class parents in the sample as a whole, Ms. Marshall's "grapevine" is rich with friends and relatives who are educators, psychologists, lawyers, and even doctors.... As a result, middle-class parents are more likely to have informal access to valuable information and advice from professionals and experts than are working-class and poor parents.

Here, in the analysis, I link the "grapevine" quote to my analytic point that middle-class parents have access to valuable information from professionals. Not unlike a hamburger, the quote is the heart of the evidence, but there is an idea (i.e., a top bun) and an interpretation (i.e., a bottom bun) that connect the quote to the overall purpose of the paper.

You need to convince the reader that your claims—your ideas—have a solid body of evidence backing them up. Of course, other kinds of researchers do this as well. Still, tables, particularly the complex tables with multiple models and interaction terms that are typical of quantitative research, may make the findings seem credible even before a reader begins to examine them—despite the fact that closer scrutiny may reveal problems. But when you are writing words instead of numbers for your evidence, you are generally not granted the same halo of authority.

Instead, you have to earn the reader's trust. You earn it by persuading the reader, step by step, that your claims are warranted. As a program officer from the National Science Foundation (NSF) once said, an ethnographer saying, "Trust me!" is not a sufficient basis for NSF to award a grant. And, it should not be sufficient for a reader to believe the findings of a study.

SO HOW DO YOU BUILD A READER'S TRUST?

LIMIT THE SCOPE OF YOUR CLAIMS

Make sure that you are not claiming too much. It is rare, for example, that qualitative research can show the impact a social process has on children's achievement, an adult's health outcome, or another significant life outcome. Writing as though it can is a rookie mistake. But your research can unpack a crucial mechanism or a process. Moreover, to be taken seriously, you do not need to show, decisively, the outcome of the process for the research. By contrast, if you try to claim something that you cannot decisively demonstrate, your research could be severely critiqued. Similarly, you usually cannot show change over time unless your research lasts a long time. A few studies are longitudinal, but most are not. You want to claim something that you are able to demonstrate with your data at hand.

Don't Introduce Too Many Ideas at Once

You want to help the reader understand only a small number of ideas. You need to group your little ideas into some big ideas. Listening to your peers, writing-group members, or teachers can help you here. Once you get clearer about your ideas, you need to be ruthless to make sure that your writing, as you revise it, does not jump from point to point in somewhat haphazard fashion (although it is appropriate and common to be hopping from point to point in a first draft of a paper). In the final work, I am fond of having only one main idea per section or paragraph, and then I spend the section providing empirical support for the claim. Too many claims can lead the reader to be confused, to believe that you do not have sufficient depth to support your claims, and to believe that you don't know what you are writing about. Having one major claim allows you to develop it, to consider various angles, to provide ample evidence to support the claim, to acknowledge disconfirming evidence, and to summarize your main points.

MAKE SURE THAT YOUR EVIDENCE PRECISELY
ALIGNS WITH YOUR CLAIMS

The evidence that you put in the final written form is just a small fraction of the evidence that you collected. Of course, it is frustrating to collect all of these data and then not have your findings see the light of day. Yet, having this depth of data is good. It means that you are certain of your claims. You can think of multiple examples for each point. You are sure. You might have favorite field note excerpts that you like to use, but you should have a lot of different pieces of fieldwork, different quotes, and different people who all point to the same conclusion. You might count how many quotes you have from different respondents so that you don't rely on some people too much. Also, a table can be an effective way to convey a great deal of data by summarizing, with brief quotes, the experiences of people in your study. (Since the table crystallizes the argument, the table is usually developed very late in the process.) Here, table 9.1 is a reprint of a table from *Unequal Childhoods* that summarized my argument.[15]

Overall, the findings section should feel solid to you, and it should feel solid to the reader. Hence, it is important to make claims only where you have research findings to back them up. In many instances, the pattern will not be present through the entire sample, but it might surface in part of the sample. You should explain this kind of pattern to the reader.

If, alas, some evidence you love does not fit into one of the many ideas of your paper, then you need to file it away to be used for a different piece of writing. Here, it simply does not matter how many hours you killed yourself collecting this lovely bit of data. You need to be clear eyed in your analysis in order to build a strong argument.

It is crucial to get feedback from friendly, constructive readers. Since I find it easier to cut than to add, I tend to write overly long first drafts. Usually, I get feedback from my writing group (which meets every three weeks). In the writing group, we tend to give each other the same feedback: this is what you seem to be saying, make this clearer, get rid of extra arguments, and analyze the data more. Armed with this feedback, I am ruthless as I edit. Although increasingly unpopular, there is compelling evidence that it is helpful for you to read a paper version of your writing rather than reading it only electronically.[16] I make sure to reread my drafts after a ruthless round of editing. (In my own writing

Table 9.1. *Typology of Differences in Child Rearing*

Child Rearing Approach

	Concerted Cultivation	Accomplishment of Natural Growth
Key elements	*Parent actively fosters and assesses child's talents, opinions, and skills*	*Parent cares for child and allows child to grow*
Organization of daily life	• multiple child leisure activities orchestrated by adults	• child "hangs out" particularly with kin
Language use	• reasoning/directives • child contestation of adult statements • extended negotiations between parents and child	• directives • rare for child to question or challenge adults • general acceptance by child of directives
Interventions in institutions	• criticisms and interventions on behalf of child • training of child to take on this role	• dependence on institutions • sense of powerlessness and frustrations • conflict between child rearing practices at home and at school
Consequences	Emerging sense of entitlement on the part of the child	Emerging sense of constraint on the part of the child

ritual, I read it on the couch, revise it, print it, and read it again.) With each reading of the revision, I cut words, get rid of jargon, improve the flow, and glean new insights. Most pieces of writing go through multiple revisions; some authors graciously have shared earlier versions of published papers so readers can see the development of the ideas.[17]

DON'T SKIMP ON EVIDENCE

In the first article that I submitted to a journal from my dissertation, I had exactly four quotes in a paper about thirty pages in length. This led one reviewer, reasonably enough, to complain that my paper was "ethnographically sparse and analytically limited," and another reviewer to note that I presented "thin and sketchy data built upon rather broad generalizations." The reviewers were right; the evidence is the heart of the enterprise. So how many quotes should a piece feature? Although it's an imperfect method, I often estimate the number of double-spaced pages my piece will be and aim for around one quote or example for every page of manuscript text (i.e., around 15 to 20 quotes in a 20-page paper or chapter).

Since you usually have a choice of many field notes or quotes to use in any written piece, you might as well go with your favorites (as long as the evidence supports the idea). It is also helpful to use quotes that have an emotional touch to them (as long as it is not overdone). Quotes that are funny, poignant, or powerful can enrich your work. Be judicious and never go beyond what you learned in the field. (In addition, you don't want to include any information that will endanger anyone or compromise anyone.) But lively text is more interesting to read. Still, you need balance here, and while you need evidence, you don't want to have too much evidence.

DON'T MAKE YOUR QUOTES TOO LONG

As you write, there is a very strong temptation to put in vast amounts of data with extremely long quotes. Partly, you may be attached to your respondents. You may want to bring their voices alive on the page. You might be mesmerized by the results. (Some of the greatest love affairs are between qualitative researchers and their data.) But, unfortunately, the reader does not need huge swaths of data.[18] The entire purpose of a piece of data is to illuminate *an idea*. You want to put in enough so that the reader understands the context, but the quotes need to be focused. Although there are no hard and fast rules here, four to eight lines is usually the right amount. A quote that is three-quarters of a page is hard for the reader to interpret, and should be broken into smaller pieces, and guided by your text so that the reader can see what *you* want them to take away from the quote. Similarly, there should not be too many ideas in one quote. If there are, it is confusing to the reader.

ACKNOWLEDGE WEAKNESSES IN YOUR INTERPRETATION

It bothers readers when you don't admit problems in your view and discuss them. Since you are writing it, and you surely know about the problems, you should admit the problems and then try to explain them away. The world is rarely neat and tidy. In most qualitative studies, it is simply not credible that all of your evidence lined up perfectly to support your claims. Sometimes people contradict themselves in thought and behavior. Some members of a group have a different view than the rest of the group. Thus, you want to be sure to say in a clear fashion, "Yes, there were signs of evidence that did not support my claim." You want to present the evidence, briefly, and then, most importantly, explain why you did not see this as fatal to your conclusions. For example, in a coauthored paper we demonstrated that many African American parents in a racially diverse elementary school were deeply distrustful of the school. The paper focuses on social class differences in how the parents expressed these concerns. Yet, in the paper, we also reported that other African American parents saw things differently:

> Moreover, not all parents shared the view that black children at the school were subjected to unequal and less favorable treatment compared to the white children. A number of [B]lack parents stated that they did not know if there were problems at the school. ... Other [B]lack parents stated that children at Quigley School were not being treated unfairly on the basis of race. Some of these parents, from a range of social-class positions, were openly hostile to the [B]lack parents who complained about racial injustice.[19]

Here, we provided additional quotes to show the vehement support some African American parents gave to the principal and their hostility to the parents who complained of racial inequality. In short, in a brief section entitled "Variation in Parents' Perceptions," we acknowledged disconfirming evidence, but the primary purpose of the paper was clear.

In discussing disconfirming evidence, you might note that it was rare, concentrated in one group, or, paradoxically, the exception that proved the rule. This discussion should be brief, but it should exist. Tone is important here. You do not want to be dismissive. Rather, you want to convince the reader that you were very willing to be persuaded by the disconfirming evidence, but it did not add up to a strong case. Of course, as noted earlier in this book, it is important that you *are* willing to have your ideas changed by the evidence you collect. After all, if you know what you are going to find before you do the study, why bother?

DON'T SUMMARIZE THE EVIDENCE, INTERPRET IT

One of the most common, but boring, things that authors do is to present an idea, present a piece of data, and then proceed to write a paragraph that simply summarizes the data that you (the reader) have just read. This is not only irritating for the reader, but also a wasted opportunity for the author. Instead of summarizing the quote, you want to go beyond it. You want to answer these questions: How does this piece of evidence support the idea? How does the idea support the thesis? What exactly in the quote led you to draw this conclusion? For example, in a paper on parent involvement, Vanessa Lopes Muñoz and I described clashes parents had with the principal over the organization of the school:

> By contrast, parents desired the school to be more personal, flexible, and fun. In short, they wanted the school to be less bureaucratic. Beth expressed an overall concern about the atmosphere during lunchtime:
> "Fun. Just needs a little fun, it's dreary in there. Tense, tense, I think it sets the overall tone there.... They have to do this manners lunch now; they have to talk in a soft whisper ... I find that they also make lunch so unfun."

We could have said, "So, the parents complained that lunch was 'unfun.'" This would have echoed a key word in the quote, but it would not give the reader any new information.

Instead, we offered this analysis by, very briefly, reminding the reader of our criticism of the literature (i.e., scholars have overstated the harmony between parents and educators) and stating our key point (the parents and the principal had different priorities):

> Researchers on parent involvement have assumed that parents and educators will be able to work in harmony with adequate levels of communication. While we found that they shared the similar generalized goal of doing what was best for the children, their different ideas about how to prioritize the needs of the children was a considerable barrier. Thus, even when working in

the best interest of the children, parents and the principal often had very different priorities.

Thus, briefly, this analysis reminds the reader why these findings matter (that previous research has generally assumed a pattern of harmony). It is crucial to be brief, but a well-placed sentence in the middle of the paper can remind the reader of why these quotes matter by connecting the data to a weakness in the literature that needs to be fixed.

You might draw the reader back to the example by pointing out aspects of it that illustrate your claim. It is a fine line to walk because you don't want to be repeating your argument over and over again. Rather, you want to help the reader understand the unique contribution that this evidence adds to your overall endeavor. Here are two examples from a paper I wrote where I provided longitudinal data on how class shaped the transition to adulthood.[20] In the example, I was telling the story (about a problem a young man had at work) as well as making an analytic point about social class and cultural knowledge. Here is an early version of one part:

> Others also reported difficulty knowing how to make their dreams come alive. For instance, for the past ten years, Mark Greely, a white young man from a poor family, worked in a Safeway grocery store. But during that time, he has wanted a job "working with computers." His goal lacks more specificity (i.e., computer repair or programming). He is stymied. In addition, he has been planning to get his driver's license for ten years. He recently passed the written test. But, in part because he has anxiety issues, achieving a driver's license is a major life goal. Nevertheless, he was able to get unemployment when he was laid off after a tiff with a manager (whom he threatened to "beat up" for insulting him), and he ultimately got his job back. But he was aided in this by a sympathetic judge who, to his surprise, was sympathetic to his anger when he heard the tale.[21] But, his threat of physical harm to the manager, while consistent with how other working-class men handle insults at work, did not comply with organizational policy.

A member of my writing group wrote: "This feels a little unclear. Maybe focus on one of these events and develop a little more?"

In the revision, the analytic point about Mark's limited cultural knowledge to manage organizational challenges is made clearer by making it the first sentence in the paragraph. In addition, I also told the story of what happened a bit more clearly:

> Others also reported difficulty in managing organizational challenges. Mark Greeley, a young white man from a poor family, has worked in a Safeway grocery store for 10 years.... Despite his long tenure, Mark had recently ... lost his job at Safeway. As he explained, when he was 30, he came to work late because of unavoidable delays on public transit. His angry manager called him into his office and said, "Yeah, if I was 21 without a high school diploma, I'd be scared to lose my job, too." Hearing this insult, Mark "snapped" and threatened to "beat up" the man. [This reaction] did not, of course, comply with organizational policy.... In summary, the working-class and poor youth had incomplete understandings of how institutions worked, had difficulty negotiating conflicts at work, felt deeply constrained in asking for help, and often failed when they sought individualized accommodations from institutions.... My argument aims to illuminate the role of noneconomic forces in both key life transitions and the little moments that build up to these transitions.

Thus, in your writing, you are trying to be as clear as possible about your results (e.g., after being insulted by the manager, Mark threatened his manager) and connect your examples to your concepts (e.g., working-class youth had incomplete understanding of how institutions worked) and to your overall argument (e.g., social class shapes cultural knowledge of institutions; this class disparity can contribute to inequality). You might look at works you admire to see how those authors draw a connection linking up the data, conceptual claims, and overarching argument.

MAKE SURE THAT ALL PARTS OF THE PAPER ARE CONNECTED TO ONE ANOTHER

In writing the individual parts of a paper or book, it is easy to lose sight of the big picture. But, you want all of the pieces to fit together tightly. Each section of the paper should be in alignment and be pointing to the same conclusion (rather than headed off in different directions). Some people reverse outline a paper (i.e., make an outline based on what they have written) to take stock of what they have. At times, it is necessary to remove an entire section to help the piece be more cohesive.

DON'T BE MORALISTIC

It is easy, in the social sciences, to be morally outraged by things you observe in your data collection. Reasonable people disagree about the stance that you should take in a written work. (See more on this issue below in the discussion of ethnographic authority.) While you always want to stay true to what your respondents report, your own tone is a different matter. For example, in your own analysis, words such as *ought, should, despicable, outrageous,* and *blame* are often a sign of your own perspective leaking into the analysis.

Why do I suggest this approach?

If you adopt a tone of moral outrage, you may lose readers who do not share this view and, more importantly, readers may come to distrust what you see and report if you make it clear that you have a strong view. After all, in qualitative research, you are the central mode of the data collection, and you see and record the data (rarely with helpers). A strong moral view of something will likely prevent you from seeing data that does not support your view (i.e., disconfirming evidence). This is not to say that any ethnographer can be completely objective or unbiased. We are social animals; this is impossible. Our social positions leak through in all social encounters, and they will guide your work.[22] There are differing schools of thought about how to proceed. My view is that it is reasonable for me to fight against my personal beliefs, be skeptical of them, put myself in situations where my ideas are often challenged, and search vigorously for disconfirming evidence. In writing, you try to help the reader understand something important. As much as possible, your goal is to communicate with readers in your writing. You don't want your word choice to lose readers when another word could easily convey your meaning. There can be challenging moments in this process. In some cases, for example, you will have quotes from respondents who show racial bigotry; their words will be offensive to many. One possibility is to acknowledge, briefly, this bigotry so that the reader will see it as the respondent's view rather than your own.

BE THOUGHTFUL ABOUT YOUR ROLE IN THE TEXT

As John Van Maanen lucidly shows in *Tales of the Field*, you can choose among many different styles of writing. In particular, you can write a "narrative" where you are absent from the scene, as Matt Desmond mostly did in his book *Evicted*. Or you can write up the results with yourself in the thick of the action so that your role in the field, and the hotly contested ethics of the situation, are clearer.[23] My own preference is for you to remind the reader, sparingly, that you were in the setting. (Jean Briggs, who spent time with an Inuit family and wrote an excellent book, *Never in Anger*, does this particularly skillfully.) You don't want to have yourself be the star of your research.

This balancing act is difficult to work out. And, there are many ways to inadvertently make yourself the star of the narrative. You can spend a lot of time talking about your experience, or you can make the narrative about your discovering process. This focus on the author can be revealing and interesting, but I find it distracts from the focus on the folks who are being studied. Others may disagree.

Writing the Discussion Section

In a musical, the overture is usually a medley of the music of the key songs that will come, informing the audience member of the arc of the performance. So too, the discussion (or, in some pieces, the conclusion) revisits the key points of the written work. Since the goal is to reprise the major points, and to discuss the implications of the findings, you don't want to introduce new data in the discussion section. Nor do you want to surprise the reader with new thoughts. Rather, all of the points you discuss should have been anticipated by the material you have presented. You might think of an undergraduate who is worried whether they have grasped the main point: you are providing reassurance that they have understood the main ideas.

Hence, you want to begin by refreshing in the reader's mind the weaknesses in the literature and the need for the study. (This you can do in a few sentences, sometimes in only one sentence.) Then you want to highlight your three or four most important points. You might briefly acknowledge any weaknesses in your study, but then explain why they are not fatal to your claims. You want to explain your contribution to the literature.

Explain your contribution to the literature succinctly (e.g., in a few sentences to a few paragraphs depending on the document). As I noted earlier, after you do this, it is common to discuss the implications. Here, you are "going bigger" and thinking more expansively. What are the implications of your study for other fields? For example, a study on how low-income women don't trust their bosses, daycare workers, or social workers, might have implications for why first-generation college students may not trust the advice they get from professors. You want to see whether your study can help illuminate social processes in other arenas.[24] You might discuss the key concepts in your study and how they relate to other important concepts. You might discuss unresolved research issues and call for additional research.

Finally, you might consider the policy implications or broader impacts of your study for daily life. Now that we have your findings, what policies should be rethought? Who should do what? What potential problems loom ahead? You may not know all of the answers, but you have spent time seriously thinking about the issues. Share what you have learned.

As you wrap up, you want to nail the ending by returning to an important theme from your study. Avoid ending with a whimper by highlighting the limitations of your study. You surely want to acknowledge those, but not at the very end of the piece. Instead, you want to leave an important idea ringing in the minds of those who read the piece. Stay within the confines of what you can claim, but speak plainly and firmly about what you have learned.

If someone were to remember your study five years from now, what is the main point that they should remember? This is what you want to emphasize in the end of your piece.

Managing Uncertainty in Writing

Some people are calm, confident, and careful writers who are not rattled by the uncertainty of the writing process. They are blessed. (They can skip reading this section.) Others, however, struggle, and some deal with their anxiety by procrastinating.[25]

Working with qualitative data can create special

> Let's be honest, writing is terrifying.
>
> Kristin Luker,
> Salsa Dancing in
> the Social Sciences

writing worries. Some of these worries are contradictory. For example, you can feel overwhelmed with your pages and pages of data and feel frustrated by the limited number of quotes that can fit in one piece of writing. Since you are swimming in data, selecting quotes can feel weighty. At the same time, you can also feel as if you don't have enough data. You can worry whether you have a basis for your claims, but then feel panic at the thought of needing to go back to collect more data. Even if you are certain about what you saw, it can seem scary to take this data and make bold claims. You may long for more data. These worries are normal, but they need to be managed, particularly since contradictory worries can surface at the same time. That can lead to paralysis.

TECHNIQUES FOR DIFFUSING ANXIETY IN WRITING

If you are an anxious writer, it can be helpful to do some reflection about what makes the writing process so difficult for *you*. Do you feel lonely? Do you feel inadequate? Do you feel worried about how your written work will be received? Knowing the source of the difficulty can help you resolve it. For example, if you are lonely (which is a common problem), then you can arrange to write (in quiet) with a friend, plan for social time before or after writing, or find some other social outlet. If you doubt the adequacy of your claims, you can interrogate the source of your doubt. Are you concerned that you don't have enough data? Are you vexed that you aren't answering the "so what" question? Are you worried that the argument isn't interesting enough? If so, you can have others read your draft and give you feedback. If you are troubled about how others will view your draft, you can try to figure out the source of your worry. Are you concerned about how the people you are describing will react? Are you concerned about the reaction of others in your discipline? Are you fretting about your positionality, particularly in terms of power and privilege? There are no one-size-fits-all answers here, but taking time to discern the source of your qualms is valuable. So is having a friend whom you can tell your fears and who will reassure you. Still, even here people can have woes, since as Pamela Richards eloquently pointed out, some people don't trust that their readers will tell them the truth. Thus, even when your informal early-review critics tell you that what you have written is good, you can fret that they are lying or being overly positive. (This is especially likely for perfectionists.)

As Luker points out, writing can be "terrifying," and learning to trust the feedback you receive, and trust the process, can be difficult.[26] But good friends will not allow you to submit pieces for review for publication if they are junk. And most critics are critical; so, if they praise something, it is reasonable to accept it. And, if you have thought through all of these issues but still find writing hard, having a "commitment schedule" and strategies for honoring your commitments can be helpful.[27]

In this process, having a group of people who will read your writing is invaluable. You can create such a group by asking people you know slightly (but who seem nice — and critical but not too critical) to meet regularly. For example, in my writing group, the three of us meet, face-to-face, every three weeks, and each of us has one-half hour to get feedback on whatever we want or to talk through an issue in data collection, recruitment, or whatever is impeding our writing. If we have a piece of writing to share, we distribute it only a couple of days before our meeting, and we give each other marginal comments and summary comments. We also share grant proposals, recruitment scripts for respondents, interview guides, coding schemes, and parts of chapters. Many times we don't have anything written, but we simply talk through a problem we are facing to get "unstuck." If something comes up between meetings then we usually make it a high priority to give immediate feedback. We also celebrate successes. Of course, there are many different ways to organize writing groups; numerous organizations provide support.[28]

> **FORGIVENESS**
> I can't write the book I want to write, but I can and will write the book I am capable of writing. Again and again throughout the course of my life I will forgive myself.
>   Ann Patchett, novelist

Finding a regular writing time also works for many people. A lot of people find *daily* writing — such as a few hours early in the morning — to be indispensable.[29] This well-worn path does not work for me, however, since I write only in spurts, often late at night. I also do something I call "outlining," in which I use paper and pen, and I sketch out possible ideas for the chapter or article. I also read over interviews and field notes and gather quotes (as noted in the previous chapter). I try to figure out my critique of other literature, my own ideas, and the quotes I will use. (I do this all from memory without looking at the computer since I don't want to get distracted, but other people prefer to look through their quotes.) After I sort of settle on the overall argument, then I begin to dig out the quotes.

Once I get going on a piece, I like to work more or less round the clock except when I have other obligations. I also find it helpful to cook when I write—such as making soup or stews where the cooking can start and stop. It is a helpful distraction, but it doesn't draw me in (as a television show, movie, or game might do). I find it is too disruptive to my flow to run errands, but emptying the dishwasher, pulling weeds, walking around the block, and other little chores are fine. And, research shows that moving around can be helpful.[30]

Once I have a draft, I read it, and revise it, and then revise it again. I have others read it, and then I revise it based on their feedback.

INDECISION AND REVISION

If you have writing anxiety, be on guard that you are not changing arguments regularly. I have seen fretful writers write an introduction and situate a piece in a literature, and then decide there are various flaws with it and then change to a new literature. Each time, they are convinced that it is a better approach—but then they change again. (This is another example of being "terrorized by the literature."[31]) I know a historian who has revised a key chapter in a book more than fifteen times over five years. Since the evidence hasn't changed in this time, and since almost all of the introductions worked well, I believe that the constant revision is about indecision and anxiety. If you have spent many weeks on settling on the main point of the paper, and you keep changing the contribution of the paper, you should reach out for help from others.[32]

Sometimes these challenges can be easier to see in others than in yourself, and misplaced indecision is a recurring pattern in life. To give one personal example from a difficult life moment, my mother had a terrible time deciding what to buy to wear to my father's memorial service when my 78-year-old father died relatively unexpectedly. (He had a massive stroke one afternoon at home and died ten days later in the hospital.) As the family planned the memorial service, my dazed and grief-stricken mother realized that she did not have anything appropriate to wear. So, my younger sister, who works in fashion, drove my mother to the mall. My mother didn't usually shop much, and her husband of 48 years had just died, and so at first it seemed reasonable that it was hard for her to find something to her liking. But, as she tried on more and more black suits—with double-breasted jackets with skirts, single-button jackets with pants, long jackets with subtle stripes with large pockets, and high-waisted shiny jackets with no pockets—and it went on, and on, and on, my sister began to have doubts. Finally, she quietly said, "Mom, I don't think it is about the suit." With a dawn of recognition, my mother realized her deep reservoir of grief might be motivating her aversion to the jackets—in a case of "magical thinking," she was hoping that if she did not choose a suit, then the memorial service, and the death itself, might be averted.[33] Armed with this insight, she bought the very next suit she tried on.

So too, in a qualitative study, these data can be used to make different arguments, but you need to choose. There are times when this choice requires you to draw on your courage. After all, as I discussed earlier, a good argument is based on criticism of other work. You are trying to point to a new way of thinking. But it is easy to worry that others might be offended. Some people imagine catastrophes that might await them, and it is true that writers are sometimes verbally attacked.[34] It is unusual since more often they are ignored, but it happens. At the time I was writing my first book, one of my good friends, a medical doctor, was also writing her first book. We were both fretting about aspects of the writing process. She wrote me something that I posted on my refrigerator: "In medicine, a bad day was when someone died. Until someone keels over and dies from my writing, I am not going to worry about it. I am going to keep writing." This is a valuable perspective. Poorly structured arguments and inferior writing are not desirable, but they won't kill anyone. The odds of being attacked are unclear, but if you are attacked, you will survive. Also, some people subscribe to the belief that there is no such thing as bad publicity for a piece of writing since even negative attention can draw readers. But sometimes you need to find your courage to write out your claims and explain why other, orthogonally related literatures have missed the point. You are trying to do something new. You think it is important. You want to speak in a clear voice.

Thus, once you select a pathway, you shouldn't second-guess the wisdom of your choice. Instead, just stick to the plan. And, if you have worries about holes in the argument, remember that you may be a lousy judge about the quality of your own work. At the very least, you should have someone else read the work and assess the weaknesses before you abandon an approach. In addition, remember that you can always acknowledge a limitation in a footnote, explain why it is not fatal, and refer the reader to other, relevant literature. One piece of writing cannot be perfect.

As you learn about your own writing rituals, you want to then organize your life—to the best of your ability—to facilitate your writing.[35] If your anxiety stops you from completing pieces, then seek professional help (e.g., cognitive behavioral therapy). A short-term therapeutic intervention (as few as eight visits) can be life changing. In addition, there are developmental editors who are professionals who can (for a fee) help you shape and strengthen a project. Hiring a professional editor (or even a "developmental" editor) can be liberating since that person can help you highlight your main points, streamline your argument, and bring polish to the piece.[36]

Finally, as you gain more experience, writing may seem less overwhelming and more manageable. You may write more and worry less. But if writing does not get easier, just accept it. Anxious writers, especially those who learn to manage their anxiety, can and do finish their papers, dissertations, and books. In fact, a lot of excellent writing has been done by anxious writers.

Coda

Your final writing becomes often shorter and clearer through the process of revision. Revision is a helpful part of the writing process.

Moreover, few of us are born with good writing skills. We have to learn these skills. And writing is a process of self-discovery that helps you learn your own strengths and weaknesses. (For example, I have learned that editing quotes is easier for me than writing the discussion section.)

Writing with qualitative data has special challenges. While qualitative researchers often have thousands of pages of data, there are tight constraints in written work; it cannot be too long. The harsh reality is that only a very small percentage of your field notes and interview transcripts will make it into the final piece. And you have to make countless decisions in writing. Most of those decisions do not have obvious answers since, for example, often one quote is just as compelling as another.

But your study can change people's minds in a way that is different from other forms of social science. A beautifully written piece of research based on participant observation and interviews brings people to life, and helps the reader understand the challenges people face. You are trying to use vivid, detailed, and compelling words to help the reader really understand the lives of the people you studied. And, you are trying to connect the lived experiences of these people to a broader conceptual point—so that the reader can understand why it matters. The experience of being fully drawn into a well-written work is a pleasure. Reading really good writing is similar to receiving a small gift from the author—a gift that you have undoubtedly received in your life and that you, even as a novice, can and should give to others.

10

Conclusion

Why Interviews and Participant Observation
Research Are Valuable

By providing vivid portraits of daily life, your interviews and participant observation can deepen our knowledge. These research approaches also can accomplish what other research often cannot. Notably, the studies can help us understand the challenges and experiences of people in a specific circumstance, capture unintended and unknown consequences of many policies, and richly show the impact of institutional forces on daily lives of individuals. Your research is done systematically, drawing on disciplinary standards of the social sciences, and yet each study is unique. The results are often deep, graphic, and illuminating—particularly because emphasis is not based on imposing a set of research questions, but on developing research questions that take into account the particularities of the setting. Studies also flesh out our portraits of people, and, even as they provide systematic data, are emotionally tinged. Thus, as in-depth interviews and participant observation expand our intellect and reach our hearts, the studies improve our understanding of the world. Of course, conceptual models vary across disciplines, but through documentation of empirical patterns, many researchers seek to understand how and why something occurs. If your research results alter how people think about a key issue, then the work can contribute to the creation of better policies.

By being immersed in the social world, you can create new forms of knowledge. Indeed, you can illuminate issues that are currently underplayed or ignored. In some cases, this can lead to the formation of new lines of research. Interviews and participant observation studies are more nimble than large-scale surveys as they adjust easily to changing times. While crucial for mapping social trends, longitudinal studies are constrained; questionnaires can't be too long, and it is difficult to add questions later or to deeply probe new directions. But in participant observation, you can keep showing up until you stop learning new things. Interviews also provide a setting to explore original questions. As a result, you can bring organizational processes and the lived experiences and perspectives of others to a broader audience, including policy makers. You can improve conceptualizations of key social processes at the organizational level, such as how organizations inadvertently impede workers' career advancement. The work also can spell out the experiences of others, including why patients do not comply with medical directives, or the ways in which parents' social class transmits advantages to children in education.

Furthermore, interviews and participant observation studies powerfully illustrate the complex interweaving of crucial social forces. Too often, social scientists focus on one institution—criminal justice systems, educational institutions, or the labor market. But the reality is that multiple institutions shape our lives at the same time. Interviews and participant observation are exceptionally suited to show, in rich detail, the ways in which these institutions reverberate across the lives of individuals—and often collide with one another. As such, you have access to complex, rich data on the ways social and structural forces intersect, shaping organizations, groups, and people. These data are all too rare.

As you write, you also have a crucial advantage. With your data, and your analysis, you create a narrative—a story—to help your reader profoundly understand the lived experiences of those you study. Narratives can be powerful. All of us have been moved by a book or movie where the characters stayed with us for a long time, helping us see our world in new ways or teaching us something about ourselves, thus throwing our own lives into fresh perspectives. Social science researchers following methodological guidelines are a far cry from the imagination of fiction authors or the work of many journalists. But interviewers and participant observers also use words, rather than numbers, to describe results; they use words to paint pictures. Stories stay with us.

These are not the only advantages, but the point is that by doing interviews and participant observation research you are engaging in important work that may help others—including people in positions of power—to see the world in different ways. Your work matters.

Mistakes and Hiccups Are Normal

Just as interviews and participant observation have unique contributions, doing this kind of work involves forging a new path, which will inevitably include some missteps. Indeed, in every research project I have done, partly because I was often doing something unfamiliar, I have made mistakes. I said something stupid. I aligned with the wrong person. I missed an important meeting. Mistakes are painful, and they are normal. Some are more serious than others: being rigid, closed-minded, domineering in interviewing, or unable to take feedback or to listen carefully are major challenges to conducting high-quality research. Nonetheless, even with these challenges, people can improve. It would take significant effort and small steps (possibly with professional help), but people can learn to become better listeners and become more intellectually flexible. They can improve their ability to take feedback. These are all crucial, nonnegotiable elements in a high-quality study. Fortunately, most mistakes are much more mundane, and sometimes things just don't go your way. Sometimes you catch someone on a bad day when their budget has been cut or they had a fight with a partner. Not everything that goes wrong is all about what you did.

Furthermore, mistakes can often be repaired. If a respondent is annoyed or resistant, listen to their concerns. Acknowledge what they say (without being defensive, explanative, correcting them, or attacking them). You say back to them what they said to you to make sure you got it right. You apologize, and you listen. Deference is key. Indeed, some research suggests that relationships with conflict, if repaired, can be closer.[1] Although you want to be as careful as possible, the reality is that you can withstand hiccups and still have a good outcome. It is wrong to take one bump in the road and "spin out," thinking, "This wasn't meant for me. I'm terrible. I should quit." Reflecting on how you could have behaved differently is helpful; beating yourself up is not. Rather, as in life itself, mistakes are inescapable. We learn from them, and life goes on.

The Gift of Being New

It can be hard to learn something new. You don't know what you are doing and can feel as if you are in over your head or don't belong. You don't even know what you don't know. Sometimes, in a bad moment, the entire enterprise can feel hopeless. It is challenging to be new and inexperienced.

Yet, researchers who are new to doing research have many special gifts to bring to the field—gifts that should not be underestimated. Often, you might look at things in a unique way. You aren't wedded to the established ideas and have more time to do the work. I once wrote a piece called "The Gift of Obscurity," where I discuss all of the professional obligations professors pick up as they become more senior. These obligations are important, and some are prestigious, but since time is a zero-sum enterprise, it also means that more established people have less time to collect data, read, think, and write. If you are getting started in your profession through a new project, sometimes you can really throw yourself into it; for participant observation, you can be there a lot to hang out. Even with the constraints in your life, you often have more time to work than more established scholars. This drive and amount of time in the field is truly wonderful. And, the payoff can be incredible as the nature of social life unfolds before you, revealing the true complexity of people's lives and uncovering powerful structural barriers that are rarely understood. This process can be transformative.

Studies have suggested that getting to know others—"the strength of weak ties"—can be helpful, but people vary in their skill and interest in networking as well as their access to people who can help them.[2] When I was early in my career, I was worried that I would not be successful in my field. I didn't know anyone. I was slow in producing work. But, as it turns out, there are meritocratic elements to the research process that are more important than connections or networking.[3] Blind peer review is key. Excellent work by unknown scholars is routinely published, and shoddy work by famous people is often rejected. Journal editors lose sleep if they don't have enough high-quality articles to fill an issue that they must publish; you are doing them a favor by submitting your piece. Furthermore, people are hungry to read high-quality work based on participant observation and interviews. When people read a fantastic study, they tell others to read it too. In sum, there is always room at the table for new people to enter the conversation. You have to take the first step; seek out feedback, listen to it, revise, focus, and repeat the process. Some of the best work is done by young, inexperienced scholars. Each day I look forward to reading more new, excellent work. You belong.

Doing Interviews and Participant Observation

Research experiences are journeys. All research projects have a beginning—ideally with some daydreaming of your hopes and ambitions. These dreams then confront realities of time, energy, money, interest, and possibilities. In this book I have taken you through the many different steps you may face in planning, collecting and analyzing data, and writing. Your true focus will unfold only over time, and you will have to make numerous hard decisions. Ideally you will be guided by something that has troubled you about prior research in the field and desire to make a "friendly amendment" to the literature. You are trying to improve our empirical knowledge and develop our conceptualization of key aspects of social life. Your study, modest as it may be, can be used as a springboard to address enduring, important issues. With clear writing, your findings will be useful not only to fellow academics in your field, but also to an intelligent college student who might read your work in a class or on their own. Your reader will see the details and big picture, thereby understanding why the study is needed.

All of us have had journeys in our lives, and you undoubtedly have accumulated experiences where you have developed some of the skills you will draw upon in your planned research. Beginning your own research journey can be challenging, even scary, but your new experiences will be exciting and interesting. And the journey will not go on forever; rather, journeys have a beginning, middle, and end, sprinkled with moments both difficult and wonderful.

I wish you well on your research journey.

Final Words

Faith:

- fidelity to one's promises: sincerity of intentions
- firm belief in something for which there is no proof: complete trust
- something that is believed especially with strong conviction;[1]

In some ways, doing research using participant observation and interviews is an act of faith.

To begin a project is an act of faith that there are good-hearted people who will allow you into their lives and let you get to know them.

To continue it, to go to a site over, and over, and over again, and to interview more and more people, is believing that you will eventually be able to figure out what you are doing.

To wrap up a study, to write up the results, draws on confidence that you have something to say, and that gatekeepers will think what you have to say is valuable.

To publish a work, is an act of conviction that readers will find it worth reading.

■

It would be nice if the people who will eventually love your project could be around to offer you support when you are in the middle of it.

But they aren't.

As a result, you need to find people to support you along the way.

Many people who have produced a good study have made mistakes, worried that it would not be any good, and generally stumbled their way through.

And you will too.

Acknowledgments

I am grateful to the outstanding professors I had when I was an undergraduate at the University of California, Santa Cruz, as well as those in the Department of Sociology at the University of California, Berkeley where I earned my doctorate. At the University of California, Berkeley, I learned a great deal from many faculty, but my interactions with Arlie Russell Hochschild and Michael Burawoy were especially formative. As a postdoc at Stanford, I audited a very helpful ethnography course with Shirley Brice Heath, Milbrey McLaughlin, and Lee Shulman. I also will always be indebted to Hugh "Bud" Mehan, Aaron Cicourel, and the late George McClure for taking me under their wings when I was a postdoctoral fellow and when I started my career at Southern Illinois University.

I have benefited enormously from my collaborations. Elliot Weininger deserves special mention for the countless times he has lent a friendly ear with incisive, skeptical questions. The writing group at Penn, where my advisees and I meet every three weeks to read work, has also been extremely helpful. The membership has waxed and waned over the years; I extend my thanks to Ashleigh Cartwright, Yi-lin Chiang, Sherelle Ferguson, Rita Harvey, Peter Harvey, Hyejeong Jo, Katharina Hecht, Blair Sackett, Doron Shiffer-Sebba, and Calvin Zimmerman for their comments on an earlier version of this manuscript. I also am grateful to Tylor Baldor, Amanda Barrett Cox, Jessica McCrory Calarco, Nora Gross, and Aliya Hamid Rao for reviewing an early version of this book, and to Patricia Berhau for the special role she played in my study that became *Unequal Childhoods*. Vanessa Lopes Muñoz, Karen Hansen, and Timothy Black were early champions of this project; they offered valuable comments along the way. The feedback of the anonymous reviewers and Amy Steinbugler, Benjamin Shestakofsky, Karolyn Tyson, Elena van Stee, and Marion Standefur made the book considerably better. Then, when the book was almost done, Robin Leidner and Leslie Paik graciously reviewed the entire book in a tight timeframe. Meghan Comstock and Lindsay Goldsmith-Markey also helped me by reading selected chapters. At the University of Chicago Press, Elizabeth

Branch Dyson patiently waited for this book and provided invaluable editorial advice. Other sociologists around the country talked with me about the book project and, in my moments of doubt, encouraged me to persevere.

Writing groups with colleagues are a great invention, and my writing group with Maia Cucchiara and Judith Levine has been an extraordinary resource. Over tea and with warmth, they have read the manuscript many times, asked pointed questions, and offered enthusiasm and helpful criticism in equal doses. Jon Wallace provided valuable feedback at an early stage. I am also deeply indebted to M. Katherine Mooney for her assiduous editing of selected chapters in this book and, indeed, of all of my books throughout my career. A group of talented undergraduates, headed by Chelsea Gardner, provided library assistance and proofing of the manuscript that I submitted for review; they include Caitlin Ang, Shawn Sangeun Kim, Nathaniel Redding, and Elom Vedomey. I am grateful to Mary Corrado for her careful copyediting; Joan-Erin Lareau, Andy Jimenez, Edward Stevens IV, and Hector Torres helpfully inspected the final proofs.

I am indebted to all of the researchers who have done such important research using interviews and participant observation, and I very much regret that space constraints do not permit me to name all of them or their works, but they have shaped me. Here in Philadelphia, colleagues who have played a special role in forming my thinking include Joy Charlton, Kimberly Goyette, David Karen, Josh Klugman, Demie Kurz, Daniel Laurison, Katherine McClelland, Janine Remillard, Lisa Smulyan, Amy Steinbugler, Elizabeth Useem, and Wesley Shumar. My colleagues at Penn and around the country have also been an invaluable source of support, and, for this project, particularly the ethnographers: the late Charles Bosk, David Grazian, Robin Leidner, and Benjamin Shestakofsky. Thanks to all of the people whose advice is shared in the book.

On our first date in 1994, Samuel Freeman was visibly shocked when I described how I had been doing participant observations in the homes of families with young children for the project that became *Unequal Childhoods*. He immediately informed me that he would *never* permit anyone to visit him in his home. He also plainly thought that the whole business of ethnography was extremely intrusive, and he was perplexed why anyone would agree to participate in it. Despite this remarkable difference in our world views, our marriage has been one of the best things in my life. This book is better because of him, and for his support of me. I am grateful to him, our children, and our grandchildren for the countless gifts they bring to my life.

Finally, I am indebted to my students, graduate and undergraduate, for all they have taught me. In courses and conversations, they have helped me see the research process with fresh eyes. I also am glad that they allowed me to share their hiccups in ethnographic research in this book. This book is dedicated to young scholars who hope to complete their own study one day.

Appendix to Chapter 3

Navigating the Institutional Review Board
for the Protection of Human Subjects:
Or, How to Manage the IRB Process

The IRB is needed because there are rogue researchers who will, in fact, harm subjects unless they are properly supervised and, more commonly, researchers who inadvertently create harm because they have not considered a wide enough array of possibilities. IRB officials also cite the possibility that a researcher might not sufficiently protect data. For example, a researcher may accidentally leave a backpack with data on the subway or not put proper protections on an online database containing sensitive information. The purpose of an IRB is to make sure that people who have graciously agreed to participate in research will not be identifiable and thus risk harm if someone gains access to poorly protected data. In addition, if a catastrophe happens (e.g., you are in a terrible car accident while you are conducting research, you are arrested, or some other unplanned negative event occurs), the IRB's formal approval provides documentation that you are conducting a university-approved activity. In some instances, your university may have liability since you are carrying out a university activity.

THE PROBLEM

The IRB is particularly suited to help medical researchers testing possible medicines that might harm research subjects. For the social and behavior researchers, the process is more challenging. Indeed, there is a "chicken or egg" problem with the process of beginning an ethnographic research study. You can't decide to do a study in a particular location unless you know that you can get permission to carry it out. You need permission from the people in the site and permission from the institutional review board for the protection of human subjects. But usually you cannot get permission to do the study unless you know what you are going to do.

Compounding the problem, your research questions are emergent as they develop across time in a specific setting. But passing through many key hurdles, including IRB proposals, research proposals, grant proposals, and hurdles put out by gatekeepers in organizations, requires that you state in precise terms exactly what you plan to do. As a result, it is stressful.

WHAT TO DO

Since you must have an IRB protocol on file, my advice is to do a "good faith" and "good enough" IRB application based on your best assessment of the nature of the proposed research question. (The only exception is if you are a registered student in a class and have no plans to ever publish or publicly present the results.) It is also in your best interest to have an IRB application on file since if a researcher is a bit out of compliance with what they have been approved to do, it is vastly better to have an IRB on file than to not have one. It is hard to stay perfectly in compliance with an IRB at every moment when the ethnographic research project is unfolding. Neither the researcher nor the IRB office wants to have the researcher contacting the IRB office on a daily basis to update and amend an IRB. Do the best you can with your initial submission and then on a regular basis, as the need arises, file an amendment consisting of a formal request for approval of these (inevitable) alterations. Small changes may be exempt. For example, at my university, changes in the wording of questions on an interview guide do not require an IRB amendment, but changes in the sample scripts for recruitment or consent forms would trigger an amendment as would the decision to add a new type of research subject to the protocol or add new forms of data collection. Usually those kinds of changes would happen once a semester. In a study where the data collection lasts two years, you might have three or so amendments.

BE BROAD

When you file an IRB, it should be as broad as possible. Try to anticipate anything that you might want to do in your study. You should also describe your research in highly general and abstract terms (that can incorporate developments of new research questions), rather than in ways that are overly narrow and can become rapidly obsolete. For example, I would start out requesting permission for a very basic form of observation (e.g., hanging out in a work setting, going to work meetings, going on trips, getting copies of emails, copying non-sensitive documents, joining lunch conversations, and tagging along with groups who go out to have a drink or a meal outside of the office). I would double or triple the number of people you hope to interview. (An interview guide for each interview usually needs to be submitted to IRB with the application.)

Since research questions evolve, I would state the research goals in a very general way, "I want to learn about turning points in a person's life including when young people, such as recent college graduates, are starting out in life," rather than in a precise way, "I will examine the impact of college on labor market experience." Similarly, many IRB offices allow you to ask general interview questions ("Tell me about your work") and list a series of probes (duties, like, dislike, sense of accomplishment, frustrations) that will be used in the interview. If you are going to bring a thank you gift, you should list a number of possible gifts and state their value: "Each respondent will receive a gift of less than $20, which might be flowers, food, a gift card, a picture frame, or some other token of appreciation. This gift depends on the circumstances, however, and it is possible, with some respondents, it would not be appropriate to give a gift and thus one will not be given."

Before granting approval, the IRB will often ask for written documentation of permission from the site that you plan to observe (e.g., schools, hospitals, or businesses). In addition, some institutions such as hospitals, prisons, and school districts have their own IRB process; your institution will usually require you to get approval from them. (But, in some cases, these other institutions will simply accept the approval of your IRB and not require a separate review.) Many IRBs will allow you to file an application and later add the information of where you will do the research. Or, you can put in the name of an organization where you hope to do the work. (The IRB will not contact them.) Then, there is almost always some "back and forth" with IRB officials as they ask you to revise sections, clarify questions, and correct errors. Because the IRB review can take a long time, it is best to start this process before finalizing all of the specific details of the project. You can get IRB approval for a study and then, at the last minute, substitute the name of a different organization. *It is better to put in a rough application and revise it than to delay the review process while trying to finalize all of the details.* When researchers finally meet the people they want to observe or interview, it is good to begin almost immediately. It is awkward to say, "Wonderful! Thank you! I'll be back after I get IRB approval!" IRB committees may require a brief letter from the field site as part of the application, but it is possible to get an IRB application very close to the final approval stage and supply this information just as you are ready to begin.

Before you submit your IRB application, you should find a role model of a successful IRB application at your institution. You can save yourself time if you talk to someone who is familiar with the procedures and (ideally) with the staff of your local IRB, ask that person to review it, and ask whether an IRB official can take a look at the forms you've filled out before you submit them (although they often resist this and they will tell the researcher to file an application first). Telephoning an IRB official or making a phone appointment will usually get you more information than email. Pick up the phone and call them, leave a message, and ask that they call you back.

CONSENT ISSUES

In some organizations, you can arrange for "passive consent" where one person in the organization gives approval, and then you inform everyone else about the study (and people can opt out). This is ideal. For example, I had passive consent to do classroom observations; the principal informed the parents the study was occurring; parents were given the opportunity to opt out. I visited the classroom, but I did not remove a child from a classroom or disrupt the educational activities. (I also helped out.) I needed to submit to the IRB the letter sent to the parents and the form that the principal signed. If you do not have passive consent, then, as part of the IRB application, each type of person in a study needs a separate consent form (e.g., teacher, principal, parent, and school secretary). Children need a verbal consent or "assent" form. Without parental consent or passive consent from an authorized person, children under 18 cannot be interviewed or disrupted from normal activities at childcare or schools. For everyone, verbal consent is very helpful, and it is legally allowed. You have to explain to the IRB how written consent gets in the way of the research goals. Also, you can have a separate consent box on the form that allows you to play an excerpt of a digital recording at a professional conference. (It is very powerful to have the voice of the respondent ring forth in a talk.) Some publishers have also insisted that research participants have signed permission for you to publish their information in a book (even without their real names); here they are often looking for an acknowledgment that it is possible (although unlikely) that someone may guess who they are in the book. This information can be woven into the main consent form ("I understand that the results of this study may be published in article or book form.") For participant observation, researchers need to file their best estimate of what they will be looking for in a research site (e.g., "In my observation I will look especially at how parents and teachers interact, moments of volunteering, discussions of children's academic progress, and moments of tension or conflict").

THE TIMEFRAME

Negotiating IRB conundrums is vastly easier if you are not in a hurry. Indeed, negotiating IRB is similar to passing through security checkpoints before you take an airplane trip. The process of being screened is intrusive, but virtually all travelers are ultimately permitted to begin their journeys. Yet, it is difficult to waltz through these checkpoints in a brief and expedited fashion; nor can you proceed according to your own time schedule. A good rule of thumb is to budget four to six months to get approval for an IRB application. In rare instances, in some institutions it can happen in three weeks, particularly if it is possible to make the case that you need a rush approval. Usually it is much longer. (But most granting agencies allow you to submit a proposal without IRB approval; the approval is needed before you can receive the grant.) The length of the IRB review process means that researchers need to file an IRB a semester or year before they hope to start the study. Some institutions have a catch-22: you cannot file an IRB until the dissertation proposal is approved. If that is the case, I would see whether there is an ongoing related study that you could join; your proposal would be an amendment to an ongoing study. It is not a huge favor to ask, and it can save months of time at a crucial moment in a career. Later, if desirable, you can usually file paperwork to amend the application so that you or someone else can become the principal investigator.[1] (Be sure to have a clear, direct conversation about the ownership of the data and potential coauthorship plans, however, before you begin.)

If you are short on time, file an IRB application to gain approval for one small piece of the research, such as interviewing people over eighteen years of age. (You need to frame this as the entire study.) In many institutions, interviewing adults who are not a vulnerable population through a snowball sample would be "exempt" and the IRB review is relatively brisk. This plan allows you to at least gain access to the field site and begin some aspect of the project. After getting approval, you can file an "amendment" to request approval to carry out additional research. Obtaining approval to conduct observations in a public space is also usually exempt or a fairly straightforward process.

With regard to IRB applications that need to go through a full board review, most IRB committees meet monthly during the academic year to discuss applications. Interactions with prisoners, children, patients, and other vulnerable populations always will require a full board review. Usually the board has questions about the project even after reading the IRB application. In some universities, the researcher can submit a revised application to the chair of the committee, who then has the power to approve it singlehandedly. If you are unlucky, it needs to go back to the committee for full board review. There are horror stories of IRBs thwarting researchers from doing their desired research. However, it is often possible to work it out. Even if the IRB initially forbids some aspect of the project, such as interviewing children, it is possible to revisit the topic later in the study. For example, one possibility is to do interviews with parents. Then, at the end of the interview, you can ask the adult whether you can interview or observe the children in a future (different) study. Always, however, it is important to "decouple" the parts of the study so that parents can participate in part A and then decline part B.

One resource for researchers is to get a National Institutes of Health (NIH) certificate of confidentiality, which is issued by the federal government. The certificate is a federal mandate protecting you from legal action (such as a subpoena) and certifying the confidentiality of your projects. NIH grant recipients are routinely given this protection. You also can obtain this certificate, even if you do not have any NIH funding, if you have some health-related questions in your study. (Some people deliberately add questions on health to their interview guide or observations questions so that they qualify.) Although designed for NIH grant recipients, social scientists with a "behavioral" component in the research qualify. The National Institutes of Health has clear instructions on "How to Get a Certificate of Confidentiality," including for "non-NIH funded research." This certificate is valuable in the unlikely event that someone tries to insist that you need to turn over your data to others.

Bureaucratic language aside, none of the IRB members I have met are interested in thwarting research. They just want to make sure that research is in compliance with the law. As they note, accidents happen. Thus, start early and, if you are in a hurry, start small. Share all of the information you are going to give to research participants. And always think about what you would want to know if you, your sibling, or your child were to be a participant in your research study.

Notes

CHAPTER ONE

1. The eleven institutions are a hospital, court, child welfare, disability, HIV/AIDS agency, public assistant, mental health agency, school, Medicaid, a drug treatment program, and church. Paik, *Trapped in a Maze*.

2. Newman, *Falling from Grace*.

3. See Michael Burawoy's vigorous defense of the conceptual contribution of ethnographic data in "The Extended Case Method" in the book *Ethnography Unbound*.

4. The terms *fieldwork, naturalistic studies*, and (sometimes) *field studies* generally are used interchangeably with ethnography. The term *ethnography* often includes participant observation supplemented with interviews (or, put differently, it includes both participant observation and interviews). As a result, to avoid confusion, I use the word *ethnography* sparingly in this book. Instead, I rely on the separate terms of *participant observation* and *interviews*. Both interviews and participant observation are extremely valuable strategies for doing ethnographic research. Sometimes these two methods collect similar types of information, but more often they collect distinctive data.

5. See White's 1979 introduction to the third edition. Strunk and White, *Elements of Style*, xvi.

6. See Denzin and Lincoln's comprehensive edited collection, *The Sage Handbook*. In addition, Flick and colleagues' work, *A Companion Guide to Qualitative Research*, includes among other entries, discussions of content analysis, "photography as a social science," conversation analysis, discourse analysis, and "deep-structure hermeneutics." For information about focus groups, see Krueger and Casey, *Focus Groups*. Portraiture, which blends "aesthetics and empiricism," was developed by Sara Lawrence-Lightfoot and is explicated in her book *The Art and Science of Portraiture*. See *The Discovery of Grounded Theory* for the classic 1967 statement by Glaser and Strauss. Michael Burawoy has elaborated the extended case method in many places, but see especially his 1998 article in *Sociological Theory*. See also Katz, "Analytic Induction," and Tavory and Timmermans, *Abductive Analysis*, for a comparison of grounded theory and the extended case method. In his book *Heatwave*, Klinenberg called his use of interviews, document analysis, and so forth a "social autopsy." In chapter 2, I briefly discuss online strategies, including "net" ethnography. For mixed methods, see Small, "How to Conduct a Mixed Methods Study."

7. There are countless examples of organizational studies. Among others, see Rivera, *Pedigree*; Shestakofsky, *Venture Capitalism*; Pollock, *Colormute*; Vaughan, *The Challenger Launch Decision*; and Wingfield, *Flatlining*.

8. Theoretical ideas can be valuable for researchers seeking to clarify why their studies' findings are important and for bolstering the move from a specific case to an analysis of a more general social pattern. A handbook or encyclopedia in your discipline will provide a summary of key theories. For example, in my field, *The Blackwell Encyclopedia of Sociology*, edited by Ritzer, has entries for institutional theory,

stratification theories, feminist theories, critical race theory, and so forth. A rich literature exists on how to apply theories to ethnographic research. Among others, see Skeggs, "Feminist Ethnography"; Ladson-Billings and Tate, "Toward a Critical Race Theory of Education"; Tavory and Timmermans, *Abductive Analysis*; Snow and colleagues, "Elaborating Analytic Ethnography"; Burawoy, "Empiricism and Its Fallacies;" Cicourel, *Cognitive Sociology*; and Ragin and Becker, *What Is a Case?*

9. Although interviews and participant observation are distinctly different methodological approaches, researchers who use them generally agree that these two practices share a logic that distinguishes them from statistical analysis of large data sets. There are, however, vigorous and at times bitter arguments among researchers who carry out in-depth interviews and participant observation on the relative merits of each approach. In their article "Talk Is Cheap," Colin Jerolmack and Shamus Khan launched an attack on interviewing, arguing that the attitudes people express are a poor way to understand what people actually do. Other scholars vehemently disagreed; Maynard wrote, for example, that Jerolmack and Khan "overstate the case and fail to discuss the ways in which interviews can be useful," and that they do not sufficiently acknowledge considerable evidence in the literature contradicting their claims (Maynard, "News from Somewhere, News from Nowhere," p. 211). Other dissenting scholars included Cerulo, "Reassessing the Problem," Vaisey, "The 'Atitudinal Fallacy' Is a Fallacy," DiMaggio, "Comment on Jerolmack and Khan," and Lamont and Swidler, "Methodological Pluralism," who reject "methodological tribalism."

10. It is ideal, and ethical, to establish some form of reciprocity with the people you are studying. The forms of reciprocity vary enormously. Some researchers focus on helping study participants (in small ways, for example by bringing harried medical residents small treats as Charles Bosk did, or large ways, by helping someone get into a drug treatment center as Timothy Black did) and paying people during the data collection part of the research. Additionally, by listening closely and without judgment to participants as they discuss significant life events, researchers may provide modest but meaningful help, particularly for people who have little occasion for receiving the complete, nonjudgmental attention of a trusted listener. Some researchers hope that their work, when introduced to the public sphere, will help to change how "thought leaders" approach a topic. (This is the goal I have aimed for.) Others strive to actively participate in organizational change or "participatory research" as part of their larger social justice orientation. These efforts to produce change work best in the context of an ongoing, committed relationship (rather than a "hit and run" approach). Still others, as one reviewer of this book pointed out, follow a desire to discover social patterns that, at times, "escape contemporary notions of what is politically or morally tractable" in an effort to help people see the limits of current approaches. There is not space here for a full hearing of these different strategies. The key point is that in the face of so many options regarding what to study and how to use the findings, reasonable people may disagree about the best choices.

11. In my own case, I began graduate school in 1976 at University of California, Berkeley as a shy, white woman from a middle-class family. My social position has shaped my research and trajectory just as social identities inevitably shape key aspects of the research process for all researchers. Although beyond the scope of this book, the broader literature on these issues, particularly the question of position-

ality, is voluminous. Among others, see Milner, "Race, Culture, and Researcher Positionality," Lacy, "The Missing Midde Class," and Hanson and Richards, *Harassed*. For an exposition of the hidden curriculum of graduate school see Calarco, *A Field Guide to Grad School*. See also the resources for students and faculty at the National Center for Faculty Diversity.

12. See Duneier, "Three Rules I Go By in My Ethnographic Research," on the "morally ambiguous" nature of ethnographic work; Black, *When a Heart Turns Rock Solid*, uses the term *exploitation*. See also work on feminist research including DeVault and Gross, "Feminist Qualitative Interviewing."

CHAPTER TWO

1. She was admitted for eight weeks only, but then, by helping the chaplain, she gained permission to stay for one year. Ellis, *In This Place Called*.

2. Lareau, *Unequal Childhoods*, and Hecht, "'It's the Value that We Bring.'"

3. The term "emic" is used to characterize an analysis from the perspective of the participants while "etic" uses external categories. Among others, see Tracy, *Qualitative Research Methods*, or Denzin and Lincoln, *Handbook*.

4. Both methods focus on the meaning of events to respondents. But they also differ. In-depth interviews provide a quiet, private moment for people to reflect and to share their beliefs and interpretations of key life experiences. Since interviews are less labor intensive than participant observation, the sample can be larger and more varied (thereby providing more opportunities for comparisons). On the other hand, the purpose of participant observation is to get accepted into a social setting, build trust, and be able to learn about crucial interpersonal and/or institutional dynamics. Using participant observation provides you with a deep, rich way to observe, firsthand, the rituals of daily life, the experiences people have, and their complex webs of social interaction. Participant observation is a particularly strong method for illuminating constraints that guide social action. In addition, because researchers who use this approach often focus on the discrepancy between established norms and practices and the actions of people in a particular social context, their work adds nuance to our understanding of critical issues. Participant observation studies yield deep, rich portraits of social processes that are less vulnerable to participants' desires to make themselves look good.

5. For a cross-national interview study of moral boundaries of upper-middle-class men in the US and France, see Lamont, *Money, Morals, and Manners* and *The Dignity of Working Men*. Mary Waters's *Black Identities* also is a comparative interview study. Roberto Gonzales shows the challenges of undocumented youth in *Lives in Limbo*; Vallejo's work, *Barrios to Burbs*, highlights hurdles in upward mobility for Latinx. In *Blue-Chip Black*, Lacy explores the varying approaches of the Black middle class to choosing a neighborhood. See Levine's *Ain't No Trust* for an account of why low-income mothers lack trust. See Dow, *Mothering while Black*, for an analysis of differences in how Black mothers manage child rearing; for experiential differences among immigrants, see Kasinitz et al., *Becoming New Yorkers*; and Steinbugler, *Beyond Loving*, for an exploration of differences in interracial relationships. Although unusual, some ethnographic studies do offer comparisons. See, among others, MacLeod, *Ain't No Makin' It*, and Willis, *Learning to Labor*, for comparisons of adolescent young men with blocked mobility. For studies using ethnographic methods comparing families on the gender division of labor, see Hoch-

schild and Machung, *The Second Shift*; and, on class and family life comparisons, see Cooper, *Cut Adrift*, and Lareau, *Unequal Childhoods*. For ethnographic comparison of gender and unemployment in professional families, see Rao, *Crunch Time*.

6. Many experienced researchers who use qualitative methods understand that changes are likely rather than exceptional, and dissertation committees, and others, can be flexible when the project shifts directions. Still, each situation is different. If your IRB application (described below) is sufficiently vague but accurate, it can cover these changes; otherwise, you need to file an amendment with the IRB. Ask peers or professors you trust for (confidential) guidance before deciding what to do. Methodological appendices in books often trace barriers to beginning a study; see also Contreras, "The Broken Ethnography."

7. Contreras, *The Stickup Kids*.

8. But see Handley, "The Unbearable Daintiness of Women."

9. Leidner, *Fast Food, Fast Talk*.

10. Luker, *Salsa Dancing*. (See also chapters 8 and 9.)

11. Becker, *Evidence*, p. 173.

12. Ferguson, "Ask Not What Your Mentor Can Do for You . . ."; Frye, "Bright Futures in Malawi's New Dawn"; Horvat and Antonio, "Hey, Those Shoes Are Out of Uniform"; Tyson, "Notes from the Back of the Room"; Hansen, *Not-So-Nuclear Families*; Sherman, *Uneasy Street*.

13. There are many discussions of the benefits of the comparative approach. Among others, see Bartlett and Vavrus, *Rethinking Case Study Research*.

14. See Rao, *Crunch Time*, for a study of unemployed professional workers where she interviewed the spouses and followed-up several months later; Chiang, *The Study Gods*, observed a group of students for an academic year and then did (multiple) interviews over seven years with twenty-eight of the students she had observed.

15. Lareau, "Schools, Housing, and the Reproduction of Inequality"; Weininger, "School Choice in an Urban Setting"; Lareau et al., "Structural Constraints and the School Choice Strategies of Black American Middle-Class Parents."

16. Steinbugler, personal communication; see also Krause, "Western Hegemony in the Social Sciences."

17. Duneier, "Three Rules."

18. See Stack, *All Our Kin*; Gans, *Urban Villagers*; and Liebow, *Tally's Corner*.

19. See Lupton, "Doing Fieldwork in a Pandemic"; Kozinets, *Netnography*; Ahlin and Li, "From Field Sites to Field Events"; Pink and Mackley, "Reenactment Methodologies"; Barker, "Electronic Support Groups"; Daniels et al., "STEER"; Klausen, "Tweeting the *Jihad*"; Laurier, "YouTube"; Stuart, "Code," and *Ballad of the Bullet*.

20. Urbanik and Roks, "GangstaLife."

21. Urbanik and Roks, "GangstaLife."

22. See Salmons, *Qualitative Online Interviewing*.

23. Deakin and Wakefield, "Skype Interviewing." See also Denscombe, *The Good Research Guide*, and Gray et al., "Expanding Qualitative Research."

24. The classic statement is by Merton, "Insiders and Outsiders." Among others, see Zinn, "Field Research"; Small, "De-exoticizing Ghetto Poverty"; Denzin and Lincoln, *The Sage Handbook*; Thapar-Björkert and Henry, "Reassessing the Research Relationship"; and Duneier and Back, "Voices from the Sidewalk."

25. Peshkin, "In Search of Subjectivity." There is a large literature on subjectivity and positionality; for an overview see Denzin and Lincoln, *The Sage Handbook*.

26. Rios, *Punished*, p. 15.

27. For example, if Rios wanted to interview local police officers, his history in the community may not have facilitated the same level of trust.

28. Lamont, *Money, Morals, and Manners* and *The Dignity of Working Men*.

29. In Weber's classic formulation, the goal is *verstehen*. See Weber, *The Theory of Social and Economic Organization*. In his thoughtful article on "De-exoticizing," Small translates Weber's concept to be "empathy." See Duneier's "Three Rules I Go By in My Ethnographic Research." The three rules are first, not assuming that you have trust with the people you are writing about (nor seeing it a precondition for a successful ethnography); second, making a commitment to being surprised, and being constantly aware that your social position "likely makes you blind to the very phenomena that might be useful to explain," and, third, consulting with your research subjects as well as those who once were in the position of the people you are studying. See also Zinn, "Field Research," as well as Denzin and Lincoln, *The Sage Handbook*.

30. Duneier, "Three Rules."

31. Researchers vary in terms of what (and when) they share of this process with the people they are studying. Some do "member checks"; others do not. (For member checks, see Hubbard et al., *Reform as Learning*; Duneier, *Sidewalk*; and Bloor, "Notes on Member Validation.") In general, the people you are studying don't want to know, or need to know, the "blow-by-blow" of how your research question is evolving. But, managing this process is highly individual, and it depends on what you promised them and what you feel is the right thing to do.

32. For example, Andrew Deener, in *The Problem with Feeding Cities*, provides an unusually clear account of his research journey. See also Lareau, *Home Advantage*.

33. Among the many who discuss this issue, Tavory and Timmerman usefully synthesize commonly used practices into something they call "the abductive approach." Tavory and Timmerman, *Abductive Analysis*.

34. Katz, "A Theory of Qualitative Methodology"; see also Burawoy's 1998 piece, "The Extended Case Method."

35. For example, many urban ethnographies have noted the premium low-income communities place on showing "respect." See, among others, Anderson, *Code of the Street*. Maia Cucchiara, in *Marketing Schools, Marketing Cities*, found a pattern similar to what Posey-Maddox reported in *When Middle-Class Parents Choose Urban Schools*. In both contexts, middle-class parents took over and transformed an urban school, marginalizing low-income parents. Of course, the historical moment, and the social position of the researchers (including their class, race, and academic training), may also contribute to how they "see" and interpret a setting. See also similar results for Gaztambide-Fernández, *The Best of the Best*, and Khan, *Privilege*. In addition, even though the families being observed in *Unequal Childhoods* liked some researchers better than others, the notes across the research team were very comparable in what they revealed.

36. Duneier, *Sidewalk*, the film.

37. Lincoln and Guba, *Naturalistic Inquiry*.

38. Pzreworski and Salomon, "On the Art of Writing Proposals." This guide is

also posted by other funding agencies to guide applicants. See also the criteria for peer review for journal articles.

CHAPTER THREE

1. Centers for Disease Control and Prevention, "Syphilis Study at Tuskegee."

2. Reyes, "Three Models of Transparency in Ethnographic Modeling"; Jerolmack and Murphy, "The Ethical Dilemmas and Social Scientific Trade-Offs of Masking in Ethnography"; Contreras, "Transparency and Unmasking."

3. Jessica McCrory Calarco, University of Indiana, personal communication.

4. Granovetter, "The Strength of Weak Ties."

5. Muñoz, "'Everybody Has to Think.'"

6. Ellis, *In This Place Called Prison.*

7. See the extensive literature on subjectivity and positionality, including Peshkin, "In Search of Subjectivity," and Denzin and Lincoln, *The Sage Handbook.*

8. McCambridge et al., "Systematic Review of the Hawthorne Effect."

9. Bourdieu, *Distinction.*

10. Black, *When a Heart Turns Rock Solid,* reports that he was "handed a shirt and cologne" before going out with the guys for a night of drinking since they did not care for his attire.

11. Reich and Bearman, *Working for Respect,* methodological appendix.

12. See Nordstrom and Robben, *Fieldwork under Fire;* Hanson and Richards, *Harassed;* Clancy, "I Had No Power to Say That's Not Okay"; and Johnson, "The Self at Stake."

13. Contreras, "Transparency and Unmasking" and "The Broken Ethnography."

14. An aunt (who was struggling with substance abuse) did swipe $20 from a research assistant's wallet while we were there, which was upsetting to the research assistant and embarrassed the family, but backpacks are also swiped regularly in the libraries of elite college campuses.

15. Lacy, "The Missing Middle Class."

16. See, among others, Huang, "Vulnerable Observers"; Hanson and Richards, *Harassed.*

17. Shamus Khan, personal communication; see also Hildalgo and Khan, "Blindsight Ethnography."

CHAPTER FOUR

1. See feminist critiques of interviewing for illumination of hierarchy and power in interviewing. For example, as DeVault and Gross write, posing interviewing as talking to people "neglects the dynamics of power involved in any empirical research: the hierarchical, often charged relations between researcher and informants, the politics of interpretation and representation, and the social consequences of making claims on the basis of science. Add to this picture a political commitment to feminism, and one begins to see the terrain of feminist interview research." DeVault and Gross, "Feminist Qualitative Interviewing," p. 235.

2. See, among others: Dunbar et al., "Race, Subjectivity, and the Interview Process"; DeVault and McCoy, "Institutional Ethnography."

3. There are many fine works on interviewing and doing ethnography. A partial list includes Weiss, *Learning from Strangers;* Gerson and Damaske, *The Science and*

Art of Interviewing; Emerson et al., *Writing Ethnographic Fieldnotes*; Nippert-Eng, *Watching Closely*; and Hammersley and Atkinson, *Ethnography*.

4. Simmel, "The Stranger," p. 404.

5. Hunt, "Police Account of Normal Force"; Sierra- Arévalo, "American Policing and the Danger Imperative."

6. Observations of the family are difficult to arrange. Doing interviews ahead of time is one method for gaining access: Lareau and Rao, "Intensive Family Observations."

7. See chapter 2 for a discussion of remote data collection.

8. Worst yet, his eyes had been dilated at the doctor's appointment, and he wore huge dark sunglasses, so I couldn't see much of his face and thereby lost crucial emotional responses when he told me about his family.

9. Sackett, "Ghosting."

10. If your IRB deems your research exempt, you may not need a consent form, or there may be someone in the organization who signs the consent form for others. Even here, however, it is good to reaffirm verbally so that people know that they are being studied.

11. I am grateful to Keith McIntosh, Temple University, for this idea.

12. Lareau, "My Wife Can Tell Me Who I Know."

13. See chapters 1, 2, and 8 for discussions of the formulation of a research question as well as many books on qualitative research. This study, and the key themes, grew out of our interest in the work of Pierre Bourdieu, especially the concept of cultural capital, and the impact of upward mobility on cultural tastes. Curl, Lareau, and Wu, "Cultural Conflict."

14. Ferguson, "Getting on the Inside Track."

15. Ferguson and Lareau, "Upwardly Mobile."

16. See, among others, The General Social Survey, Panel Study of Income Dynamics, and Early Childhood Education Study. The National Opinion Research Center (NORC) and the National Center for Educational Statistics are two of many highly reputable sources for surveys.

17. In *Making Ends Meet* Edin and Lein reveal that once the low-income women became convinced the interviewers were not there to scrutinize them or take away government benefits, the women were eager to talk. In my own work, I have found a similar pattern.

18. I find the question, "How much was your downpayment?" as overly direct. I think it smooths it out a bit to ask the question with a percentage.

19. Tourangeau and Smith, "Asking Sensitive Questions"; Krumpal, "Determinants of Social Desirability Bias"; Gerbert and colleagues, "When Asked, Patients Tell"; Perlis and colleagues, "Audio-Computerized Self-Interviewing Versus Face-to-Face Interviewing"; Phillips and colleagues, "A Systematic Review." Others use a "screener-survey" when they are recruiting people to the study; they ask sensitive questions at that point. I have worried about the impact of screen-surveys on recruitment, since it is creating more work for the respondent, but some researchers have found them to be very helpful.

20. https://otranscribe.com/.

21. Levine, "Landing a Job."

CHAPTER FIVE

1. It's hard work to make a lengthy, in-depth interview seem like a polite—or better yet—a friendly exchange of information. This takes practice and skill. You might find it helpful to look at television news programs where a television anchor coordinates among four or five news commentators; or you could watch talk shows whose hosts interview a wide variety of people. Listening to radio interview programs such as *Fresh Air* (distributed by National Public Radio) also might prove useful.

2. Shamus Khan, personal communication.

3. My research focused on how parents from different classes and racial backgrounds raise children. I was particularly interested in differences in children's leisure activities, parents' and children's language use in the home, and parents' intervention in children's experiences in organizations such as schools, clinics, and doctors' offices.

4. As the Principal Investigator, I had undertaken a month-long training of the research assistants, but this first-semester doctoral student had not taken any undergraduate or graduate courses on research methods. Arguably I should have provided her with more training or met with her more often. If I were to do it again, I would hire students who had already completed at least one semester of course work on qualitative methods; have all interviews transcribed within 24 hours of being completed (provided the project had sufficient funding); and during the project's early stage, spend an hour each week carefully reviewing each interview conducted by each novice assistant until we both were satisfied with the student's baseline interviewing skills.

5. Her husband is the father of Tyrec and his older sister, Anisha, who is in seventh grade. Ms. Taylor also has an older son (Malcolm) who is out of school and has a different father.

6. As I explain in *Unequal Childhoods*, middle-class parents saw their children as a project and they engaged in "concerted cultivation" to develop children's talents and skills, while working-class parents, including Ms. Taylor, used scarce resources to care for their children, but then presumed that children would spontaneously grow and thrive. Ms. Taylor saw football as something Tyrec wanted to do, which took a lot of her time, but not something to help him develop a set of valuable life skills. See Lareau, *Unequal Childhoods*.

7. Howie Becker, 2021, http://www.howardsbecker.com/articles/improv.html.

CHAPTER SIX

1. For ethnographies on one group, see, among others, Gans, *Urban Villagers*; Liebow, *Tally's Corner*; Contreras, *Stickup Kids*; Ho, *Liquidated*; Black, *When a Heart Turns Rock Solid*; and Stack, *All Our Kin*. See also Viscelli, *The Big Rig*, for an ethnography of truck drivers; Hoang, *Dealing in Desire*, for a study of nightclubs and financial transactions in Vietnam; and many school ethnographies including, Cucchiara, *Marketing Cities, Marketing Schools*, and Chiang, *The Study Gods*. For books based on both observations and interviews, see among others, Clair, *Privilege and Punishment*; Pattillo's works, *Black Picket Fences* and *Black on the Block*, on the heterogenous nature of Black communities and neighborhood life; Ferguson, *Bad Boys*, on the role of public schools in shaping Black masculinity, and many others.

For example, in her article, "Police Accounts of Normal Force," Jennifer Hunt demonstrates how, despite a formal training program that showed new officers how to prevent police brutality, workplace dynamics among police officers continued to reward the use of excessive force. See also Sierra-Arévalo, "American Policing and the Danger Imperative."

2. Most methods book discuss coding, for a particularly helpful discussion of "open" and "focused" coding see Emerson et al., *Writing Ethnographic Fieldnotes*.

3. There is a vast literature on this question. Among others, see Katz, "On Becoming an Ethnographer"; Hoang, "Dealing in Desire"; Lofland et al., "Analyzing Social Settings"; and Denzin and Lincoln, *Handbook*.

4. Muñoz, "Everybody Has to Think."

5. See Lareau and Rao, "Intensive Family Observations."

6. Bringing the basketball did change the dynamic, and I considered not doing it for that reason, but, I rationalized that the kids did have a basketball from time to time, just not regularly. I also bought and brought some water guns since this was a common game the children enjoyed. I would not have brought in any items for a game they did not normally play.

7. From Harvey and Lareau, "Studying Children Using Ethnography."

8. Ellis, *In This Place Called Prison*.

9. There is an extensive literature on the kinds of relationships participant observers develop with people they study, and many forge deep, long-term relationships. In some cases, however, relationships can be disrupted when the participants read the results of the research. In my own case, some families were fine with the study, and I continue to be in touch with them around the holidays, but since others were hurt and angry, they severed our tie. I have a lengthy discussion of this issue in the appendix to the second edition of *Unequal Childhoods*.

10. I had been told that by someone, but I never investigated it. There may have been a way to work out the university regulations, but, given my research goals, it was a moot point.

11. Sackett, "The Instability of Stable Poverty."

12. For a longer discussion of this issue, see Lareau and Rao, "Intensive Family Observations."

13. Peshkin, "In Search of Subjectivity."

14. Malinowski, *A Diary in the Strict Sense of the Term*. Lansdown's essay on Malinowski's diary notes that "it was his incuriosity that was most at issue in the *Diary*, where his nastiness seemed practically triumphant, where his own feelings preoccupied him more than almost anything else at hand, where his powers of sympathy were almost completely in abeyance." See Lansdown, "Crucible or Centrifuge?" Curiosity is a crucial aspect of ethnographic research, and readers were shocked by Malinowski's lack of it.

15. Research shows that educators uniformly try to talk parents into the value of reasoning with their children (rather than hitting them), but some parents, particularly low-income parents, are likely to disagree. See, among others, Cucchiara, "'Sometimes You Have to Pop Them,'" as well as Lareau, *Unequal Childhoods*.

16. Heath, "The Madness(es) of Reading and Writing Ethnography"; Duneier, "Three Rules," p. 100.

17. Katz, "Analytic Induction."

18. Muñoz, personal communication, and "Everyone Has to Think."

19. For discussions of researchers' role in the field see Lofland et al., *Analyzing*

Social Settings; Denzin and Lincoln, *The Sage Handbook*; Hanson and Richards, *Harassed*; and countless methodological appendices including Lareau and Shultz, *Journeys through Ethnography*. See also journals such as *Ethnography*, *Qualitative Sociology*, and *Journal of Contemporary Ethnography*.

20. Whyte, *Street Corner Society*.

21. See Erickson, "Taught Cognitive Learning."

22. Lareau and Rao, "Intensive Family Observations."

23. Lareau and Rao, "Intensive Family Observtions."

CHAPTER SEVEN

1. Harvey, "Make Sure You Look Someone in the Eye."

2. Anderson, *A Place on the Corner*, p. 196.

3. The research assistants and I carried openly displayed recorders during our visits and had consent to use them. This excerpt is from Lareau, *Unequal Childhoods*, 2nd ed., p. 96. This moment was painful for the research assistant to observe. On non-intervention, see *Unequal Childhoods*, 358–359.

4. Black, *When a Heart Turns Rock Solid*, pp. 110 and 112.

5. Mears, *Pricing Beauty*, p. 108.

6. Robin Leidner, *Fast Food*, p. 71.

7. Ferguson, "Getting on the Inside Track."

8. Harvey and Lareau, "Studying Children Using Ethnography."

9. http://www.psychpage.com/learning/library/assess/feelings.html.

10. In this case, I had carried out months of observation in two public schools in different classrooms. Then, I conducted about one-half of the interviews with the parents in 88 families. Faced with the reality that it was impossible for me, alone, to conduct the study I wanted to carry out, I worked with a racially diverse team of research assistants. First, they helped me finish the interviews. Then, guided by conceptual categories, we selected families who represented key themes that had emerged from the interviews. I then contacted the families (by mail or in person) to broach the idea of them being in an intensive family observation. If they agreed, the families were visited, usually daily, for about three weeks. They were paid for their participation (after the study was over) the equivalent of $500 in current dollars. I asked 19 families, and a total of 12 families ultimately agreed—divided equally by class (middle-class, working-class, and poor) and race (white and African-American). Given the intrusiveness of the request, I considered this to be a reasonable response rate. I did fieldwork in all of the families; I was the lead fieldworker in two families. See Elliott et al., "Marking Time in Ethnography."

11. Lareau and Rao, "Intensive Family Observations."

12. In the end of the study, as we were completing data collection on two families, Patricia Berhau (a white woman who was an advanced doctoral student who worked as a project manager) took over the task of nightly phone calls with the research assistants for three weeks while I was out of the country. She did not, however, conduct field visits in the families.

CHAPTER EIGHT

1. Srivastava and Hopwood, "A Practical Iterative Framework."

2. Of course, others have their own suggestions for how to proceed with data analysis. See among others, Tavory and Timmermans on *Abductive Analysis*, Tim-

mermans and Tavory, *Surprise!*, Miles et al. on *Qualitative Data Analysis*, and Luker, *Salsa Dancing*, as well as handbooks, textbooks, and works on specific genres such as grounded theory or institutional ethnography.

3. See Snow and colleagues, "Elaborating Analytic Ethnography," for a discussion of different theoretical ambitions you might have, such as discovery, extension, and reconstruction. Lofland, "Analytic Ethnography"; Abramson and Gong, *Beyond the Case*; and Luker, *Salsa Dancing*.

4. Burawoy, "Empiricism and Its Fallacies," italics in the original, pp. 51 and 52.

5. For an especially thoughtful work on the process of framing a study, see Luker, *Salsa Dancing*.

6. See Grazian, "Thank God It's Monday."

7. Becker, *Writing for Social Scientists*.

8. Anderson, *Code of the Street*.

9. See the case of Leona Helmsley where her dog was given a trust fund with 12 million dollars when she died in 2007, and the dog was part of the legal dispute over the will. Jeffrey Toobin, "Rich Bitch."

10. Fresh Air Interview, "To Make *The Godfather* His Way."

11. There were significant ethical concerns. The immigrants were a vulnerable population. Since it was an undergraduate class project that he did not ever intend to publish, he did not need the permission of the institutional review board for the protection of human subjects. But, given their vulnerability, it was very problematic for him—an inexperienced student doing a class project—to write notes that could be subject to subpoena or could create harm to the immigrants he observed. When I learned of his specific goals, I called a meeting where I expressed my concerns; he agreed to focus on the experience of legal immigrants.

12. See Hofferth, "Response Bias."

13. Dow, *Mothering while Black*.

14. A heavily revised version of this paper was subsequently published. Lareau et al., "Parental Challenges."

15. This statement was made by an editor in charge of accepting or rejecting book manuscripts for a university press; the editor found that authors could be crestfallen when they learned there was still more work to do with a book manuscript.

16. See Luker, *Salsa Dancing*, p. 19.

17. See Timmermans and Tavory, *Surprise!*, for an in-depth analysis of coding.

18. Hirsch and Khan, *Sexual Citizens*, p. 287.

19. Miles et al., *Qualitative Data Analysis*.

20. Among others, see Erickson, "Taught Cognitive Learning," and Emerson et al., *Writing Ethnographic Fieldnotes*. Other people have different approaches. Jessica Calarco offers her own "flexible coding," developed in conversation with a piece by Deterding and Waters, "Flexible Coding of In-Depth Interviews."

21. But see Emerson et al., *Writing Ethnographic Field Notes*, pp. 186–194. They note that editing is not simple: "The process of editing is not a straightforward, simple task. On the one hand, shortening and editing for clarity forwards the smooth flow of the overall ethnographic story: too long excerpts bog the reader down in extraneous details. On the other hand, one always loses some of the vividness and complexity of the original fieldnotes in the editing process" (p. 192).

22. Lareau, *Unequal Childhoods*, p. 171.

23. Not all of the edited quotes end up in the text. Sometimes I simply move key

phrases into the text, set off by quotation marks, and then eliminate the quote. It can be more efficient. If you reserve your quotes for more vivid phrases it can help the "color" and flow of the manuscript.

CHAPTER NINE

1. Kidder and Todd, *Good Prose*, p. xviii.

2. Of course, journalists are often excellent writers. In addition, there sometimes is overlap between very detailed journalistic accounts (such as long-form articles or radio stories) and in-depth interview and participant observation studies. But, in general, social science research follows different methodological steps than journalism, including a review by an institutional review board (IRB), a longer period and broader scope of data collection, a systematic comparison and analysis of the relevant social processes, and a theoretical contribution to a disciplinary body of ideas. By contrast, journalistic studies tend to be conducted rapidly, to be more superficial analytically, to be more focused on a single case, and to be newsworthy in the short term rather than intended to contribute to long-term abstract understanding of social mechanisms. For excellent journalistic accounts of topics similar to those of social science researchers see, among others, Jason DeParle's books *American Dream* and *A Good Provider*. But, these works were not reviewed by an IRB, do not have a transparent methodology, and do not offer systematic comparison typical of work done by social scientists. His goals also do not include improving our abstract models.

3. See Lamont, *Bird by Bird*; or Elbow's *Writing without Teachers*.

4. See Webster's Dictionary definition of "iterative" at https://www.merriam-web ster.com/dictionary/iterative.

5. The piece was by Anyon, "Social Class and School Knowledge," which used observational data to show social class differences in the use of the curriculum across five elementary schools.

6. Belcher, *Writing Your Journal Article*.

7. Becker, *Writing for Social Scientists*, p. 53. Becker quotes a "model introduction" at length.

8. Hughes is quoted in Becker's book *Writing for Social Scientists*, p. 50.

9. Mantz, "The Best Crime Tours of Chicago"; and Chicago Architecture Center, "Get Your Guide."

10. Luker, *Salsa Dancing*.

11. As Benjamin Shestakofsky pointed out to me, the literature review argument mirrors the structure of the findings. But, instead of presenting quotes as evidence, you are presenting other articles to support your claims. Then, after you briefly describe the articles, you provide an interpretation.

12. Rawls, *Lectures on the History of Political Philosophy*. Rawls quotes John Stuart Mills in his review of Alfred Sedgwick: "A Doctrine is not Judged At All Until It Is Judged in Its Best Form," xiii.

13. Ferrell, *Billionaire Wilderness*, has a response rate of 18 percent, but he also did not routinely ask respondents about the size of their net worth.

14. Czajka and Beyler, "Declining Response Rates."

15. Lareau, *Unequal Childhoods*, p. 31. See Blair-Loy, *Competing*, to see a table highlighting her thesis.

16. Barshay, "Evidence Increases for Reading on Paper."

17. See Jessica Calarco's blog posting "Revise and Resubmit," http://www.jessica calarco.com/tips-tricks/2021/1/2/revise-and-resubmit.

18. Still, others strongly believe in including longer passages with the voices of participants to more fully represent the voice and agency of the participant. But since the author (not the participant) selects the longer passage for the reader, the role of the researcher cannot be avoided. Moreover, it can be hard for readers to grasp the point of a long quote (since a long quote often has many points), and the reader can become confused or distracted from the author's purpose.

19. Lareau and Horvat, "Moments of Social Inclusion and Exclusion."

20. Lareau, "Cultural Knowledge and Social Inequality."

21. The article provides a longer account of the events. Lareau, "Cultural Knowledge and Social Inequality."

22. Peshkin, "In Search of Subjectivity," p. 17.

23. As Margery Wolf writes, some "critics question the very possibility of ethnographers representing the experience of another culture, and others question the ethics of even attempting to do so, seeing the process itself as an exercise in colonialism (domination)." *A Thrice-Told Tale*, p. 5.

24. Levine, *Ain't No Trust*.

25. Lieberman, "Why You Procrastinate."

26. Luker, *Salsa Dancing*, p. 22.

27. I thank Sarah Quinn for bringing to my attention this quote from Ann Patchett, "The Getaway Car."

28. For example, some universities support writing groups. See National Center for Faculty Development and Diversity. There are numerous blogs on writing, including http://getalifephd.blogspot.com/.

29. Writers like to write about writing, so there is an extensive literature on this topic. For an unusually rigid writing schedule, see *Clockwork Muse* by Zerubavel. See also Valian, "Learning to Work."

30. Korkki, "To Stay on Schedule, Take a Break."

31. See Becker, *Writing for Social Scientists*. He offers an analogy of walking into a room in a cocktail party where a number of small group conversations are going on in different subfields. Which one do you want to join?

32. One reader pointed out that this anxiety can be justified since ethnographers can get feedback from reviewers that they admire the data, but "don't think the framing works."

33. See Joan Didion's moving memoir following her husband's sudden death, *The Year of Magical Thinking*.

34. See the attacks by Steven Lubet, who has never done ethnography, on a number of scholars: *Interrogating Ethnography*.

35. See Zerubavel, *Clockwork Muse*; and Valian, "Learning to Work."

36. Developmental editors are especially helpful when you have a lot of data, and you have an argument, but you need help clarifying your main points. Since I have a bad habit of repeating myself (as well as changing tenses within one paragraph), I have worked with a professional editor in all of my major works (including selected chapters for this book). For most of my career, I paid for it out of my personal funds. Since editors are always thanked in the acknowledgments, it is a good place to look for one. Or, if you ask around, you will discover people who use editors (including many international scholars). It is a good idea to do a sample edit with

the editor before making a commitment. You need to feel safe with the person, and you want to feel as if the person's input makes your writing better. Otherwise, find another editor.

CHAPTER TEN

1. Although the specifics are different in research relationships, the principle of acknowledgment and "repair" for couples offers valuable insights: Benson, "Repair Is the Secret Weapon."

2. McPherson et al., "Birds of a Feather."

3. This is not to say that there are no benefits to people from positions of privilege. See Calarco's *Field Guide for Grad School* for an exposition of the "hidden curriculum" in university life. But the point is that people can bring fresh insights. To give only one example, Matt Desmond's family lost their home when he was young. As a young scholar he brought fresh insight to this understudied arena of social life in *Evicted*. Many other studies followed.

FINAL WORDS

1. See definition of "faith" in the Merriam-Webster Dictionary, https://www.merriam-webster.com/dictionary/faith.

APPENDIX TO CHAPTER 3

1. In some universities, students are not allowed to be the principal investigator of their studies; only a faculty member can play this role. Still, students usually fill out all of the paperwork and then ask the faculty member to review it. Also, many departments require the approval of a departmental chair or representative for an IRB application. It is critical to give these representatives a heads-up that an application will be crossing their path in the coming week. If the department representative is out of town, it is reasonable to ask whether there is someone who could sign during this absence. Students have been known to have their applications delayed by two weeks as they wait to gain a departmental signature; a prior arrangement can trim these delays.

Bibliography

Abramson, Corey M., and Neil Gong, eds. *Beyond the Case: The Logics and Practices of Comparative Ethnography*. New York: Oxford University Press, 2020.

Abrego, Leisy J. *Sacrificing Families: Navigating Laws, Labor, and Love across Borders*. Palo Alto: Stanford University Press, 2014.

Ahlin, Tanja, and Fangfang Li. "From Field Sites to Field Events: Creating the Field with Information and Communication Technologies (ICTs)." *Medicine, Anthropology and Theory* 6, no. 2 (2019): 1–24.

Anderson, Elijah. *A Place on the Corner*. Chicago: University of Chicago Press, 2003.

Anyon, Jean. "Social Class and School Knowledge." *Curriculum Inquiry* 11, no. 1 (1981): 3–42.

Barker, Kristin K. "Electronic Support Groups, Patient-Consumers, and Medicalization: The Case of Contested Illness." *Journal of Health and Social Behavior* 49, no. 1 (2008): 20–36.

Barnes, Riché J. Daniel. *Raising the Race: Black Career Women Redefine Marriage, Motherhood, and Community*. New Brunswick: Rutgers University Press, 2015.

Barshay, Jill. "Evidence Increases for Reading on Paper Instead of Screens." *Hechinger Report*, August 12, 2019. https://hechingerreport.org/evidence -increases-for-reading-on-paper-instead-of-screens/.

Bartlett, Lesley, and Frances Vavrus. *Rethinking Case Study Research: A Comparative Approach*. London: Taylor & Francis, 2016.

Becker, Howard S. *Evidence*. Chicago: University of Chicago Press, 2017.

Becker, Howard S. *Writing for Social Scientists: How to Start and Finish Your Thesis, Book, or Article*. 3rd ed. Chicago: University of Chicago Press, 2020.

Belcher, Wendy Laura. *Writing Your Journal Article in Twelve Weeks: A Guide to Academic Publishing Success*. Chicago: University of Chicago Press, 2019.

Benson, Kyle. 2017. "Repair Is the Secret Weapon of Emotionally Connected Couples." *Gottman Institute*, February 23, 2017. https://www.gottman.com /blog/repair-secret-weapon-emotionally-connected-couples/.

Black, Timothy. *When a Heart Turns Rock Solid: The Lives of Three Puerto Rican Brothers On and Off the Streets*. New York: Pantheon, 2009.

Black, Timothy, and Sky Keyes. *It's a Setup: Fathering from the Social and Economic Margins*. New York: Oxford University Press, 2020.

Blair-Loy, Mary. *Competing Devotions: Career and Family among Women Executives*. Cambridge, MA: Harvard University Press, 2003.

Bloor, Michael J. "Notes on Member Validation." In *Contemporary Field Research: A Collection of Readings*, edited by Robert M. Emerson, 156–172. 1st ed. Prospect Heights, IL: Waveland Press, 1983.

Bosk, Charles L. *Forgive and Remember: Managing Medical Failure*. Chicago: University of Chicago Press, 2003.

Bourdieu, Pierre. *Distinction: A Social Critique of the Judgement of Taste*. Translated by Richard Nice. Harvard University Press, 1984.

Bourgois, Philippe. *In Search of Respect: Selling Crack in El Barrio*. Cambridge: Cambridge University Press, 2003.

Briggs, Jean L. *Never in Anger*. Cambridge, MA: Harvard University Press, 1971.

Burawoy, Michael. "Empiricism and Its Fallacies." *Contexts* 18, no. 1 (2019): 47–53.

Burawoy, Michael. "The Extended Case Method." In *Ethnography Unbound: Power and Resistance in the Modern Metropolis*, edited by Michael Burawoy, Alice Burton, Ann Arnett Ferguson, Kathryn J. Fox, Joshua Gamson, Nadine Gartrell, Leslie Hurst, Charles Kurzman, Leslie Salzinger, Josepha Schiffman, and Shiori Ui, 271–287. Berkeley: University of California Press, 1991.

Burawoy, Michael. "The Extended Case Method." *Sociological Theory* 16, no. 1 (1998): 4–33.

Burawoy, Michael. *Manufacturing Consent: Changes in the Labor Process under Monopoly Capitalism*. Chicago: University of Chicago Press, 1982.

Burton, Linda M. "Black Grandparents Rearing Children of Drug-Addicted Parents: Stressors, Outcomes, and Social Service Needs." *Gerontologist* 32, no. 6 (1992): 744–751.

Burton, Linda M. "Seeking Romance in the Crosshairs of Multiple Partner Fertility: Ethnographic Insights on Low-Income Urban and Rural Mothers." *Annals of the American Academy of Political and Social Science* 654, no. 1 (2014): 185–212.

Calarco, Jessica McCrory. *A Field Guide to Grad School: Uncovering the Hidden Curriculum*. Princeton: Princeton University Press, 2020.

Calarco, Jessica McCrory. "Flexible Coding for Field Notes." *Scatterplot*, March 29, 2019. https://scatter.wordpress.com/2019/03/29/flexible-coding-for-field -notes/.

Calarco, Jessica McCrory. *Negotiating Opportunities: How the Middle Class Secures Advantages in School*. New York: Oxford University Press, 2018.

Cartwright, Ashleigh. "'He Was Always Neat and Clean': Observing Selection Practices for Racial Integration to Reconsider Bourdieu's Cultural Capital Framework." Unpublished manuscript, University of Pennsylvania, 2021.

Centers for Disease Control and Prevention. "U.S. Public Health Service Syphilis Study at Tuskegee." Accessed May 26, 2020. https://www.cdc.gov/tuskegee /index.html.

Cerulo, Karen A. "Reassessing the Problem: Response to Jerolmack and Khan." *Sociological Methods & Research* 43, no. 2 (2014): 219–226.

Charmaz, Kathy. *Constructing Grounded Theory*. 2nd ed. London: Sage Publications, 2014.

Cherlin, Andrew J., Tera R. Hurt, Linda M. Burton, and Diane M. Purvin. "The Influence of Physical and Sexual Abuse on Marriage and Cohabitation." *American Sociological Review* 69, no. 6 (2004): 768–789.

Chiang, Yi-Lin. *The Study Gods: How the New Chinese Elite Prepare for Global Competition*. Princeton: Princeton University Press, forthcoming.

Chiang, Yi-Lin. "When Things Don't Go as Planned: Cultural Capital and Parental Strategies for Elite College Enrollment." *Comparative Education Review* 62, no. 4 (2018): 503–521.

Cicourel, Aaron V. *Cognitive Sociology: Language and Meaning in Social Interaction*. New York: Free Press, 1974.

Clair, Matthew. *Privilege and Punishment: How Race and Class Matter in Criminal Court*. Princeton: Princeton University Press, 2020.

Clancy, Kate. "I Had No Power to Say That's Not Okay: Reports of Harassment and Abuse in the Field." *Scientific American*, April 13, 2013. https://blogs.scientificamerican.com/context-and-variation/safe13-field-site-chilly-climate-and-abuse/.

Clergy, Orly. *The New Noir: Race, Identity, and Diaspora in Black Suburbia*. Berkeley: University of California Press, 2019.

Collins, Randall. *Interaction Ritual Chains*. Princeton: Princeton University Press, 2005.

Contreras, Randol. "The Broken Ethnography: Lessons from an Almost Hero." *Qualitative Sociology* 42, no. 2 (2019): 161–179.

Contreras, Randol. *The Stickup Kids: Race, Drugs, Violence, and the American Dream*. Berkeley: University of California Press, 2013.

Contreras, Randol. "Transparency and Unmasking Issues in Ethnographic Crime Research: Methodological Considerations." *Sociological Forum* 34, no. 2 (2019): 293–312.

Cooper, Marianne. *Cut Adrift: Families in Insecure Times*. Berkeley: University of California Press, 2014.

Coppola, Francis Ford. "To Make *The Godfather* His Way, Francis Ford Coppola Waged a Studio Battle." Interview by Terry Gross. *Fresh Air*, NPR, November 15, 2016. https://www.npr.org/2016/11/15/502250244/to-make-the-godfather-his-way-francis-ford-coppola-waged-a-studio-battle.

Cucchiara, Maia. "Culture and Control in Alternative Schools." Unpublished manuscript, Temple University, 2021.

Cucchiara, Maia Bloomfield. *Marketing Schools, Marketing Cities: Who Wins and Who Loses When Schools Become Urban Amenities*. Chicago: University of Chicago Press, 2013.

Cucchiara, Maia. "'Sometimes You Have to Pop Them': Conflict and Meaning-Making in a Parenting Class." *Social Problems*, spaa045, https://doi-org.proxy.library.upenn.edu/10.1093/socpro/spaa045.

Curl, Heather, Annette Lareau, and Tina Wu. "Cultural Conflict: The Implications of Changing Dispositions among the Upwardly Mobile." *Sociological Forum* 33, no. 4 (2018): 877–899.

Czajka, John L., and Amy Beyler. "Declining Response Rates in Federal Surveys: Trends and Implications." *Mathematica Policy Research*, June 15, 2016. https://aspe.hhs.gov/system/files/pdf/255531/Decliningresponserates.pdf.

Daniels, Nicola, Patricia Gillen, Karen Casson, and Iseult Wilson. "STEER: Factors to Consider When Designing Online Focus Groups Using Audiovisual Technology in Health Research." *International Journal of Qualitative Methods* 18 (2019): 1–11.

Davis, Dána-Ain, and Christa Craven. *Feminist Ethnography: Thinking through Methodologies, Challenges, and Possibilities*. Lanham: Rowman & Littlefield, 2016.

Deakin, Hannah, and Kelly Wakefield. "Skype Interviewing: Reflections of Two PhD Researchers." *Qualitative Research* 14, no. 5 (2013): 603–616.

Deener, Andrew. *The Problem with Feeding Cities: The Social Transformation of Infrastructure, Abundance, and Inequality in America*. Chicago: University of Chicago Press, 2020.

Deener, Andrew. "The Uses of Ambiguity in Sociological Theorizing: Three Ethnographic Approaches." *Sociological Theory* 35, no. 4 (2017): 359–379.

Deener, Andrew. *Venice: A Contested Bohemia in Los Angeles*. Chicago: University of Chicago Press, 2012.

Denscombe, Martyn. *The Good Research Guide: For Small-Scale Social Research Projects*. London: McGraw-Hill Education, 2014.

Denzin, Norman K., and Yvonna S. Lincoln. *The Sage Handbook of Qualitative Research*. 5th ed. Thousand Oaks, CA: Sage Publications, 2018.

DeParle, Jason. *American Dream: Three Women, Ten Kids, and a Nation's Drive to End Welfare*. New York: Penguin Books, 2005.

DeParle, Jason. *A Good Provider Is One Who Leaves: One Family and Migration in the 21st Century*. New York: Penguin Books, 2019.

Desmond, Matthew. *Evicted: Poverty and Profit in the American City*. New York: Crown, 2016.

Deterding, Nicole, and Mary C. Waters. "Flexible Coding of In-Depth Interviews: A Twenty-First Century Approach." *Sociological Methods & Research* 20, no. 10 (2018): 1–32.

DeVault, Marjorie L. *Feeding the Family: The Social Organization of Caring as Gendered Work*. Chicago: University of Chicago Press, 1994.

DeVault, Marjorie L., and Glenda Gross. "Feminist Qualitative Interviewing: Experience, Talk, and Knowledge." In *Handbook of Feminist Research*, edited by Sharlene Nagy Hesse- Biber, 206–235. Thousand Oaks, CA: Sage Publications, 2012.

DeVault, Marjorie L., and Liza McCoy. "Institutional Ethnography: Using Interviews to Investigate Ruling Relations." In *Handbook of Interview Research: The Complexity of the Craft*, edited by Jaber Gubrium and James Holstein, 751–776. Thousand Oaks, CA: Sage Publications, 2002.

Didion, Joan. *The Year of Magical Thinking*. New York: Vintage, 2007.

DiMaggio, Paul. "Comment on Jerolmack and Khan, 'Talk Is Cheap' Ethnography and the Attitudinal Fallacy." *Sociological Methods & Research* 43, no. 2 (2014): 232–235.

Dow, Dawn Marie. *Mothering while Black: Boundaries and Burdens of Middle-Class Parenthood*. Berkeley: University of California Press, 2019.

DuBois, W. E. B. *The Philadelphia Negro: A Social Study*. New York: Oxford University Press, 2007.

Dunbar, Christopher, Dalia Rodriguez, and Laurence Parker. "Race, Subjectivity, and the Interview Process." In *Handbook of Interview Research: Context and Method*, edited by Jaber F. Gubrium and James A. Holstein, 279–298. Thousand Oaks, CA: Sage Publications, 2002.

Duneier, Mitchell. "How Not to Lie with Ethnography." *Sociological Methodology* 41, no. 1 (2011): 1–11.

Duneier, Mitchell. *Sidewalk*. New York: Farrar, Straus and Giroux, 1999.

Duneier, Mitchell. *Sidewalk*. Directed by Barry Alexander Brown. Princeton: Princeton University, 2010. https://www.thesociologicalcinema.com/videos /ethnographic-filmmaking-and-the-social-life-of-a-sidewalk.

Duneier, Mitchell. "Three Rules I Go By in My Ethnographic Research on Race and Racism." In *Researching Race and Racism*, edited by M. Bulmer and J. Solomos, 92–102. New York: Routledge, 2004.

Duneier, Mitchell, and Les Back. "Voices from the Sidewalk: Ethnography and Writing Race." *Ethnic and Racial Studies* 29, no. 3 (2006): 543–565.

Duneier, Mitchell, Philip Kasinitz, and Alexandra Murphy, eds. *The Urban Ethnography Reader*. London: Oxford University Press, 2014.

Edin, Kathryn, and Maria Kefalas. *Promises I Can Keep: Why Poor Women Put Motherhood before Marriage*. Berkeley: University of California Press, 2005.

Edin, Kathryn, and Laura Lein. *Making Ends Meet: How Single Mothers Survive Welfare and Low-Wage Work*. New York: Russell Sage Foundation, 1997.

Elbow, Peter. *Writing without Teachers*. 2nd ed. New York: Oxford University Press, 1998.

Elliott, Sinikka, Josephine Ngo McKelvy, and Sarah Bowen. "Marking Time in Ethnography: Uncovering Temporal Dispositions." *Ethnography* 18, no. 4 (2016): 1–21.

Ellis, Rachel. *In This Place Called Prison: Religion and the Social World of Incarcerated Women*. Berkeley: University of California Press, forthcoming.

Emdin, Christopher. *For White Folks Who Teach in the Hood … and the Rest of Y'all Too: Reality Pedagogy and Urban Education*. Boston: Beacon Press, 2016.

Emerson, Robert, ed. *Contemporary Field Research: Perspectives and Formulations*. 2nd ed. Long Grove, IL: Waveland Press, 2001.

Emerson, Robert M., Rachel I. Fretz, and Linda L. Shaw. *Writing Ethnographic Fieldnotes*. 2nd ed. Chicago: University of Chicago Press, 2011.

Erickson, Frederick. "Definition and Analysis of Data from Videotape: Some Research Procedures and Their Rationales." In *Handbook of Complementary Methods in Education Research*, edited by J. Green, G. Camilli, and P. Elmore, 177–192. Washington, DC: American Educational Research Association, 2006.

Erickson, Frederick. "Taught Cognitive Learning in Its Immediate Environments: A Neglected Topic in the Anthropology of Education." *Anthropology & Education Quarterly* 13, no. 2 (1982): 149–180.

Erikson, Kai. *Everything in Its Path: Destruction of Community in the Buffalo Creek Flood*. New York: Simon and Schuster, 1976.

Evans, Shani Adia. *The World Was Ours: Race, Memory, and Resistance in the Gentrified City*. Chicago: University of Chicago Press, forthcoming.

Ferguson, Ann Arnett. *Bad Boys: Public Schools in the Making of Black Masculinity*. Ann Arbor: University of Michigan Press, 2010.

Ferguson, Sherelle. "Ask Not What Your Mentor Can Do for You … : The Role of Reciprocal Exchange in Maintaining Student-Teacher Mentorships." *Sociological Forum* 33, no. 1 (2018): 211–233.

Ferguson, Sherelle. "Getting on the Inside Track: Class, Race, and Undergraduates' Academic Engagement." Unpublished paper, University of Pennsylvania, 2021.

Ferguson, Sherelle, and Annette Lareau. "Upwardly Mobile College Students' Estrangement: The Importance of Peers." Unpublished paper, 2021.

Ferrell, Justin. *Billionaire Wilderness: The Ultra-wealthy and the Remaking of the American West*. Princeton: Princeton University Press, 2020.

Fine, Gary Alan. *Gifted Tongues: High School Debate and Adolescent Culture.* Princeton: Princeton University Press, 2001.

Fine, Gary Alan. *Kitchens: The Culture of Restaurant Work.* Berkeley: University of California Press, 2008.

Fine, Gary Alan. *With the Boys: Little League Baseball and Preadolescent Culture.* Chicago: University of Chicago Press, 1987.

Flick, Uwe, Ernst Von Kardorff, and Ines Steinke. *A Companion to Qualitative Research.* Thousand Oaks, CA: Sage Publications, 2004.

Frye, Margaret. "Bright Futures in Malawi's New Dawn: Educational Aspirations as Assertions of Identity." *American Journal of Sociology* 117, no. 6 (2012): 1565–1624.

Gans, Herbert J. *The Urban Villagers: Group and Class in the Life of Italian-Americans.* Updated ed. New York: Simon and Schuster, 1982.

Gaztambide-Fernández, Rubén A. *The Best of the Best: Becoming Elite at an American Boarding School.* Cambridge, MA: Harvard University Press, 2009.

Gerbert, Barbara, Amy Bronstone, Steven Pantilat, Stephen McPhee, Michael Allerton, and James Moe. "When Asked, Patients Tell: Disclosure of Sensitive Health-Risk Behaviors." *Medical Care* 37, no. 1 (1999): 104–111.

Gerson, Kathleen, and Sarah Damaske. *The Science and Art of Interviewing.* New York: Oxford University Press, 2020.

Get Your Guide. "Chicago Architecture Center." https://www.getyourguide.com /discovery/chicago-architecture-center-l97377/?utm_force=0.

Glaser, Barney G., and Anselm L. Strauss. *The Discovery of Grounded Theory: Strategies for Qualitative Research.* Chicago: Aldine, 1967.

Goffman, Erving. *The Presentation of Self in Everyday Life.* New York: Double Day Anchor Books, 1959.

Golann, Joanne W. *Scripting the Moves: Culture and Control in a "No Excuses" Urban Charter School.* Princeton: Princeton University Press, 2021.

Gonzales, Roberto G. *Lives in Limbo: Undocumented and Coming of Age in America.* Berkeley: University of California Press, 2016.

Granovetter, Mark S. "The Strength of Weak Ties." *American Journal of Sociology* 78, no. 6 (1973): 1360–1380.

Gray, Lisa M., Gina Wong-Wylie, Gwen R. Rempel, and Karen Cook. "Expanding Qualitative Research Interviewing Strategies: Zoom Video Communications." *Qualitative Report* 25, no. 5 (2020): 1292–1301.

Grazian, David. *American Zoo: A Sociological Safari.* Princeton: Princeton University Press, 2015.

Grazian, David. "Thank God It's Monday: Manhattan Coworking Spaces in the New Economy." *Theory and Society* 49, no. 5–6 (2020): 991–1019.

Gross, Nora. "Brothers in Grief: The Stages of Grieving for a School and Its Students Following Three Shooting Deaths of Black Teenage Boys." PhD diss., University of Pennsylvania, 2020.

Gubrium, Jaber F., and James A. Holstein, eds. *Handbook of Interview Research.* Thousand Oaks, CA: Sage Publications, 2001.

Hammersley, Martyn, and Paul Atkinson. *Ethnography: Principles in Practice.* 3rd ed. London: Routledge, 2007.

Handley, Kate. "The Unbearable Daintiness of Women Who Eat with Men."

Society Pages, December 27, 2015. https://thesocietypages.org/socimages
/2015/12/27/the-unbearable-daintiness-of-women-who-eat-with-men/.

Hansen, Karen. *Not-So-Nuclear Families: Class, Gender, and Networks of Care.*
New Brunswick: Rutgers University Press, 2004.

Hanson, Rebecca, and Patricia Richards. *Harassed: Gender, Bodies, and
Ethnographic Research.* Berkeley: University of California Press, 2019.

Harvey, Peter. "Make Sure You Look Someone in the Eye: Socialization and
Classed Comportment in Two Elementary Schools." Unpublished paper. Paper
presented at the American Sociological Association Annual Meeting, 2018.

Harvey, Peter Francis, and Annette Lareau. "Studying Children Using
Ethnography: Heightened Challenges and Balancing Acts." *Bulletin of
Sociological Methodology/Bulletin de Méthodologie Sociologique* 146, no. 1
(2020): 16–36. [published in English and French]

Head, Emma. "The Ethics and Implications of Paying Participants in Qualitative
Research." *International Journal of Social Research Methodology* 12, no. 4
(2009): 335–344.

Heath, Shirley Brice. "The Madness(es) of Reading and Writing Ethnography."
Anthropology & Education Quarterly 24, no. 3 (1993): 256–268.

Heath, Shirley Brice. *Ways with Words: Language, Life and Work in Communities
and Classrooms.* Cambridge: Cambridge University Press, 1983.

Hecht, Katharina. "'It's the Value That We Bring': Performance Pay and Top
Income Earners' Perceptions of Inequality." Unpublished paper, London School
of Economics, 2021.

Hesse-Biber, Sharlene Nagy, ed. *Handbook of Feminist Research: Theory and
Praxis.* 2nd ed. Thousand Oaks, CA: Sage Publications, 2011.

Hidalgo, Anna, and Shamus Khan. "Blindsight Ethnography and Exceptional
Moments." *Etnografia e Ricerca Qualitativa* 2, no. 2 (2020): 185–193.

Hirsch, Jennifer S., and Shamus Khan. *Sexual Citizens: A Landmark Study of Sex,
Power, and Assault on Campus.* New York: WW Norton & Company, 2020.

Ho, Karen. *Liquidated: An Ethnography of Wall Street.* Durham, NC: Duke
University Press, 2009.

Hoang, Kimberly Kay. *Dealing in Desire: Asian Ascendancy, Western Decline, and
the Hidden Currencies of Global Sex Work.* Berkeley: University of California
Press, 2015.

Hochschild, Arlie Russell, and Anne Machung. *The Second Shift: Working
Families and the Revolution at Home.* Rev. ed. New York: Penguin, 2012.

Hofferth, Sandra. L. "Response Bias in a Popular Indicator of Reading to
Children." *Sociological Methodology* 36, no. 1 (2006): 301–315.

Horvat, Erin McNamara, and Anthony Lising Antonio. "'Hey, Those Shoes Are
Out of Uniform': African American Girls in an Elite High School and the
Importance of Habitus." *Anthropology & Education Quarterly* 30, no. 3 (1999):
317–342.

Huang, Mingwei. "Vulnerable Observers: Notes on Fieldwork and Rape."
Chronicle of Higher Education, October 12, 2016. https://www.chronicle
.com/article/Vulnerable-Observers-Notes-on/238042.

Hubbard, Lea Ann, Mary Kay Stein, and Hugh Mehan. *Reform as Learning:
School Reform, Organizational Culture, and Community Politics in San Diego.*
Routledge, 2013.

Hunt, Jennifer. "Police Accounts of Normal Force." *Urban Life* 13, no. 4 (1985): 315–341.

Jerolmack, Colin. *Up to Heaven and Down to Hell: Fracking, Freedom, and Community in an American Town*. Princeton: Princeton University Press, 2021.

Jerolmack, Colin, and Shamus Khan. "Talk Is Cheap: Ethnography and the Attitudinal Fallacy." *Sociological Methods & Research* 43, no. 2 (2014): 178–209.

Jerolmack, Colin, and Alexandra K. Murphy. "The Ethical Dilemmas and Social Scientific Trade-Offs of Masking in Ethnography." *Sociological Methods & Research* 48, no. 4 (2017): 801–827.

Jo, Hyejeong. "Diverging Paths: Three Essays on the Transitions of Working-Class Young People in South Korea." PhD diss., University of Pennsylvania, 2017. ProQuest: 10690671.

Johnson, Alix. "The Self at Stake: Thinking Fieldwork and Sexual Violence." *Savage Minds*, March 16, 2016. https://savageminds.org/2016/03/16/the-self-at-stake-thinking-fieldwork-and-sexual-violence/.

Jones, Nikki. *Between Good and Ghetto: African American Girls and Inner-City Violence*. New Brunswick: Rutgers University Press, 2009.

Kaplan, Elaine Bell. *Not Our Kind of Girl: Unravelling the Myths of Black Teenage Motherhood*. Berkeley: University of California Press, 1997.

Kasinitz, Philip, John H. Mollenkopf, and Mary C. Waters, eds. *Becoming New Yorkers: Ethnographies of the New Second Generation*. New York: Russell Sage Foundation, 2004.

Katz, Jack. "Analytic Induction." In *International Encyclopedia of the Social and Behavioral Sciences*, edited by Neil and Paul B. Baltes, 480–484. Oxford: Pergamon Press, 2001.

Katz, Jack. "Armor for Ethnographers." *Sociological Forum* 34, no. 1 (2019): 264–275.

Katz, Jack. "On Becoming an Ethnographer." *Journal of Contemporary Ethnography* 48, no. 1 (2019): 16–50.

Katz, Jack. "A Theory of Qualitative Methodology: The Social System of Analytical Fieldwork." In *Contemporary Field Research*, edited by Robert Emerson, 127–148. Prospect Heights, IL: Waveland Press, 1983.

Khan, Shamus. *Privilege: The Making of an Adolescent Elite at St. Paul's School*. William G. Bowen Series 56. Princeton: Princeton University Press, 2012.

Khan, Shamus. "The Subpoena of Ethnographic Data." *Sociological Forum 34*, no. 1 (2019): 253–263.

Kidder, Tracy, and Richard Todd. *Good Prose: The Art of Nonfiction*. New York: Random House, 2013.

Klausen, Jytte. "Tweeting the *Jihad*: Social Media Networks of Western Foreign Fighters in Syria and Iraq." *Studies in Conflict & Terrorism* 38, no. 1 (2015): 1–22.

Klinenberg, Eric. *Heat Wave: A Social Autopsy of Disaster in Chicago*. Chicago: University of Chicago Press, 2002.

Korkki, Phyllis. "To Stay on Schedule, Take a Break." *New York Times*, June 16, 2012. https://www.nytimes.com/2012/06/17/jobs/take-breaks-regularly-to-stay-on-schedule-workstation.html.

Kozinets, Robert V. "The Field behind the Screen: Using Netnography for

Marketing Research in Online Communities." *Journal of Marketing Research* 39 (2002): 61–72.

Kozinets, Robert V. *Netnography: Redefined.* 2nd ed. Thousand Oaks, CA: Sage Publications, 2015.

Krause, Monika. "'Western Hegemony' in the Social Sciences: Fields and Model Systems." *Sociological Review* 64, no. 2 (2016): 194–211.

Krueger, Richard A., and Mary Anne Casey. *Focus Groups: A Practical Guide for Applied Research.* Thousand Oaks, CA: Sage Publications, 2014.

Krumpal, Ivar. "Determinants of Social Desirability Bias in Sensitive Surveys: A Literature Review." *Quality & Quantity* 47, no. 4 (2013): 2025–2047.

Lacy, Karyn R. *Black like Me.* New York: Russell Sage Foundation, forthcoming.

Lacy, Karyn R. *Blue-Chip Black: Race, Class, and Status in the New Black Middle Class.* Berkeley: University of California Press, 2007.

Lacy, Karyn R. "The Missing Middle Class: Race, Suburban Ethnography and the Challenges of 'Studying Up.'" In *Urban Ethnography: Legacies and Challenges, Research in Urban Sociology,* vol. 16, edited by Richard E. Ocejo and Ray Hutchinson, 143–155. Bingley, UK: Emerald Publishing, 2019.

Ladson-Billings, Gloria, and William F. Tate. "Toward a Critical Race Theory of Education." *Teachers College Record* 97, no. 1 (1995): 47–68.

Lamont, Anne. *Bird by Bird: Some Instructions on Writing and Life.* New York: Anchor, 1995.

Lamont, Michèle. *The Dignity of Working Men: Morality and the Boundaries of Race, Class, and Immigration.* Cambridge, MA: Harvard University Press, 2002.

Lamont, Michèle. *Money, Morals, and Manners: The Culture of the French and the American Upper-Middle Class.* 2nd ed. Chicago: University of Chicago Press, 1999.

Lamont, Michèle, and Ann Swidler. "Methodological Pluralism and the Possibilities and Limits of Interviewing." *Qualitative Sociology* 37, no. 2 (2014): 153–171.

Lane, Jeffrey. "The Digital Street: An Ethnographic Study of Networked Street life in Harlem." *American Behavioral Scientist* 60, no. 1 (2015): 43–58.

Langford, David R. "Developing a Safety Protocol in Qualitative Research Involving Battered Women." *Qualitative Health Research* 10, no. 1 (2000): 133–142.

Lansdown, Richard. "Crucible or Centrifuge? Bronislaw Malinowski's *A Diary in the Strict Sense of the Term.*" *Configurations* 22, no. 1 (2014): 29–55.

Lareau, Annette. "Cultural Knowledge and Social Inequality." *American Sociological Review* 80, no. 1 (2015): 1–27.

Lareau, Annette. "The Gift of Obscurity." *Footnotes* 25 (May/June 1997). https://sociology.sas.upenn.edu/people/annette-lareau.

Lareau, Annette. *Home Advantage: Social Class and Parental Intervention in Elementary Education.* 2nd ed. Lanham: Rowman & Littlefield Publishers, 2000.

Lareau, Annette. "My Wife Can Tell Me Who I Know: Methodological and Conceptual Problems in Studying Fathers." *Qualitative Sociology* 23, no. 4 (2000): 407–433.

Lareau, Annette. "Schools, Housing, and the Reproduction of Inequality:

Experiences of White and African-American Suburban Parents." In *Choosing Homes, Choosing Schools*, edited by Annette Lareau and Kimberly Goyette, 169–206. New York: Russell Sage Foundation, 2014.

Lareau, Annette. *Unequal Childhoods: Class, Race, and Family Life.* 2nd ed. Berkeley: University of California, 2011.

Lareau, Annette, and Vanessa Lopes Muñoz. "'You're Not Going to Call the Shots': Structural Conflict between Parents and a Principal in a Suburban Elementary School." *Sociology of Education* 85, no 3 (2012): 201–218.

Lareau, Annette, and Erin McNamara Horvat. "Moments of Social Inclusion and Exclusion: Race, Class, and Cultural Capital in Family-School Relationships." *Sociology of Education* 72, no. 1 (1999): 37–53.

Lareau, Annette, and Aliya Hamid Rao. "Intensive Family Observations: A Methodological Guide." *Sociological Methods & Research* (April 2020). doi:10.1177/0049124120914949.

Lareau, Annette, and Jeffrey Shultz. *Journeys through Ethnography: Realistic Accounts of Fieldwork.* Boulder: Westview, 1996.

Lareau, Annette, Elliot B. Weininger, and Amanda Barrett Cox. "Parental Challenges to Organizational Authority in an Elite School District: The Role of Cultural, Social, and Symbolic Capital." *Teachers College Record* 120, no. 1 (2018): 1–46.

Lareau, Annette, Elliot Weininger, and Catherine Warner. "Structural Constraints and the School Choice Strategies of Black American Middle-Class Parents." *British Journal of Sociology of Education* 42, no. 4 (2021).

LaRossa, Ralph. "Thinking about the Nature and Scope of Qualitative Research." *Journal of Marriage and Family* 74, no. 4 (2012a): 678–687.

LaRossa, Ralph. "Writing and Reviewing Manuscripts in the Multidimensional World of Qualitative Research." *Journal of Marriage and Family* 74, no. 4 (2012b): 643–659.

Laurier, Eric. "YouTube: Fragments of a Video-Tropic Atlas." *Area* 48, no. 4 (2016): 488–495.

Lawrence-Lightfoot, Sara, and Jessica Hoffman Davis. *The Art and Science of Portraiture.* San Francisco: Jossey-Bass, 1997.

Leidner, Robin. *Fast Food, Fast Talk: Service Work and the Routinization of Everyday Life.* Berkeley: University of California Press, 1993.

Levine, Judith A. *Ain't No Trust: How Bosses, Boyfriends, and Bureaucrats Fail Low-Income Mothers and Why It Matters.* Berkeley: University of California Press, 2013.

Levine, Judith A. "Landing a Job: Moving from College to Employment in the New Economy." Unpublished manuscript, Temple University, 2020.

Lieberman, Charlotte. "Why You Procrastinate (It Has Nothing to Do with Self-Control)." *New York Times*, March 25, 2019. https://www.nytimes.com/2019/03/25/smarter-living/why-you-procrastinate-it-has-nothing-to-do-with-self-control.html.

Liebow, Elliot. *Tally's Corner.* Boston: Little, Brown, and Company, 1967.

Lincoln, Yvonna S., and Egon G. Guba. *Naturalistic Inquiry.* Newbury Park, CA: Sage Publications, 1985.

Lofland, John. "Analytic Ethnography: Features, Failings, and Futures." *Journal of Contemporary Ethnography* 24, no. 1 (1995): 30–67.

Lofland, John, David A. Snow, Leon Anderson, and Lyn H. Lofland. *Analyzing Social Settings: A Guide to Qualitative Observation and Analysis*. 4th ed. Belmont: Wadsworth Publishing, 2005.

Lubet, Steven. *Interrogating Ethnography: Why Evidence Matters*. New York: Oxford University Press, 2018.

Luker, Kristin. *Salsa Dancing into the Social Sciences: Research in the Age of the Info-Glut*. Cambridge, MA: Harvard University Press, 2009.

Lupton, Deborah, ed. "Doing Fieldwork in a Pandemic (Crowd-Sourced Document)." 2020. https://nwssdtpacuk.files.wordpress.com/2020/04/doing-fieldwork-in-a-pandemic2-google-docs.pdf.

Lynd, Robert Staughton, and Helen Merrell Lynd. *Middletown: A Study in American Culture*. New York: Harcourt Brace, 1965.

MacLeod, Jay. *Ain't No Makin' It: Aspirations and Attainment in a Low-Income Neighborhood*. London: Routledge, 2018.

Malinowski, Bronislaw. *A Diary in the Strict Sense of the Term*. Palo Alto: Stanford University Press, 1989.

Mantz, Annalise. "The Best Crime Tours of Chicago." *Timeout*, March 26, 2018. https://www.timeout.com/chicago/things-to-do/best-crime-tours-of-chicago.

Matthews, Stephen A., James E. Detwiler, and Linda M. Burton. "Geo-ethnography: Coupling Geographic Information Analysis Techniques with Ethnographic Methods in Urban Research." *Cartographica* 40, no. 4 (2005): 75–90.

Maynard, Douglas W. "News from Somewhere, News from Nowhere: On the Study of Interaction in Ethnographic Inquiry." *Sociological Methods & Research* 43, no. 2 (2014): 210–218.

McCambridge, Jim, John Witton, and Diana R. Elbourne. "Systematic Review of the Hawthorne Effect: New Concepts Are Needed to Study Research Participation Effects." *Journal of Clinical Epidemiology* 67, no. 3 (2014): 267–277.

McPherson, Miller, Lynn Smith-Lovin, and James M. Cook. "Birds of a Feather: Homophily in Social Networks." *Annual Review of Sociology* 27, no. 1 (2001): 415–444.

McTavish, Jill R., Melissa Kimber, Karen Devries, Manuela Colombini, Jennifer C. D. MacGregor, C. Nadine Wathen, Arnav Agarwal, and Harriet L. MacMillan. "Mandated Reporters' Experiences with Reporting Child Maltreatment: A Meta-synthesis of Qualitative Studies." *BMJ Open* 7, no. 10 (2017).

Mears, Ashley. *Pricing Beauty: The Making of a Fashion Model*. Berkeley: University of California Press, 2011.

Mears, Ashley. *Very Important People: Status and Beauty in the Global Party Circuit*. Princeton: Princeton University Press, 2020.

Menjívar, Cecilia. *Fragmented Ties: Salvadoran Immigrant Networks in America*. Berkeley: University of California Press, 2000.

Merton, Robert K. "Insiders and Outsiders: A Chapter in the Sociology of Knowledge." *American Journal of Sociology* 78, no. 1 (1972): 9–47.

Miles, Matthew B., A. Michael Huberman, and Johnny Saldana. *Qualitative Data Analysis: A Methods Sourcebook*. 3rd ed. Thousand Oaks, CA: Sage Publications, 2014.

Milner, H. Richard. "Race, Culture, and Researcher Positionality: Working Through Dangers Seen, Unseen, and Unforeseen." *Educational Researcher* 36, no. 7 (2007): 388–400.

Morgenstern, Julie. *Organizing from the Inside Out: The Foolproof System for Organizing Your Home, Your Office and Your Life.* New York: Holt, 2004.

Muñoz, Vanessa Lopes. "'Everybody Has to Think—Do I Have Any Peanuts and Nuts in My Lunch?' School Nurses, Collective Adherence, and Children's Food Allergies." *Sociology of Health and Illness* 40, no. 4 (2018): 603–622.

Murphy, Kate. *You're Not Listening: What You're Missing and Why It Matters.* New York: Celadon Books, 2019.

National Institutes of Health. "Certificates of Confidentiality (CoC)—Human Subjects." *Policy & Compliance, Human Subjects, NIH Central Resource for Grants and Funding Information, U.S. Department of Health and Human Services.* Washington, DC. Accessed May 26, 2020. https://grants.nih.gov/policy/humansubjects/coc.html.

Newman, Katherine S. *Falling from Grace: Downward Mobility in the Age of Affluence.* Berkeley: University of California Press, 1999.

Nippert-Eng, Christena. *Watching Closely: A Guide to Ethnographic Observation.* London: Oxford University Press, 2015.

Nordstrom, Carolyn, and Antonius C. G. M. Robben, eds. *Fieldwork under Fire: Contemporary Studies of Violence and Culture.* Berkeley: University of California Press, 1995.

Paik, Leslie. *Trapped in a Maze: How Social Control Institutions Drive Family Poverty and Inequality.* Berkeley: University of California Press, forthcoming.

Patchett, Ann. "The Getaway Car: A Practical Memoir about Writing and Life." In *This Is the Story of a Happy Marriage,* 19–60. London: Bloomsbury, 2013.

Pattillo, Mary. *Black on the Block: The Politics of Race and Class in the City.* Chicago: University of Chicago Press, 2010.

Pattillo, Mary. *Black Picket Fences: Privilege and Peril among the Black Middle Class.* 2nd ed. Chicago: University of Chicago Press, 2013.

Perlis, Theresa E., Don C. Des Jarlais, Samuel R. Friedman, Kamyar Arasteh, and Charles F. Turner. "Audio-Computerized Self-Interviewing Versus Face-to-Face Interviewing for Research Data Collection at Drug Abuse Treatment Programs." *Addiction* 99, no. 7 (2004): 885–896.

Peshkin, Alan. "In Search of Subjectivity—One's Own." *Educational Researcher* 17, no. 7 (1988): 17–21.

Phillips, Anna E., Gabriella B. Gomez, Marie-Claude Boily, and Geoffrey P. Garnett. "A Systematic Review and Meta-analysis of Quantitative Interviewing Tools to Investigate Self-Reported HIV and STI Associated Behaviours in Low- and Middle-Income Countries." *International Journal of Epidemiology* 39, no. 6 (2010): 1541–1555.

Pink, Sarah, and Kerstin Leder Mackley. "Reenactment Methodologies for Everyday Life Research: Art Therapy Insights for Video Ethnography." *Visual Studies* 29, no. 2 (2014): 146–154.

Pollock, Mica. *Colormute: Race Talk Dilemmas in an American School.* Princeton: Princeton University Press, 2009.

Posey-Maddox, Linn. *When Middle-Class Parents Choose Urban Schools: Class,*

Race, and the Challenge of Equity in Public Education. Chicago: University of Chicago Press, 2014.

Psych Page. "List of Feeling Words." Psychpage.com. Accessed May 31, 2020. http://www.psychpage.com/learning/library/assess/feelings.html.

Pugh, Allison J. "What Good Are Interviews for Thinking about Culture? Demystifying Interpretive Analysis." *American Journal of Cultural Sociology* 1, no. 1 (2013): 42–68.

Pzreworski, Adam, and Frank Salomon. "On the Art of Writing Proposals." *Social Science Research Council,* [1988] 1995 rev., accessed May 26, 2020. https://www.ssrc.org/publications/view/the-art-of-writing-proposals/.

Ragin, Charles C., and Howard Saul Becker, eds. *What Is a Case? Exploring the Foundations of Social Inquiry.* Cambridge: Cambridge University Press, 1992.

Rao, Aliya Hamid. *Crunch Time: How Married Couples Confront Unemployment.* Berkeley: University of California Press, 2020.

Rawls, John. *Lectures on the History of Political Philosophy.* Edited by Samuel Freeman. Cambridge, MA: Harvard University Press, 2008.

Ray, Victor. "A Theory of Racialized Organizations." *American Sociological Review* 84, no. 1 (2019): 26–53.

Reich, Adam, and Peter Bearman. *Working for Respect: Community and Conflict at Walmart.* New York: Columbia University Press, 2018.

Reich, Jennifer A. *Calling the Shots: Why Parents Reject Vaccines.* New York: NYU Press, 2016.

Reich, Jennifer A. *Fixing Families: Parents, Power, and the Child Welfare System.* New York: Routledge, 2005.

Reyes, Victoria. "Three Models of Transparency in Ethnographic Research: Naming Places, Naming People, and Sharing Data." *Ethnography* 19, no. 2 (2018): 204–226.

Richards, Pamela. "Risk." In *Writing for the Social Sciences: How to Start and Finish Your Thesis, Book, or Article,* 3rd ed., edited by Howard S. Becker, 98–109. Chicago: University of Chicago Press, 2020.

Rios, Victor M. *Punished: Policing the Lives of Black and Latino Boys.* New York: NYU Press, 2011.

Ritzer, George, ed. *The Blackwell Encyclopedia of Sociology,* vol. 1479. New York: Blackwell Publishing, 2007.

Rivera, Lauren A. *Pedigree: How Elite Students Get Elite Jobs.* Princeton: Princeton University Press, 2016.

Rubin, Lillian B. *Worlds of Pain: Life in the Working-Class Family.* New York: Basic Books, 1976.

Sackett, Blair. "Ghosted: Disappearance in Qualitative Research in the Digital Era." Unpublished paper, University of Pennsylvania, 2021.

Sackett, Blair. "The Instability of Stable Poverty: Economic Shocks, Network Shocks, and Economic Insecurity in a Refugee Camp." Unpublished paper, 2021.

Sackett, Blair, and Annette Lareau. *Seeking Refuge, Finding Inequality.* Berkeley: University of California Press, forthcoming.

Salmons, Janet. *Qualitative Online Interviewing: Strategies, Design, and Skills.* 2nd ed. Thousand Oaks, CA: Sage Publications, 2015.

Sánchez-Jankowski, Martín. *Islands in the Street: Gangs and American Urban Society.* Berkeley: University of California Press, 1991.

Scheper-Hughes, Nancy. *Death without Weeping: The Violence of Everyday Life in Brazil.* Berkeley: University of California Press, 1993.

Sherman, Rachel. *Uneasy Street: The Anxieties of Affluence.* Princeton: Princeton University Press, 2019.

Shestakofsky, Benjamin J. *Venture Capitalism: Startups, Technology, and the Future of Work.* Unpublished book manuscript, University of Pennsylvania, 2021.

Shiffer-Sebba, Doron. "Trust Fund Families: Government Policy and Elite Social Reproduction." Unpublished paper, University of Pennsylvania, 2021.

Shklovski, Irina, and Janet Vertesi. "'Un-Googling': Research Technologies, Communities at Risk and the Ethics of User Studies in HCI." In *The 26th BCS Conference on Human Computer Interaction* (2012): 1–4.

Sierra-Arévalo, Michael. "American Policing and the Danger Imperative." *Law & Society Review* 55, no. 1 (2021): 70–103.

Simmel, George. "The Stranger." In *The Sociology of Georg Simmel*, translated by Kurt Wolff, 402–408. New York: Free Press, [1908] 1950.

Skeggs, Beverly. "Feminist Ethnography." In *Handbook of Ethnography*, edited by Paul Atkinson, Amanda Coffey, Sara Delamont, John Lofland, and Lyn Lofland, 426–442. Sage Publications, 2001. https://www.doi.org/10.4135/9781848608337.

Small, Mario L. "De-exoticizing Ghetto Poverty: On the Ethics of Representation in Urban Ethnography." *City & Community* 14, no. 4 (2015): 352–358.

Small, Mario Luis. "'How Many Cases Do I Need?' On Science and the Logic of Case Selection in Field-Based Research." *Ethnography* 10, no. 1 (2009): 5–38.

Small, Mario Luis. "How to Conduct a Mixed Methods Study: Recent Trends in a Rapidly Growing Literature." *Annual Review of Sociology* 37 (2011): 57–86.

Small, Mario Luis. *Someone to Talk To.* New York: Oxford University Press, 2017.

Small, Mario Luis. *Unanticipated Gains: Origins of Network Inequality in Everyday Life.* New York: Oxford University Press, 2009.

Smiley, Jane. "Five Writing Tips: Jane Smiley." *Publishers Weekly*, October 3, 2014. https://www.publishersweekly.com/pw/by-topic/industry-news/tip-sheet/article/64221–5-writing-tips-jane-smiley.html.

Snow, David A., Calvin Morrill, and Leon Anderson. "Elaborating Analytic Ethnography: Linking Fieldwork and Theory." *Ethnography* 4, no. 2 (2003): 181–200.

Srivastava, Prachi, and Nick Hopwood. "A Practical Iterative Framework for Qualitative Data Analysis." *International Journal of Qualitative Methods* 8, no. 1 (2009): 76–84.

Stacey, Judith. "Can There Be a Feminist Ethnography?" *Women's Studies International Forum* 11, no. 1 (1988): 21–27.

Stack, Carol B. *All Our Kin: Strategies for Survival in a Black Community.* New York: Harper and Row, 1975.

Steinbugler, Amy C. *Beyond Loving: Intimate Racework in Lesbian, Gay, and Straight Interracial Relationships.* Oxford: Oxford University Press, 2012.

Strauss, Anselm L. *Qualitative Analysis for Social Scientists.* Cambridge: Cambridge University Press, 1987.

Strunk, William, Jr., and E. B. White. *The Elements of Style.* 3rd ed. New York: Penguin, 2005.

Stuart, Forrest. *Ballad of the Bullet: Gangs, Drill Music, and the Power of Online Infamy.* Princeton: Princeton University Press, 2020.

Stuart, Forrest. "Code of the Tweet: Urban Gang Violence in the Social Media Age." *Social Problems* 67, no. 2 (2020): 191–207.

Tavory, Iddo, and Stefan Timmermans. *Abductive Analysis: Theorizing Qualitative Research.* Chicago: University of Chicago Press, 2014.

Thapar-Björkert, Suruchi, and Marsha Henry. "Reassessing the Research Relationship: Location, Position and Power in Fieldwork Accounts." *International Journal of Social Research Methodology* 7, no. 5 (2004): 363–381.

Timmermans, Stefan, and Iddo Tavory. *Surprise! Abductive Analysis in Action.* Chicago: University of Chicago Press, forthcoming.

Toobin, Jeffrey. "Rich Bitch," Annals of Law, *New Yorker*, September 29, 2008.

Tourangeau, Roger, and Tom W. Smith. "Asking Sensitive Questions: The Impact of Data Collection Mode, Question Format, and Question Context." *Public Opinion Quarterly* 60, no. 2 (1996): 275–304.

Tracy, Sarah J. *Qualitative Research Methods: Collecting Evidence, Crafting Analysis, Communicating Impact.* 2nd ed. Hoboken, NJ: Wiley Blackwell, 2020.

Tyson, Karolyn. *Integration Interrupted: Tracking, Black Students, and Acting White after Brown.* New York: Oxford University Press, 2011.

Tyson, Karolyn. "Notes from the Back of the Room: Problems and Paradoxes in the Schooling of Young Black Students." *Sociology of Education* 76, no. 4 (2003): 326–343.

Tyson, Karolyn, "When Trust Hurts." Unpublished book manuscript, University of North Carolina, 2021.

Urbanik, Marta-Marika, and Robert A. Roks. "GangstaLife: Fusing Urban Ethnography with Netnography in Gang Studies." *Qualitative Sociology* 43 (2020): 1–21.

Vaisey, Stephen. "The 'Attitudinal Fallacy' Is a Fallacy: Why We Need Many Methods to Study Culture." *Sociological Methods & Research* 43, no. 2 (2014): 227–231.

Valian, Virginia. "Learning to Work." In *Working It Out: 23 Women Writers, Artists, Scientists, and Scholars Talk about Their Lives and Work*, edited by S. Ruddick and P. Daniels, 162–178. New York: Pantheon Books, 1977.

Vallejo, Jody. *Barrios to Burbs: The Making of the Mexican American Middle Class.* Palo Alto: Stanford University Press, 2012.

Van Maanen, John. *Tales of the Field: On Writing Ethnography.* 2nd ed. Chicago: University of Chicago Press, 2011.

Vaughan, Diane. *The Challenger Launch Decision: Risky Technology, Culture, and Deviance at NASA.* Chicago: University of Chicago Press, 1996.

Viscelli, Steve. *The Big Rig: Trucking and the Decline of the American Dream.* Berkeley: University of California Press, 2016.

Waters, Mary C. *Black Identities: West Indian Immigrant Dreams and American Realities.* Cambridge, MA: Harvard University Press, 1999.

Weber, Max. *Economy and Society: An Outline of Interpretative Sociology.* Edited by Guenther Roth and Claus Wittich. Berkeley: University of California Press, 2013.

Weber, Max. *The Theory of Social and Economic Organization*. Edited by Talcott Parsons. Translated by A. M. Henderson and T. Parsons. New York: Free Press, 1997.

Weininger, Elliot B. "School Choice in an Urban Setting." In *Choosing Homes, Choosing Schools*, edited by Annette Lareau and Kimberly Goyette, 268–294. New York: Russell Sage Foundation, 2014.

Weiss, Robert S. *Learning from Strangers: The Art and Method of Qualitative Interview Studies*. New York: Simon and Schuster, 1995.

Whyte, William F. *Street Corner Society: The Social Structure of an Italian Slum*. 3rd ed. Chicago: University of Chicago Press, 1981.

Williams, Christine L. *Still a Man's World: Men Who Do Women's Work*. Berkeley: University of California Press, 1995.

Willis, Paul E. *Learning to Labour: How Working-Class Kids Get Working-Class Jobs*. Legacy ed. New York: Columbia University Press, 2017.

Wingfield, Adia Harvey. *Flatlining: Race, Work, and Health Care in the New Economy*. Berkeley: University of California Press, 2019.

Wolf, Margery. *A Thrice-Told Tale: Feminism, Postmodernism, & Ethnographic Responsibility*. Palo Alto: Stanford University Press, 1992.

Young, Alford. "Uncovering a Hidden 'I' in Contemporary Urban Ethnography." *Sociological Quarterly* 51, no. 4 (2013): 51–65.

Zerubavel, Eviatar. *The Clockwork Muse: A Practical Guide to Writing Theses, Dissertations, and Books*. Cambridge, MA: Harvard University Press, 1999.

Zimmermann, Calvin Rashaud. "Looking for Trouble: How Teachers' Disciplinary Styles Perpetuate Gendered Racism in Early Childhood." Unpublished paper, University of Notre Dame, 2020.

Zinn, Maxine Baca. "Field Research in Minority Communities: Ethical, Methodological and Political Observations by an Insider." *Social Problems* 27, no. 2 (1979): 209–219.

Index

analysis, tools for: analytic contribution, highlighting of, on first page of field notes, 164–66; analytic priorities, setting of, in writing field notes, 177–79; data collection, pausing to figure out focus, 19; memos, value of, 55–56; silences and things that didn't happen, highlighting of, 169–79. *See also* emergent; intellectual contribution; memos

Anderson, Elijah, 168, 288n2, 283n35, 289n8

anxiety: about asking sensitive questions, 84–85; at beginning of a study, 37; as inevitable, 57; as justified, 57–58; about positionality, 37; and rejection, 57; and techniques for diffusing anxiety in writing, 253–58; and unclear procedures, 58; and worry that study is a "big mess," 4

autoethnography, 8

Becker, Howard: on interviewing as similar to improvisation, 138, 286n7; on introductions as a "road map," 231, 290n7, 290n8; on "no one right way," 200, 287n7; on "saturation," 18, 282n11; terrorized by literature, 17, 207, 256, 291n31

Belcher, Wendy Laura, 230, 290n6

Benson, Charles, 229, 230

bias, efforts to minimize: and asking a research question without knowing the answer, 191, 203; complete objectivity, impossibility of, 251; and considering competing answers, 196; in data analysis, 213, 215; in describing the study, 47; as a garment which cannot be removed, 151; and interrogating own assumptions,

151–53; in interview questions, 113; and learning from the data, 214–16; and memos, use of, 215–16; by not guiding answers, 75; by not ignoring disconfirming evidence, 214; and openness to being surprised, 63, 153; and providing sufficient data for the claims, 199, 204; reactivity, 33–34; reliability, 33–34; replicability, 33–34; representativeness, 33–34; social desirability bias in interviews, 64; in writing, 251

Black, Timothy: on clothing, 284n10; example of an ethnography, 286n1; on power imbalances, 281n12, 288n4; on reciprocity, 280n10; on reporting inaction in fieldnotes, 169–70

Bosk, Charles, 146, 280n10

Bourdieu, Pierre, 284n9, 285n13

Briggs, Jean, 252

Burawoy, Michael: extended case method, 283n34; on theory, 16, 197, 280n8, 289n4; on value of analytic rather than chronological account, 225

Calarco, Jessica McCrory: earlier versions of published papers, 291n17; on flexible coding, 289n20; on "hidden curriculum," 281n11, 292n3; on masking individuals in study, 41, 284n3

cancellation: and asking to follow up, 68; frequency of, 68; of interviews, 19, 65, 68; and prioritizing invitations in the field, 142; and recruiting someone after being ghosted, 68–69

challenges: and false starts, 58; and feeling overwhelmed, 225; as inevitable, 2–3, 35, 58, 262, 265; from

challenges (*cont.*)
    lack of data, 13–14; as not equally
    significant, 35, 58; from overly gen-
    eral interviews, 101–19; in respond-
    ing to critiques, 33–35; usually not
    fatal, 3; from vague field notes, 181–
    87. *See also* bias, efforts to mini-
    mize; mistakes
Chiang, Yi-Lin, 282n14, 286n1
children, methodological decisions:
    challenges of studying, 174; de-
    ciding on an age group, 236; and
    entertaining children, 121; IRB and
    consent with, 274; playing with,
    145–46; presence of, during an
    interview, 123; swiping researchers'
    belongings, 174–75
"Choosing Homes, Choosing Schools"
    (Lareau and Weininger): design
    decisions, 23, 282n15; demographic
    questions from interview guide,
    81–82; gaining access to school dis-
    tricts, 43–47; and "Parenting Chal-
    lenges," 289n14
Clair, Matthew, 2, 286n1
class: and clothing of researcher, 49–
    50; in family life, especially child
    rearing, 201, 206–7, 217–25; in-
    sider/outsider issues and, 28–29;
    and overview of Lareau's argument
    on class and child rearing, 245; and
    participant observation, avoiding
    highlighting in, 147; and partici-
    pant observation, shaping own view
    of, 151–53; and race, 207; upward
    mobility and cultural tastes study
    interview guide, 76–79. See also
    Unequal Childhoods (Lareau)
clothing, 49–51
coding. *See* data analysis
confidence: in asking sensitive ques-
    tions, 83–84; projecting when clue-
    less, 5–6
confidentiality: accidental revelation
    of a confidential site, 40; and code
    name, 40; and code name, chang-
    ing, 40; confidentiality agreement,
    for research assistants, 89; deciding

    early about, 40–42; and explain-
    ing to participants, 44–45; over-
    view, 40–42; transcripts, deidentify-
    ing before coding, 88–89. *See also*
    masking
consent: asking for, 70, 95; and not co-
    ercing, 69; and recording, announc-
    ing when, 95; reiterating key points,
    70; respondent's contact informa-
    tion, obtaining it on form, 70. *See
    also* Institutional Review Board for
    the Protection of Human Subjects
    (IRB)
content analysis, 8
Contreras, Randol: example of an eth-
    nography, 286n1; on importance of
    trust, 282n6, 282n7; "insider" per-
    spective of, 27; on trust from mask-
    ing research site, 51, 282n7, 284n2,
    284n3
Cooper, Marianne, 282n2
Coppola, Francis Ford, 203, 204
Cucchiara, Maia, 16, 55, 283n25, 286n1
Curl, Heather, 76, 285n13

Damaske, Sarah, 285n3
data analysis: abductive approach,
    279n6, 283n33; and alternative ex-
    planations to consider, 195, 215–16;
    and analytic memos, rereading all,
    198; as anxiety inducing, 199–200;
    and Atlas.ti and other programs,
    212–13; and changing research
    question easier than changing site,
    204–5; as chaotic process, 199; and
    coding scheme, example of, 210–13;
    creating a file of quotes, 214–15;
    data, learning from, 214–16; and
    data collection, happening through-
    out, 195; and data matrices, 213;
    definition of, 195; eloquence, not
    being swayed by, 214; exposition of
    process of editing quotes, 216–25;
    and focus as letting go of other
    possibilities, 204; and forgetting
    to think, 196; and formal coding,
    209–16; and forming a focus early,
    197–98; and going deep and step-

ping back, 209–10; iterative, 195; listening to data, importance of, 197; mechanisms for figuring out focus, 195–225; moving from topic to research question, 196; multiple pieces of evidence for a claim, looking for, 213; overview of, 195–225; patterns, looking for, 214; research question, refining of, 198–204; rigorously considering disconfirming evidence, 215; seeking variation in data, 214–15; and self-knowledge, as key in decisions, 204; silences, listening for, 213; software programs, choosing to forgo use of, 212; and stepping back for perspective, 199, 214–15; steps of, 30–31; transcripts and field notes, poring over, 212–13; and writing, blurry boundary with, 197

data management: code names, use of in file names, 54–55; code names, use of in conversation, 164–65; data collection, keeping meticulous records on, 53–55, 166; file names, examples of, 54–55; file names, highlighting identifying features of participants, 54; keeping back-up of notes, 166; keeping it simple, 53; losing track of, 52; memos as critical, 55–56; multiple forms of data, managing, 53; organizing system, creating, 53–54; overview of, 52–56; record keeping, keeping track of the number of interviews, 90; summary page on field notes, 164–66; total amount of data often collected, 197–98; total hours in the field, and recording hours spent doing participant observation, 166; uploading interviews immediately, 88; value of interview profiles, 90

Deener, Andrew, 15, 283n32

Denzin, Norman K.: on different qualitative research methods, 279n6; on emic and etic, 281n3; on one's role in the field, 287n3, 288n19; on positionality and subjectivity, 282n24,

283n25, 28; on reducing bias in a study, 284n7; on verstehen, 283n29

DeParle, Jason, 290n2

design: choosing where to do research, 24–26; criteria for making decisions, 15; decisions to make, 15, 17–27; duration of data collection, 18; examples of, 21; goals of, 13; hard choices in, 15, 21, 23; keeping study small, 23–24; normal to make changes in, 13; overview, 11–27; size of a study, 19, 21; time available, considering amount of, 12; value of reading to help focus, 16; varying by career stage, 12

Desmond, Matt, 148, 252, 292n3

details: example of an interview that yielded more details, 119–39; example of an overly general interview with suggestions for improvement, 103–20; and feeling as if you are on the shoulder of the researcher, 91; importance of, 91; interviewer training the respondent in terms of how much detail to give, 107–9; a more vivid set of field notes, 187–94; notes without sufficient detail, 180–87; writing detailed field notes, 163–94. *See also* field notes; interviewing; participant observation

developmental editors, 291n36

digital diaries, 26, 282n19

DiMaggio, Paul, 280n9

disconfirming evidence: as characteristic of excellent work, 36; in coding, 209–10, 213; importance of keeping an open mind in data collection, 167, 251; importance of seeking, 153, 167; looking for it in data collection, 209; needing to share with reader, 227–28; as part of research journey, 31–32; reliability and, 33; in taking stock of data, 213–16; in writing, 243, 247

don't know what you are doing: focus is unclear, 5; and importance of confidence, 6; as normal, 2, 4, 263; during participant observation, 162;

don't know what you are doing (*cont.*) when there are multiple directions, 202

dominant groups, dangers of making their experiences normative, 23

Dow, Dawn Marie, 207, 281n5, 289n13

dreaming: elements of, 12; overview of, 11–13; as part of process, 58; value of, 12

Duneier, Mitchell: on being surprised, 153; dissertations, as best ethnographies, 24; on mistakenly assuming trust, 28, 29, 283n30; on "morally ambiguous" nature of ethnographic work, 281n12; on "three rules," 282n17, 287n16; "Voices from the Sidewalk," 35, 283n24, 283n31, 284n36

economic position of the researcher: earning a living while doing participant observation, 154; lack of grants, 24; paying bills during data collection, 18

Edin, Kathryn, 121, 285n17

elevator speech: bad introductory speeches, 48; being vague but accurate, 47–49, 159–60; better speeches, 48; components of, 47; developing a second, 159–60; practicing delivery, 49; preparation of, for entry to the field, 141. *See also* recruitment and gaining access

Ellis, Rachel: on gaining access to a prison, 12, 47, 281n1, 284n6; on helping out, 146, 287n8; on writing vivid field notes, 176–77

Emdin, Christopher, 51

emergent: acting confident, 5–6; analogy with photography, 2–4; as chaotic process, 199; continuing to read during data collection, 17; data analysis, taking place throughout data collection, 195; finding focus in data collection, 6, 76, 98, 139, 159, 161–62, 197–207; finding focus through data analysis, 195–225; iterative process, 214–15;

lacking data from all respondents, 13–14; learning as you go, 262; mistakes and hiccups as normal, 262; no one right way, 200; normal to make changes, 13, 15, 22; reading data, thinking about literature, 214; repairing mistakes, 262; research plan being contingent, 6; research questions shifting, 32; saturation, 18; thinking as you go, 7; uncertainty as inevitable, 37; value of a pause in data collection, 19. *See also* uncertainty

Emerson, Robert M., 163, 285n3, 287n2, 289n20, 289n21

emic and *etic*, 281n3

Erickson, Frederick, 288n21, 289n20

Erikson, Kai, 1

ethnography: using interviewing and participant observation instead of, 279n3. *See also* interviewing; participant observation

ethics: acknowledging disconfirming evidence, 216; being mindful of power dynamics, 99; clarifying your role in the field to make ethical challenges clearer, 252; and ethnographers representing the views of others in another culture, 291n23; following spirit of informed consent, 70, 99, 162; guiding interview without pressuring or coercing, 99; IRB as protecting human subjects from harm, 271–77; principle of beneficence, 37; project must be ethical, 11; reciprocity as important form of, 280n10; recording secretly, refraining from, 158; and refraining from coercion, 68, 69, 84; student project with ethical concerns, 205, 289n11; unethical, refraining from being, 156

excellence in research: agreement on standards of, 35; both as insiders and as outsiders, 29; data set, likely uneven in, 33; journal editors yearning for, 263; people telling others about, 263; qualities of,

35–36; too many to list, 8; unclear procedures, 58; work that falls short of, 2

exciting: beginnings, 11, 37; ideas, reflecting, 37; intellectual journeys, 9, 57, 264; interviewing as, 87, 92; field work as more than writing field notes, 194; learning what others see as, 56; as principle for focusing research question, 144, 196, 198, 203; writing analytic memos, 159

exhaustion: adjusting pace of reading literature during data collection, 17; contributing to pitiful field notes, 177–78; at end of interview, 88; fieldwork leading to, 154; imperative to write field notes even if battling, 194; planning rest, 154; research leading to, 9, resting improves memory, 159

extended case method, 8, 279n3, 279n6, 283n34

faith, 265

feedback. *See* listening, to feedback

Ferguson, Ann Arnett, 286n1

Ferguson, Sherelle, 80, 172–73, 282n12, 285n14, 288n7

field notes: amount of time needed to write, 158, 159–60, 166, 175; capturing inaction, 169–70; capturing passage of time, 170–71; capturing reactions of multiple participants around a focal point, 168, 186; chronology on first page, 164–66; considering your intellectual goals, 167; dialogue, keeping to a minimum, 173–74; do's and don'ts in writing field notes, 172–73; first page of notes, 164–66; floodlight vs. flashlight, 163–64, 167, 192; focusing on light, smells, noise, colors, 167, 171, 176–77, 190; getting better with more experience, 158, 194; as good investment, 159; highlighting silences, 169–70; imperative to write after each visit, 151, 154, 166; improving notes through feedback,

194; as lifeblood of a project, 140, 194; making as comprehensive as possible at first, 167; making very detailed but succinct, 159; method for marking progress while writing, 179; as more accurate than memory, 140; needing time to write, 18–19; not skipping a step, 170–71, 172–73; overview of issues involved in writing high-quality notes, 163–94; presenting emotion, nonverbal behavior, 171–72, 173, 183, 186, 187–88; prioritizing observations linked to your key questions, 177–79; showing, not telling, 171–72, 228; some days as better than others, 159, 163–64; stopping observation until notes are written, 158; strong set of notes, 181–82, 187–93; as tedious to write, 194; uneven set of field notes, example of, 181–87; using a thesaurus, 178–80, 189; WRITE, 166–72; writing lushly, 163, 166. *See also* memos; participant observation, role in the field

findings, reported in words, not numbers, 23, 91

Fine, Gary Alan, 15

flexibility: appearing flexible even under stress, 67; aspiring to, 262; and being systematic, 9, 55; being "vague but accurate" in IRB application leads to, 282n6; Calarco and Deterding and Waters on flexible coding, 289n20; crucial importance of mental flexibility and keeping an open mind, 153; and food choices, 150; importance of, in research design, 13; IRB requirements, making research question broad to give yourself, 40; understanding need for, 282n6. *See also* emergent

focus, pausing data collection to figure out, 19

focus groups, 8, 26

food: accepting offers of, 149–50; fieldwork, eating before, 149–50; interviews, bringing to, 71; interviews, food (*cont.*)

useful gift for, 73–74; never eating in front of respondents who are not eating, 150; recruitment, strategy for, 46, 47, 68–69; as a ritual for writing field notes, 154

4 R's: definitions of, 33–35; examples of, 34

Fretz, Rachel I., 163, 285n3, 287n2, 289n20, 289n21

Frye, Margaret, 282n12

Gans, Herbert J., 282n18, 286n1

Gaztambide-Fernández, Rubén A., 283n35

gender: in design decisions, 23; feminist critiques of interviewing, 284n1; and housework in an interview, 97; participant observation, shaping view of, 151–53

Gerson, Kathleen, 285n3

goals of this book: as friendly companion, 9; guide for usage, 9–10; overview, 3

Godfather, The (film), 203–5

Grazian, David, 15, 289n6

Gross, Nora, 50

grounded theory, 279n6, 288n2

guidelines, for interviewing: balancing digging deep and moving on, 101; being proactive, 94–95; being realistic, 102–3; controlling overly talkative respondents, 99–100; do's and don'ts of interviewing, 94; double checking that all of questions were asked, 103; doubling back to a theme, 98, 136; expecting overly succinct respondents, 100; focusing on subjective meanings, 96–97; goals of the study, focusing on, 94; listening carefully, 94; listening for great quotes, 102–3; no right or wrong answers, assuring respondent of, 95; overview of, 93–103; deflecting questions, 101–2; power inequalities, being mindful of, 99; reusing effective probes, 96; selecting experts on topic, 93–93; talk-

ing as little as possible, 94; thinking while listening, 97–98; using own knowledge, 97; using participant's own words, 95–96

guidelines, for participant observation: developing a second elevator speech, 159–60; issues on recording notes openly or not, 157–58; managing entry to field, 141–43; needing to make instant decisions, 155–56; not wanting to go to the field, 154–55; overview of, 140–62; recording data, 156–59; role in field, always eating ahead of time, 149–50; role in field, keeping an open mind, 153; role in field, managing requests for help, 148–49; role in field, placing self in space, 144–46; role in field, positionality, 143–44; role in field, small talk, 146–47; role in field, visiting early and often, 150–51; role in field, who you are shapes what you see, 151–53; transitioning in and out of fieldwork, 154–55; work-life balance issues, 160–61; writing notes from very beginning, 156–57

Hansen, Karen, 282n12

Hanson, Rebecca, 281n11, 284n12, 284n16, 288n19

hard choices: in choosing location, 24; during fieldwork, 185; in finding the focus of study, 239; guidelines for making, 19–24; in interviewing, 81, 97–98; as part of the process, 15, 23, 58; understanding one study cannot do everything, 195; in *Unequal Childhoods*, 22; weighing of, 23

Harvey, Peter, 165–66, 174–76, 287n7, 288n1, 288n8

Heath, Shirley Brice, 153, 287n16

Hecht, Katharina, 12, 281n2

Hoang, Kimberly Kay, 16, 286n1, 287n3

Hochschild, Arlie Russell, 4, 146, 282

Horvat, Erin McNamara, 291n19, 282n12

Hubbard, Lea Ann, 283n31

Hughes, Everett, 231, 290n8

humor: challenges of invoking, 51; with food, 150; use of, to show interview is not interrogation, 95; valuable in interviewing, 61; valuable in participant observation, 147, 156; as way to ask or deflect, 42, 101

imposter syndrome, 57; and best work, some done by inexperienced scholars, 263–64. *See* novice researcher

income: asking about, 81, 82, 83–84; avoiding coercion, 84; importance of looking calm and assured, 83–84; questions to learn wealth, 84–85; and short silences, 84; use of computer, more accurate for sensitive questions, 85, 285n19. *See also* interview guide; interviewing

informed consent. *See* consent

insider/outsider issues, 27–29; benefits of insider and outsider status, 28; risks of misunderstanding when crossing race and class boundaries, 28; thinking through one's perspective, 29; vulnerable to criticism, regardless of position, 29

Institutional Review Board for the Protection of Human Subjects (IRB): application, being broad, 272–74; application, confidence in, 5, 271–77; application, and considering what you would want to know if the study involved you or your family member, 277; application, importance of following principles of, 162; application, navigating process, 272; application, patience with approval, 39–40; application, presenting range of possible gifts, 73, 273; application, sequence of steps, 40; application, timeframe of, 275; core goals of, 39; consent and, 273; culture clash with emergent nature of research, 39, 271–73; legal protections of confidentiality certificates, 276–77; purpose of, 38–39, 271;

rough application, submitting early, 273; Tuskegee, 38

intellectual contribution: always multiple options, 4; figuring out focus about one-half to two-thirds of the way through data collection, 6, 76, 98, 197; linking evidence to idea in the literature, 248; mechanisms for clarifying, 198–207; reading the literature to figure out, 17; study as a "friendly amendment" to the literature, 264; unclear initially, 4; value of memos in discerning, 55–56, 180. *See also* emergent; "so what"

interview guide: asking income last, 81; asking neutral, open-ended questions, 75; asking sensitive questions, 83–85; as capturing the key themes of the study, 79–81; checklist, value of giving to respondents, 80–81; demographic questions, 79; example of interview guide on cultural tastes and upward mobility, 76–79; examples of demographic questions, 81–82; first question, as easily answerable, 74; first questions, as general, 74; ideal types of questions, 75; number of questions, 74, 91; overview of, 74–82; reviewing ahead of time, 72. *See* income; interviewing; value of interviewing and participant observation

interviewing: acknowledging power dynamics, 62, 99; as an analytic search for information, 63; announcing when recording beings, 95; answers, as providing multiple possible pathways for next step, 92, 126, 131; asking for consent, 95; asking income and other sensitive questions, 82–85; asking one question at a time, 116, 126; asking only part of a sample a question, 13–14; bad interviews, 100; balancing digging deep and moving on, 101, 125; beginning of, 121–22; being mindful of power inequalities, 99; being open to being surprised, 63; being pro-

interviewing (*cont.*)

active, 94–95; being realistic, 102–3; as boring, 62; choosing respondents who are experts on topic, 75, 93–94; and collaboration not working well, 104; common mistakes, 120; confirming interview location and time, 67–68; creating an interview bag with key materials, 71–72; data, keeping track of, 89; data management of files, 88–89; deciding on interview location, 65–66; deflecting questions, 101–2; do's and don'ts for interviewing, 94; double checking questions, 103; doubling back to a theme to gain more information, 98; example of interviewing defendants, 60–62; example of interview lacking detail, 103–20; exciting and stressful to make instant decisions, 92; first question as opening gambit, 61; focusing on subjective meanings, 96–97; on following up later to ask a question, 102; goal of, 120; guiding interview without pressuring or coercion, 199; hard choices in interviews, 97–98; importance of details, 91; importance of first fifteen minutes, 91, 110, 138, 194; as improvisation, 138; interview questions, changing over time, 13; intimacy of, 63; items to carry; 71–72; keeping in mind goals of study, 94; keeping recorder on after interview is over, 85–86; as less time consuming than participant observation, 64; limits of, 14, 64; listening carefully, 94; listening for great quotes, 102–3; needing to make instant decisions, 92; no more than two interviews per day, 67; no right or wrong answers, assuring respondent of, 95; obtaining detailed answers, 119, 121, 127, 128; offering a range of options, 134, 136; okay to use own knowledge, 97; one answer providing five different possible next steps, 104–5; one great quote per interview, 103; overview of guidelines for interviewing, 93–103; particularly good at, 14; as partnership, 63, 94, 106, 121, 138; purpose of, 63; questions inviting open-ended answers, 107, 112, 118; recruiting others after interview is over, 86–87; respondents discussing experiences of others, 131; respondents too talkative or too succinct, 92, 99–100; reusing effective probes, 96; reviewing questions, as acceptable, 13; scheduling time between interviews, 66–67; sensitive information, asking for, 100; as showing respondent's perspectives, 63; similarities with participant observation, 8; stumbling in asking, 133; taking risks, 97; talking as little as possible, 94, 120; thank you gifts for participants, 73–74; thinking while listening, 97–98; transcription, 88–89; turning points in, 97, 109, 127–28, 131; unfolding unexpectedly, 91; using participant's own words, 95–96, 104, 134; value of, 1, 14, 63–64; varying wording across interviews, 75–76; when to arrive, 72; working to build rapport, 95, 120; writing a memo after interview, 88–89; writing out directions in case of no cellular service, 71–72. *See also* guidelines, for interviewing; interview guide; probes

iterative: definition of, 195, 290n4; looking at data and literature and thinking about the contribution, 214–16, 227–28; in writing, 228

Jerolmack, Colin, 142, 280n9, 2284n2

journalists: as excellent writers, 290n2; not following same methodological standards, 261, 290n2; objecting to masking of site, 40; sharing similar topics as social scientists, 235, 290n2

journeys, research: critique of literature as key element of, 209; establishing goals for, 36; obstacles as routine, 38, 199; overview of research journey, 29–33, 30–31; table 2.2; phases of research journey, 264; as pleasurable, 37; preparing for, 38–59; presentation of, in writing, 225; as process of moving from research topic to research question, 196, 200–204; project as a journey, 9; steps in beginning, 11–37, 161–62. *See also* emergent

Katz, Jack, 33–34, 279n6, 287n17, 283n34, 287n3
Khan, Shamus: on having a mental health plan, 58; on last question asked in interview, 98, 284n17; on not using a data analysis program, 289n18; on outlining, 228; on parallel findings in *Privilege* and *The Best of the Best*, 283n35; "Talk Is Cheap," 280n9
Kidder, Tracy, 226, 290n1
Kim, Sangeun "Shawn," 46
Klinenberg, Eric, 279n6

Lacy, Karyn R., 52, 281n5, 284n15
Lamont, Michèle, 28, 280n9, 281n5, 283n28
Lareau, Annette: book of methodological appendices, 288n19; examples of blurry and clearer introduction, 231–33; job after college interviewing defendants, 60–61; method of intensive family observations, 285n6, 287n12, 288n11, 288n22, 288n23, 288n22, 288n23; methodological appendix to *Home Advantage*, 32, 283n32; positionality, 280n11; prior research projects, 8; study with Ferguson of first-generation students, 80, 285n14; variable reactions of parents towards school, 291n19. *See also* "Choosing Homes, Choosing Schools" (Lareau and Weininger); *Unequal Childhoods* (Lareau)
Lawrence-Lightfoot, Sara, 279n6

Leidner, Robin, 17, 171–72, 282n9, 288n6
Lein, Laura, 287n17
Levine, Judith A., 89, 101, 281n5, 285n21, 291n24
Liebow, Elliot, 282n18, 286n1
Lincoln, Yvonna S.: bias in a study, on reducing, 284n7; on different qualitative research methods, 279n6; on emic and etic, 281n3; field, on one's role in, 287n3, 288n19; on positionality and subjectivity, 282n24, 283n25, 28; on verstehen, 283n29
listening, general: benefits of, 3; importance of, 3
listening, to data: in conducting interviews, 91–139; definition of, 3; in formal coding, 209–13; learning during participant observation, 153; patterns emerging in data analysis, 195–213; quote, what it is really saying, 213–25; requests for help from participants, 148–49. *See also* field notes; interviewing; participant observation
listening, to feedback: accepting, 262; anxiety, as way to help with, 58, 255; as "baked into" an intellectual journey, 30, 32; as crucial in writing, 208, 244; in data analysis, 199, 208; and excellent work, 264; feedback, seeking out, 208–9; and field notes, improving, 194; getting feedback early and often, 36, 160, 194, 208; helping set priorities, 32, 56, 159, 243; ignoring, 12; improving skills in, 94; and interesting arguments, 254; in making design decisions, 20; memos as pathway for, 56, 180; negative feedback, examples of, 208; overview, 3; and research question, focusing of, 202; talking to others for support while in the field, 155–56; writing process, as step in, 256. *See also* writing groups
listening, to literature: discerning your conversation partners, 17, 193, 198, 200, 206–8; good studies being de-

frequently, 56; writing weekly, during data collection, 19. *See also* data analysis; intellectual contribution

mistakes: and false starts, 58; and good studies, 3; on inevitability of, 2–3, 58, 265; not always significant, 58

mixed methods, 8, 279n6

Morgenstern, Julie, 53

Muñoz, Vanessa Lopes, 154, 248, 284n5, 287n4, 287n18

Murphy, Kate, 94

net ethnography, 25–27. *See also* online

Newman, Katherine, 2, 279n2

novice researchers: and best ethnographies, 24; example of an interview by, 103–20; field notes improving with feedback, 194; gifts of, 263–64; good results despite hard problem, 3; and good writing, 259; hard to be, 263; room at the table for new scholars, 264; set of field notes done by, 181–87

online: advantages of research using, 26–27; comparison with face-to-face interviews, 26–27; interviewing, 25; IRB risks, 271; normally good to avoid for recruitment, 43; quality issues, 26; searches, can reveal site, 41; searching your own name to see what participants see, 45; strengths and weaknesses of, 26–27; as tool for recruitment, 43, 46

Paik, Leslie, 1, 279n1

pandemic, COVID-19, 25

paradoxes: data analysis, going deep and stepping back, 209–10; digging deep in an interview but also moving on to cover topics, 100, 125, 133, 137; earliest stages filled with many, 37; participant observation, list of some involved in, 162; systematic and flexible, 9; valuable in showing disconfirming evidence which proves the rule, 247

participant observation: accessing, easier through sponsorship, 43, 237; and challenges similar to interviewing, 11; collecting distinctive data from interviewing, 279n4; collecting feedback during data collection, 153, 159; consent, 141, 142–43; debate about openly taking notes, 157–59; debate about relative value compared to interviewing, not elaborated here, 9, 280n9; early visits as especially important, 194; elevator speech, 47–49, 141; examples of, 15–16; field notes, as more accurate than memory, 140; first days in field, 141–42; food and, 149–50; frequency of visits during, 18–19; gifts to participants, 149; good for showing social processes, 1, 15; helping out, 146; humor, as valuable, 147, 156; importance of keeping an open mind, 153, 167; important to take vantage point of participant, 193; instant decisions, 155–56; learning how to do, 140–62; "make familiar strange," 157; making decisions guided by goals, 143–44; managing requests for help, 148–49; notes getting better over time, 158; not going back until notes are done, 158; not good for, 14; only going can write notes, 151; particularly good for, 14–15; physical placement in site, 144–45; playing with kids, 145–46; positionality and, 151–52; questions to ask to help focus, 159; reflexivity, importance of, 151–53; reluctance to go to the field, 154–55; researchers, needing social support, 155–56; rituals as helpful, 154; role in the field, 143–56; seeking disconfirming evidence, 153; similarity with interviewing, 8; sometimes not much happens, 166–67; synonyms for, 279n4; tem-

in interviews, 99; power of race to shape social interactions and identity, 49–51; scholars of color, dressing to feel legitimate, 50; scholars of color, facing racial hostility from respondents, 52; segregated neighborhoods, and whites exaggerating danger in, 52; tensions between number of groups and sample size, 22–24

Rao, Aliya Hamid: being open about note-taking, 157, 288n23; examples of blurry and clearer introductions, 231–33; longitudinal interview study, published as *Crunch Time*, 262n14; method of intensive family observations, 285n6, 287n12, 288n11, 288n22, 288n23; taking notes during family observations, as not viable, 157, 288n22

rapport: assessing impact of actions on, 150; building in interview, 95, 120, 121; building online, 26; building rapport with overly succinct interviewee, 99; building via clothing, 50–51; limits to, 29; stories about yourself, telling participants, 101

Rawls, John, 235, 290n12

reciprocity: ethical nature of, 280n10; helping out, 146; in recruitment, 44; requests for help, listening carefully to, 148–49; thanking interview respondents, 73

recorders: consent, obtaining, 69, 95; field work, displaying openly in, 288n3; field work, use in, 15; keeping in waterproof bag, 71; keeping on after interview ends, 85–87; microphones improving sound quality, 69; police recorders, distinguishing from, 64; public space, reducing sound quality in interviews, 67; technical disasters with, 70; using phone, 69; using two recorders, 69–70

recruitment and gaining access: asking others for help, 42; bringing food, 46; business cards, as helpful,

70; checking if they have referral, 87; details, 43; examples of recruitment requests, 43–47; how to ask, 42; how to present yourself, 45; via letter, 46; limiting requests, 68; listing references, 47; overview, 42–47; phone call, asking for, 43, 46; power dynamics, 42; via public Instagram, 46; showing interest in respondents, 49; speech for a snowball sample, 86; sponsorship, as helpful, 43, 237; telling participants what you want them to do, 49; via texting, 42; waiting for answer, 42; website, as valuable tool, 45; whom to exclude, 42. *See also* elevator speech; interviewing

reenactment videos, 26, 282n19

reflexivity: considerations in, 254, 284n7; importance of, 151–53; and positionality, 27–29, 193. *See also* role in the field

reliability, 33–35

replicability, 33–35

representativeness, issues to consider: and advancing theoretical ideas, 16, 36, 264; assessing how typical site is, 238–39; being methodical and systematic in design, 12–37; goal of study, on selection of research site, 236–37; overview, 33–34. *See also* bias, efforts to mitigate

research question: alignment process, 204–9; choice of question involves emotion, 200; choosing one you want to answer, 9; examples of research questions, 30–31; figuring out conversation partners, 200; framing, while collecting data, 209; initial, emergent, and ultimate research question, 30–31; meeting strengths of the method; 9; not knowing answer when beginning, 203; question changing in a typical research journey, 30–31; refinement of, 198–204. *See also* data analysis; emergent

respondents. *See* participants

Reyes, Victoria, 284n2
Richards, Pamela, 254
rigor, qualities of excellence in research, 35–36. *See also* disconfirming evidence; systematic
Rios, Victor, 27, 28, 283n26
Ritzer, George, 279n8
Rivera, Lauren A., 279n7
role in the field: clothing, 49–51; critiques about, responding to, 34;
difficult moments in field, 169,
288n3; eating ahead of time, 149–
50; keeping an open mind, 153;
making instant decisions, 155–56;
managing requests for help, 148–49;
not wanting to go to the field, 154–
55; placing self in space, 144–46;
positionality, 27–29, 143–44; reactivity, 33–34; small talk, 146–47;
researcher, frustrated, 152, 171–72,
172–74; transitioning in and out of
fieldwork, 154–55; visiting early and
often, 150–51; who you are shapes
what you see, 151–53. *See also* in-
sider/outsider issues; participant
observation

Sackett, Blair, 148, 285n9
safety, 51–52; feigning illness and
leaving if feeling threatened, 52;
in the field, 155–56
sample. *See* design
self-presentation: in clothing, 49–51;
and insider/outsider status, 27–29;
in introducing yourself to participants, 47–49; in stories you share
about yourself, 101
sexual harassment, by respondents of
the interviewer, 61
Shaw, Linda L., 163, 285n3, 287n2,
289n20, 289n21
Sherman, Rachel, 282n12
Shestakofsky, Benjamin, 208, 210–13,
279n7, 290n11
shyness: participant observation, as
challenging, 152; and role of enjoy-
able topic in respondents relaxing,
100

Sierra-Arévalo, Michael, 285n5, 287n1
Simmel, George, 63, 285n4
Small, Mario Luis, 20, 279n6, 282n24,
283n29
Smiley, Jane, 240
snowball sample: asking at end of
interview, 86–87; asking respondent
for contact information, 87; thank
you note, nudging a respondent to
ask, 45
social class. *See* class
"so what": and analytic memos, 193;
as conceptual contribution, 240,
253; as element of outstanding research, 35; as goal in writing, 229,
239, 253; as key part of data analysis, 200; as part of "soul" of a piece,
240; as potential source of anxiety,
254; struggling to find, 206–8; and
theory, valuable role of, 196. *See also*
intellectual contribution
sponsorship: assisting sponsor, 146;
connections, asking for, 43; often
crucial for admittance to research
site, 237; for organizations, 43–44;
valuable, as they can vouch for you,
42
Stack, Carol B., 282n18, 286n1
Steinbugler, Amy, 23, 281n5, 282n16
Strunk, William, Jr., 5, 6, 279n5
Stuart, Forrest, 282n19
surprise: Duneier rule, and commitment to, 283n29; look for, 56, 63,
153
systematic: in collecting data on
issues of interest, 32, 56, 209;
in design, 20; in having robust
data to support claims, 244–45,
246; in keeping meticulous records
of data collection, 52–55; need for
being, 9; in probing for additional
details in interviews, 91–139; in
searching for disconfirming evidence, 209–10, 210–13; in using
code names in file system, 54–55;
in writing detailed field notes, 163–
95. *See also* disconfirming evidence;
flexibility

Tavory, Iddo, 279n6, 280n8, 283n33, 288n2, 289n2
terrorized by the literature, 17, 207, 256
theory: limited discussion of, 9, 197; role of, 279n8; value of, 279n8. *See also* emergent; intellectual contribution; "so what"
think as you go. *See* data analysis; emergent; intellectual contribution; uncertainty
time: allowing time for IRB approval, 39; amount needed to write field notes, 18–19, 158, 166; arrival time for interviews, 72–73; availability of, in shaping design, 15; doing field work at different times, 33, 151; factors influencing length of study, 18; focus, long uncertainty about, 4; interviews, requiring less than participant observation, 64; marking time in field notes, 164–65, 170–71; need for, in completing study, 12–13, 18–19; participants sustaining golden manners, difficulty of, over long period of, 34; rejuggling to make time, 18; scheduling buffer times, 67–68; specifying how much, with respondents, 48; spent on reading, minimal, 17; to think, 17; time budgets for field work, 19; visiting often, 151; and writing field notes, 158–59, 175; younger scholars, often having more, 24
Timmermans, Stefan, 279n6, 280n8, 283n33, 288n2, 289n2
Todd, Richard, 226, 290n1
topic vs. research question, 15–16, 196; parallel in filmmaking, 203–4
transcription: art of controlling an interview revealed by transcripts, 99; in coding, poring over, 209, 213; errors, in automatic systems, 88; small percentage making it into the final piece, 258; time consuming, 88; time consuming, as part of data management, 196; transition from transcripts to edited quotes, 216–25;

using code names for file names, 88; word-for-word, invaluable in data analysis; 88. *See also* data analysis; data management
transformative potential of research on researcher, 10, 162
trust: and Duneier rule, 283n29; essential component, 14; interview where trust building was difficult, example of, 103–20; questions to establish trust, 105. *See also* rapport; role in the field
tweets, 26
Tyson, Karolyn, 16, 282n12

uncertainty: as inevitable, 3–6; linked to contingency, 6; in participant observation, 153; thinking as you go, 7; and unclear procedures, 58; about visit unfolding, 149–50
Unequal Childhoods (Lareau): challenges in, 50; church visit in Carroll family, 181–85; costly error to interview fathers, 75, 285n12; danger of neighborhood exaggerated due to racial bias, 51–52; design decisions for, 12, 21–22, 236, 288n10, 288n12; example of how participants misrepresent purpose of study, 142; example of inaction spelled out in field notes, 169; example of not knowing where to sit, 145; experience of Mark Greely on social class and cultural knowledge, 249, 291n20, 291n21; field notes similar across research team, 283n35; gaining access to research sites, 236; homework battle and dinner visit in Handlon family, 187–93; on how parents view children's activities, 137, 286n6; involving different literature, 17; Marshall family on finding a gymnastics program, 217–25, 241–43, 289n22; naysayers, 12, 281n2; overnight with Tallingers, 177–79; recorders in, use of, 158, 288n3; recruiting families for, 42–43; researchers' backgrounds shaping what they